YOU'RE PAID WHAT
YOU'RE WORTH

YOU'RE PAID WHAT YOU'RE WORTH

AND OTHER MYTHS OF THE MODERN ECONOMY

JAKE ROSENFELD

THE BELKNAP PRESS *of*
HARVARD UNIVERSITY PRESS

Cambridge, Massachusetts
London, England

2021

First printing

Library of Congress Cataloging-in-Publication Data

Names: Rosenfeld, Jake, 1978– author.
Title: You're paid what you're worth : and other myths of the
    modern economy / Jake Rosenfeld.
Description: Cambridge, Massachusetts : The Belknap Press of
    Harvard University Press, 2021. | Includes bibliographical references
    and index.
Identifiers: LCCN 2020022460 | ISBN 978-0-674-91659-3 (cloth)
Subjects: LCSH: Pay equity. | Equality. | Performance standards. |
    Wages and labor productivity. | Merit pay.
Classification: LCC HD6061 | DDC 331.2/153—dc23
LC record available at https://lccn.loc.gov/2020022460

To Erin McGaughey
For making it all worth it

CONTENTS

PART I: QUESTIONS ABOUT PAY

1 What Does Determine Our Pay?   3

2 What Do We Think Determines Our Pay?   26

PART II: PAYING FOR PERFORMANCE?

3 Employers Against the Free Market   57

4 Mismeasuring Performance and the Pitfalls of Paying for Merit   87

5 The Bosses' Boss   115

PART III: PAYING FOR THE JOB?

6 When Good Jobs Go Bad   147

7 Bad Jobs Can Be Good   185

PART IV: TOWARD A FAIRER WAGE

8 Rethinking Inequality   221

9 Toward a Fairer Wage   243

Epilogue: What Foot Soldiers Deserve   268

Notes   273   Acknowledgments   337   Index   341

YOU'RE PAID WHAT YOU'RE WORTH

PART I

QUESTIONS ABOUT PAY

1 WHAT DOES DETERMINE OUR PAY?

UNITED AIRLINES' EIGHTY THOUSAND EMPLOYEES earned extra pay when the company met certain performance targets, such as besting rivals in on-time departures and lost luggage rates. In March of 2018, the company decided to scrap its incentive plan and replace it with a lottery that awarded cash prizes, vacation packages, and fancy cars to lucky employees chosen at random. Reaction from the workforce was swift and unambiguous. An internal company forum exploded with comments blasting the change. One worker posted: "This is NOT a way to boost morale! It does quite the opposite. I wonder what kind of bonus was given to those in the big tower who came up with this nonsense."[1] Another summed up the dominant viewpoint: "Sometimes you guys get it right, sometimes you get [it] wrong. This . . . one wasn't even close." It didn't help that the total cash value of the lottery awards amounted to tens of millions of dollars less than the company had awarded in performance bonuses. Many workers saw the change as an underhanded way to cut their pay. Management backed away from the new system within days.[2]

Wells Fargo also had a long-standing incentive plan in place for its tellers and personal bankers. A portion of pay depended on performance goals, with "performance" defined largely by the number of accounts a worker persuaded customers to open with the colossal San Francisco-based bank. The incentive system worked extremely well: in 2013, Wells Fargo's retail customer households held an average of six of the bank's products (for example, IRAs, CDs, savings accounts, credit cards), far higher than the industry norm.[3] Branch managers received daily quotas from higher-ups, often accompanied by threatening language: "We were constantly told we would end up working for McDonald's," one Florida manager recalled.[4] Managers passed the pressure down the hierarchy, exhorting their tellers and personal bankers—whose take-home pay varied by how many products they sold—to meet the branches' targets. When not enough customers responded to their pitches, some employees found another way to hit their numbers by forging signatures, making up new email addresses, and collectively opening millions of accounts without customers' knowledge or approval.[5] To date, the bank has paid over $4 billion in settlements resulting from the workers' and other company malfeasance.[6] In 2017, the firm announced an overhaul in how it handles incentive pay to its hundreds of thousands of employees, measuring performance not by the sheer number of accounts opened but by how actively customers use their existing accounts. At the same time, a greater fraction of compensation was shifted to base salary, away from performance-based pay. Amidst the turmoil, the company's top executive quit, having made over $37 million during his short tenure in the role.[7]

"Who gets what and why?" has preoccupied workers, employers, and those of us who study them for centuries. Debates about increasing inequality, stratospheric executive pay, and minimum-wage legislation dominate contemporary economic discourse among experts and policymakers. A rising level of worker activism, from the Fight for $15 among fast-food and retail workers to the teacher strikes that roiled one state after another in the spring of 2018, demonstrate grassroots attention to the crucial issue of pay-setting in our economy. Yet traditional explanations of what determines our pay, both commonsense and academic, focus on impersonal market forces or intrinsic characteristics of our jobs. These answers to the question of who gets what and why are empirically inadequate and increasingly unhelpful as guideposts toward a fairer future.

In 2013, President Obama proclaimed: "I believe this is the defining challenge of our time: Making sure our economy works for every working American."[8] As we enter the 2020s, the challenge remains urgent. A future in which the economy works for all requires an accurate understanding of how today's economy actually works. This book provides an important part of that by offering a perspective on pay-setting grounded in the day-to-day, routine actions of people in organizations.

In our organizations—whether large, multinational firms, government agencies, or tiny nonprofits—we negotiate over the appropriate distribution of organizational revenue. We stake claims, sometimes explicitly, often implicitly, on a slice of the organization's pie. We make these claims based on a set of available resources, and other actors within and beyond the organization validate certain sets of these claims over others.[9] These negotiations don't occur in a vacuum, and the resources that we bring to them aren't predetermined. They are dynamically shaped by four key elements: power, inertia, mimicry, and equity. Together, these channel our efforts to receive a greater share of our organization's revenue.

This account of pay-setting is rooted in organizations—with all their power dynamics and established habits, tendencies toward imitation, and equity concerns of people within them—and recognizes the many peculiarities and paradoxes we see in real-world wage disparities. Most important, it provides a pathway to a more equitable future. Why do construction workers today earn about $10,000 less per year than they did in the 1970s? Why does a Burger King worker in Denmark earn over twice as much as one in the United States? What happened to the so-called "good jobs" we have heard about in every campaign season? How have we ended up with levels of economic inequality at heights unscaled since the Gilded Age? How should a company define "performance," and how much of workers' pay should be tied to it? The account of pay-setting this book provides answers to these questions, and many more.

POWER, INERTIA, MIMICRY, AND EQUITY

Power is the ability to get one's way even in the face of opposition. All wage and salary determination involves the exercise of power and represents the outcome of past and sometimes ongoing power struggles. Power has the force to settle claims made in organizations over slices of the pie. We marshal our available resources to augment our power in wage and salary negotiations. The old Joe Hill song and labor rallying cry, "There is Power in a Union," gets at something fundamental about our workplaces: unequal power relationships. Cheery bromides about the boss's open-door policy or Walmart's "associate" label for every worker in the company can't mask a truth about the hierarchical bureaucracies in which most paycheck-drawing Americans work: some people in the building have a greater ability to get their way than others, including their way with the organization's revenue.

Power comes in various forms. Coercive power is at work when, despite a bone-deep belief that you're being underpaid, you don't openly question your salary because your boss is a vindictive tyrant who punishes any dissent. You may "consent" to your pay level by not explicitly challenging it, but you certainly don't believe it's legitimate. But when you accept your salary based on trust that your boss has your interests and those of the broader organization in mind—that's legitimate power. Power in workplaces becomes legitimated when those who are subject to it give it their consent. Lack of overt conflict does not imply, therefore, that power is absent. Indeed, the ability to instill in others a belief that the organization's pay structure "makes sense" is a core component of legitimate power.[10]

Legitimate power is an essential feature of modern workplaces, at least healthy ones, allowing us to go about our working day without being consumed with frustration or spite, or planning reprisals against our supervisors.

Over time, as power struggles play out, and especially as the outcomes are widely viewed as legitimate, inertia sets in—the second basic element underlying pay-setting. Organizational inertia is a well-documented general phenomenon.[11] Specifically with regard to pay, it is the tendency for a compensation rate associated with a given job to persist over time. For many of us, the overt, conflictual battles over pay occurred prior to our arrival at our workplace. Upon hire, we were either told exactly what we would be making or offered some small room to negotiate. This is inertia, a property of workplaces where claims made and validated in the past—before you ever started the job—determine what your job pays. Here, pay attached to particular jobs assumes a "taken-for-granted-ness," a sense that, say, the $22 per hour offered for a starting line mechanic is a legitimate wage for that particular job. You're paid what you're paid because your organization has decided that's what your job gets. Inertia doesn't mean that ongoing power dynamics are absent, just that the overt claims-making process has been temporarily settled. When workers start to believe pay levels for various jobs are just common sense, and make no explicit claims to change them, that's legitimated power helping to quell any calls for a greater share of organizational revenue. Inertia sets in, we go about our daily business, taking for granted that the numbers on our paycheck and a coworker's in the nearby cubicle make some sense.

Inertia at one organization often leads to mimicry by others. Mimicry, the third basic element influencing many of our paychecks, describes a common process through which your employer pays the going rate for your position in your industry. Many employers set their pay scales after surveying other organizations and copying their practices. Interviews with nearly five thousand employers in late 2019 and early 2020 found that three-quarters had surveyed other firms about pay within the past year; one in five reported referencing market data for one job title or another on a daily or weekly basis.[12] What this translates to is that firms in the same industry often offer similar pay for the same job titles. That $22 hourly wage for a line mechanic that has been the going rate at Ray's Best Equipment for years influences what startup Sally's Even Better Equipment offers its workers, too, because Sally commissions a market study of her competitors. In this way, a claims-making process that occurred at a workplace in the past settles into inertia and the wage level it yielded diffuses to other workplaces, thanks to imitative employers, and comes to be seen as the "natural" rate for line mechanics.

Wage surveys are one tried-and-true tactic employers use to mimic one another. For new hires, employers often use a less labor-intensive one: they simply ask you what you made in your last job. Nearly fifty percent of US workers report that their current employer used their past salary as a factor when negotiating a starting offer.[13] This constitutes another way in which inertia diffuses across workplaces. Pay rates spread across firms based on information provided by prospective employees without the employer having to conduct any further investigations into what her competitors pay. Asking about salary history is so commonplace that some states, of late, have enacted legislation to ban the practice.[14] The concern is that basing a new hire's pay on what she was paid in the past will only perpetuate a gender or racial pay gap, if the worker was discriminated against in her prior position.

Mimicry is what's going on when employers say they "pay the market rate." They may indeed do just that—but note how invoking the "market" conjures up images of implacable forces beyond human control, thereby shutting down any possible negotiation. Given that markets are unstable sites of ongoing power struggles (more on this later), a market rate, whatever it may be, can and often does change rapidly. How the market is defined, moreover, is rarely straightforward. What is determined to be part of the relevant market can make a big difference to your pay. This is certainly true for those lucky few who sit at the top of our organizational pyramids—the chief executive officers (CEOs).

One fact of our modern economy is astronomical CEO pay. We know that CEO pay is high—and we know which CEOs receive the most—because publicly traded firms and tax-exempt organizations are obligated to disclose that information. At these enterprises, boards of directors set executive compensation, and must justify the numbers they settle on to shareholders and other funders. This transparency around pay and the justifications for it have provided researchers with a wide-open arena to study market-making among our executive class. In one study, researchers from the University of Illinois and University of Wisconsin found that, in many cases, corporate boards base their pay recommendations on what CEOs in a company's core industry make—mimicry at work among our corporate titans. That's a reasonable approximation of the relevant market-based benchmarking standard. But that doesn't always happen. When boards (which are disproportionately composed of others from the executive class) feel their pay decisions are under particular legitimacy pressure—for example, when a company performs poorly or a CEO is especially highly paid, they are more likely to "selectively define peers in self-protective ways," constructing a relevant market that justifies their decisions.[15] They may do the same in situations where a company's whole industry is booming. A CEO overseeing a highly profitable company loses some of her luster—and justification for a huge raise—if the company's performance was just on par with the rest of the sector. Pulling more firms from other industries into the set used for salary comparisons can restore some of the sheen. So claiming you "pay the market rate" obscures more than it illuminates, and lends a gloss of technical wizardry to what is often a rather subjective process, and one that can involve a fair bit of creativity. Better simply to say the organization mimicked what its peers were doing.

Employers don't only mimic what other companies are doing in pay-setting because it's an easy shortcut through an otherwise winding, thorny pathway to determining who deserves what (as we'll see in Chapter 4). They also mimic to maintain a notion of equity among their workers. Equity—the notion of paying fairly—is the final basic element underlying pay-setting. As the organizational psychologist J. Stacy Adams wrote over a half-century ago, "The fairness of an exchange between employer and employee is not usually perceived by the former purely and simply as an economic matter. There is an element of relative justice involved that supervenes economics and underlies perceptions of equity or inequity."[16] Offering new employees a starting annual salary $10,000 less than what your competitors pay for the same position may make business sense from a pure accounting standpoint: your payroll costs will no doubt be lower than your peers'. But good luck luring applicants to accept your offer. Many won't, feeling that your pay is unfair.

Equity concerns affect pay determination in a range of ways. The workers at United Airlines were enraged that the company would make a portion of pay a matter of sheer luck, challenging norms of deservedness. As one United employee vented on the company's internal discussion forum: "Imagine your dismay when a colleague of yours wins through the lottery system and you know they are one of the laziest unmotivated people."[17] We think it's unfair when an undeserving colleague receives a bonus—or a shiny new Mercedes—

despite lackluster effort on the job. The old adage, "A fair day's pay for a fair day's work" gets at this notion that rewards should be tied to actual effort.

We also think it's unfair when our pay goes down. In 2017, the Missouri state legislature voted to override a decision by St. Louis's Board of Aldermen to increase that city's minimum wage, which had already been effect for three months. When the new wage law was struck down, a curious thing happened—or rather, didn't happen: many employers, now free to go back from $10 to $7.70 per hour for their lowest-paid employees, chose not to. One would think that a profit-maximizing firm faced with such a gift would jump at the opportunity to slash its operating expenses, yet over a hundred businesses didn't budge. An owner of a diner explained his decision to keep wages where they were: "It makes business sense for retention and morale."[18] Other employers did accept the gift from the state legislature to reduce their payroll costs. Predictably, the pay cut left their workers feeling (literally) shortchanged. A local McDonald's franchisee was one business owner that reverted back to the prior minimum wage. Bettie Douglas, who had worked there for ten years, had quickly grown used to her $10 per hour wage, and didn't hold back about her employer's decision: "It's horrible. It's ridiculous. It's just ridiculous." Her perspective was that "I'm not asking them for anything I haven't earned. I've earned $10 after 10 years."[19]

The feeling of unfairness we have when asked to take a pay cut is what makes wages "sticky," in economists' colorful phrasing. Wage stickiness challenges textbook formulations of pay determination, which predict that, as demand falls for your firm's goods or services, your pay should as well. In reality, cutting pay erodes morale—it takes away something we believe we've rightfully earned, as Bettie Douglas asserted—and so employers are reluctant to do it. In fact, when the economic climate turns sour, many employers choose layoffs over pay cuts. As one employer told Truman Bewley, a Yale University economist, in Bewley's investigation into wage rigidity: "I know something real. Never cut wages. If you do, you make enemies."[20] Better instead to make friends of the remaining employees thankful they're still working, and working without any reduction in pay.

For so many of us, what we get paid is bound up in our sense of self. Cutting our pay is a form of moral injury, as another employer Bewley interviewed made clear: "A pay cut is like a criticism or an insult. Pay is so closely associated with self-worth that a cut is taken personally."[21] When setting pay, then, employers must grapple with whether the worker will find the offered wage equitable—whether she will think it's fair. Recent surveys suggest many employers are failing at this task. In one survey from late 2016, approximately half of employers reported that their workers felt they were paid fairly. One problem: only twenty percent of the workers surveyed agreed.[22]

Our sense of equity—of what's right and wrong when it comes to compensation levels—goes beyond our feelings about our own pay. Equity concerns extend to what our peers are making. Leaving my pay the same while offering raises to all my coworkers is likely to instill the same sense of unfairness as a pay cut. Minimum wage increases reverberate upward as employers scramble to adjust not only the lowest-paid employees' earnings, but also the pay of employees who were earning a bit more than the previous minimum. Maintaining relative differentials is important to satisfying many workers' equity concerns and, conversely, when these differentials are upset, some workers get upset. This is exactly what happened at Walmart after its widely praised move to raise minimum pay in 2015. Following an initial honeymoon period in the press, further reporting revealed that the retail behemoth hadn't accounted for equity concerns, and some long-standing workers were frustrated. "It took me four years to get to $10.80," one Walmart associate complained. "When minimum wage goes up we don't receive a pay increase unless we are under the minimum. . . . Apparently experience doesn't get rewarded."[23]

Equity concerns illuminate the seeming paradox that arises when firms face backlash for making what are ostensibly worker-friendly moves. Mud Bay is an employee-owned company that operates a chain of pet-supply stores in the Pacific Northwest. After Seattle increased its hourly minimum wage to $12 per hour, Mud Bay duly raised its starting pay to meet the new requirement. With new workers now starting out at a pay level that veteran workers had only recently achieved, some veteran employees called the move unfair. As the district manager summed things up, "As you're raising that bottom, it's affecting everybody."[24]

Dan Price, founder of Seattle-based credit card processor Gravity Payments, had little reason to worry about his city's minimum wage rate. Most of Gravity's employees easily cleared the old wage floor. Nonetheless, hearing from an angry employee who was struggling to keep up with Seattle's rising cost of living led Price to come up with a novel idea: instituting a minimum salary within his own company. He knew that, for someone to live in the vicinity and have a decent life, they would need more than the median household income of the rest of the United States, so he set the floor at $70,000 a year. While he was at it, he cut his own salary to that same amount. The free publicity came quickly. For his audacity, talk shows booked him, newspapers ran profiles of him, Rush Limbaugh insulted him. And many employees were thrilled—especially those whose prior salaries were far below the new minimum. For them, Price was validating an equity norm: the idea that a full-time worker should be paid enough to live comfortably, even in a high-cost city.

But not all of Price's workers were pleased. A different set of fairness concerns motivated two top employees to leave the firm, illustrating how our notions of equity can vary even within the same organization. Why? As one departing employee said, "He gave raises to people who have the least skills and are the least equipped to do the job, and the ones who were taking on the most didn't get much of a bump."[25] His perspective, that those benefiting the most from the policy change deserved it the least, was similar to the worries that United Airlines' rank-and-file employees expressed about its lottery system. A web developer quit, too, complaining that "Now the people who were just clocking in and out were making the same as me."[26]

Price's workers were making horizontal comparisons: workers levying moral judgments about the pay of their peers. While research finds that workers vary in terms of whom they compare themselves to, many of us pay particular attention to peers within our same organizations—using what scholars refer to as internal referents.[27] Discovering that Kathy in the adjacent cubicle makes more than we do can quickly lower our satisfaction with our pay, and may lead us to ask for a raise.[28] And we are more likely to quit when Kathy's raise exceeds our own.[29] Sometimes these lateral comparisons extend beyond the walls of our own workplace. Other research finds that comparisons with similar workers in different organizations also drive levels of pay satisfaction.[30]

We make vertical comparisons, too. In a recent experimental study on attitudes toward CEO pay, Esra Burak Ho finds that Americans tend to think of high CEO pay as fair only when CEOs have delivered exceptional returns for their firms.[31] Participants indicated that annual salaries above $1 million were unfairly high for average-performing CEOs. What is average CEO pay for the largest US firms today? Approximately $15.6 million, or over fifteen times what Americans think of as fair.[32] Evidently, power can trump pay equity norms, at least for those at the top of our economic pyramid. This discrepancy between what we think CEOs should make and their actual earnings shows up in other recent surveys of Americans' attitudes toward CEO pay. One from 2015 found that three-quarters of respondents felt that CEO pay was too high.[33]

The feelings of unfairness that arise from these vertical comparisons can be consequential. Lower-level managers are more likely to quit their jobs if the distance between their pay and that of the CEO grows too large.[34] Bewley's interviews with over one hundred employers suggest that, if you absolutely have to cut your workers' pay, you had better plan to cut yours, as well: "It was accepted that the pay of ordinary workers could not be cut without cutting the pay of managers proportionately by as much or more."[35] Donald J. Carty, former CEO of American Airlines, learned this lesson the hard way. When the company's unions spread the news that he had granted large executive pay increases after workers agreed to significant concessions, the resulting uproar forced the company to retract the bonuses—Carty's own would have exceeded $1.5 million—and renegotiate the concession package. Carty's resignation soon followed.[36]

Horizontal and vertical comparisons—and the norms of equity we bring to them—are an integral feature of the pay-setting process. As Carty discovered, employers ignore them at their peril. This can be tricky since, as the case of Gravity Payments shows, different people hold different ideas about what's equitable. But certain norms are pretty consistent, rooted in deep-seated psychological tendencies such as loss aversion—the idea that "losses loom larger than gains."[37] Because workers are more likely to react negatively to pay cuts than positively to increases, most employers are reluctant to cut worker pay even in the most adverse business environment.

Other notions of fairness can be quite widespread but vary across place and time. Japanese manufacturing employees who earn significantly more than their coworkers in the same plant report feelings of discomfort; workers with similar advantages in US factories don't.[38]

As we'll explore in detail in Chapter 5, when George Romney was chairman and president of American Motors Corporation, he rejected salary increases that his board approved for him, believing that out-earning his workers by a huge margin was unprincipled. Perhaps other business leaders of his era felt similarly, as the typical ratio of top to average salaries in organizations back then pales in comparison to what we see today. The subsequent explosion of executive compensation has plenty of causes, but one is a rather dramatic shift in our corporate elite's "pay norms."[39] Thanks to changing notions of what's equitable, a level of compensation once regarded as offensively high is now considered the CEO's just desserts.

POWER, INERTIA, MIMICRY, AND EQUITY are the four basic elements shaping our pay. Of the four, power drives decisions most, since a change in power relations can upend existing inertial practices, re-shaping what gets mimicked and what's considered equitable. Yet, as we'll see, all four elements are central to understanding who gets what in our modern economy. Their dynamic forces play out in organizations, as workers, employers, and other actors stake claims to portions of the organizational revenue. Often, organizational inertia prevails: our room to negotiate is limited by past power struggles that, over time, legitimize a salary or wage for a particular job. Organizational inertia is evident when we think of a job as "naturally" paying a certain amount. Mimicry, meanwhile, simplifies the pay-setting process for employers while simultaneously assuaging core equity concerns. Paying the going rate in a particular labor market helps stave off workers' claims that the salary on offer is unfair. But pay norms change and vary among workers, meaning that no employer can expect to be wholly free of disgruntled workers who believe they're not receiving their fair share.[40]

Plenty of people in the world have devoted serious thought to pay. What can a new approach add to the prominent academic and lay understandings of the topic? Quite a lot. Chapter 2 explores how his four-element model diverges from other explanations of pay-setting. Dominant understandings fall into two broad camps. One suggests that earnings stem from individual performance—that, broadly speaking, our paychecks reflect the value we add to our organizations. The academic anchor for this understanding is the human capital theory of wages and salaries. From the classic human capital model we are taught that workers' pay is commensurate with their productivity—their contributions to their workplace.[41] From this influential perspective, individual contributions—potential and realized—to our workplace's revenue constitute *the* key factor determining what we take home at the end of the day. I challenge this model of pay. My account, by foregrounding the importance of organizations and relations within them, relegates human capital—our job-relevant skills and experience—to a lesser role, just one factor among many influencing our share of the pie.

The second camp emphasizes the importance of occupations in structuring pay distributions. The occupation itself, meaning the type of job we do, and the training, education, and licensing required to obtain and perform that job—that's what determines our pay. Engineers get paid a lot, comparatively speaking, while fast-food workers get paid a little. This camp's emphasis is not incompatible with the focus of the first dominant camp. The second would point out that engineers, on average, earn more than fast-food employees, perhaps because of the greater training and skills required to become an engineer, but adherents of the human capital model could still emphasize that some engineers earn a lot more than others, perhaps because they contribute more to their workplaces than engineers earning less. A common shorthand to capture both these presumptions is to say we're

paid our market value. Our pay reflects the supply of and deman
for workers in our occupation, combined with how well we perform in that occupation. Both explanations are widely accepted
and both tell us something about pay determination in the moder
economy. But this book is about their flaws.

Obviously, individual performance matters. If I were to sneak
into an orthopedic surgeons' unit and manage to pass myself off as
physician, my pay would soon plummet to zero based on abysma
performance in a job for which I lack all relevant skills. The skill
that determine our workplace performance provide an important justification for claiming a greater share. But skill is just one potentia
factor among many. Our pay is determined likewise by varying level
of competition in product and labor markets. These forces set constraints on the claims-making process. If my firm produces a produc
for which the market dries up and its revenue plummets below zero
no amount of claims-making resources will legitimize my deman
for a giant bonus. And if, in a period of high unemployment, employers have a glut of potential replacements at the ready, my clair
for a greater share isn't likely to succeed. Like the skill sets worker
bring with them to the job, these market forces are simply potentia
sources of legitimacy, among many others, that actors within organizations can use in negotiating shares of available revenues.

While my account departs from these two prominent explanations of pay, it is anchored in theoretical and empirical work across
range of disciplines. Most notably, I adopt the relational inequality
perspective, with its attention to inter- and intra-organizational dynamics and its emphasis on power struggles as a fundamental force
shaping inequality—in my case, by applying this lens to wage and salary
inequality.[42] Recent empirical research on the importance of firms in
determining pay helps substantiate the relational inequality contention that organizations are the central sites of pay-setting.[43] I share
with a growing number of labor economists the conviction that labo

market imperfections are not anomalies to be set aside, but rather the norm. These scholars' emphases on employers' inherent market power in wage-setting, and the various ways in which employers generate power from frictions in labor markets, influence my own explorations into employers' efforts to restrict labor market competition.[44] Organizational scholars' ideas about path-dependence, the stability of organizational forms, and "founding effects" motivate the inclusion of pay inertia in my account.[45] A different strain of organizational scholarship focuses on the "isomorphism"—or imitation—so common in organizational fields.[46] I document an analogous process of mimicry in pay-setting. Equity concerns in pay-setting have long interested scholars. In particular, certain versions of the efficiency wage theory—labor economists' explanations for why firms pay above-market wages—focus on equity issues in workplaces.[47]

The fundamental building blocks of this account can be traced to prior work, but nowhere have these been combined in one overarching explanation for pay. It's an account that differs from prevailing viewpoints not only within the academy, but among the broader public, as well. It's relatively simple to document what academics believe about pay determination—we write for a living, so it's just a matter of working one's way through some thickets of abstruse prose and formulas. Capturing what the public believes about pay-setting is trickier. With few exceptions, we haven't asked workers or their employers how they understand their pay. So that's what I did: I commissioned a survey of approximately 1,100 full-time workers, asking them to reflect on why they earn what they earn. I then fielded a survey of 161 senior human resource managers and other executives whose responsibilities include setting pay, asking how they go about making compensation decisions. Would these managers, if given the chance, change anything about pay determination? To find out, I included a question about whether their current practices aligned with their ideals about pay-setting.

The findings of these surveys are detailed in the second half of Chapter 2. They reveal that standard academic and common understandings of wage and salary determination align pretty well. Workers and pay-setters generally agree that workers' pay is driven by their market value—some combination of individual skills and experience and the jobs in which they are employed. These taken-for-granted assumptions are widespread, often uncontested, and quite misleading.

This introductory chapter has already asserted that prevailing explanations for why we earn what we earn are inadequate and distorted accounts of pay-setting in modern economies. The chapters in Parts II and III detail exactly why. Chapters 3 through 5, comprising Part II, explore all the ways in which the "pay for performance" understanding of wages and salaries presents an incomplete picture of contemporary pay-setting. This human capital model of pay determination rests on the assumption of a more-or-less free and fair labor market—one with open competition, in which workers are aware of their value and the value of others and are free to take their services to the organization willing to pay them the most. Chapter 3 highlights an important and often-overlooked fact of our economy. Employers act to restrict competition, obscure workers' value, and impede their mobility. These efforts extend well beyond the comparatively well-known maneuvers to stifle competition in product and service markets. There are also numerous ways in which companies limit competition in labor markets. Of late, many of these tactics have successfully shifted power away from workers toward their employers in claims-making over shares of organizational revenue. They include rampant use of noncompete clauses in contracts, no-hire rules quietly agreed upon among competing firms, and secrecy policies that inhibit workers from finding out what their peers make. The consequences are felt in paychecks, especially as employers mimic one another, diffusing these competition-stifling practices throughout entire industries.

Chapter 4 investigates the ongoing quest in many organizations to measure and track pay, and peg it to individual performance, and the unintended consequences that often follow. Many of us are employed in jobs in which our contributions to our workplace are intertwined with the efforts of others. Disentangling our individual value-added is impossible, not because we haven't created the right measure yet but because the right measure can never exist. Equally important, in modern workplaces measures of individual productivity are rarely objective and widely agreed upon. This opens up space for definitional disputes that devolve into power struggles over what skills and work experiences fuel productivity and should be deemed worthy of high pay. At Wells Fargo, until recently, the skills deemed most pay worthy were the ones required to maximize the number of accounts held by each customer. That changed when it became clear, within and outside the organization, that this particular definition of worker productivity had created the incentive for rampant fraud. We see such fights in every kind of "knowledge worker" occupation, from disputes in journalism over how to quantify reporters' performance to battles roiling schools over how to measure teachers' contributions to their students' achievement. The difficulty of teasing apart individual contributions in many types of work, and the fights over what productivity means in others, haven't soured all employers on the idea of pay-for-performance. Chapter 4 closes with a look at the consequences. It turns out that ranking and stacking employees and paying them based on proxy measures for productivity can lead to infighting, decreased cooperation, and general breakdowns of workplace cohesion. The quest to motivate high achievement by pegging pay to individual performance can cause overall performance to suffer.

Not all the actors influencing pay are within the four walls of the organization. The rise of "shareholder capitalism" has had many hotly debated consequences for our economy. In Chapter 5 I investigate one: what the mantra of "shareholders know best" has meant for average worker pay. In recent decades, investors' successful calls for maximal returns have left workers at many companies scrambling for crumbs. This fundamental shift in power among organizational claimants upended long-standing ways of doing business and destabilized existing notions of equity, leading to a whole new set of practices for organizations to mimic. Paying workers for the value they add gets harder when the boss's bosses on Wall Street want more of that value to go to shareholders.

Part III turns to the idea that pay is an inherent feature of the jobs that we do. Chapter 6 tackles the myth of "good jobs," like manufacturing and mining work, examining the variation in wages and working conditions associated with these jobs in different times and places. What is rarely mentioned in all the political rhetoric about resurrecting the so-called good jobs that once formed the backbone of America's middle class is that plenty have already returned. The problem is, most aren't so good. Many are downright awful. There is nothing inherent about a job that makes it good or bad—the wages and working conditions attached to the job are what make all the difference. In recent decades, the power dynamics, norms of equity, mimicry, and inertia practices have fundamentally altered the daily experience of workers in jobs still commonly conceived as "good." Many of these jobs are anything but.

If good jobs can be bad, then the upside is that bad jobs can be made good. Chapter 7 explores how. Cross-national comparisons reveal a wide range of pay and working conditions attached to many jobs currently understood as bad in the United States. A look at our own recent history suggests some of the bad jobs of today used to be pretty good. And that's a good thing too, because, contrary to the political promises of many elected officials, there is little reason to believe that manufacturing and mining firms are going to employ the large share of the workforce they once did. What then are the jobs of the future? Given an aging population and the continued expansion of education, our government predicts a need for millions of nurses, home healthcare aides, and educators of all kinds. We'll also need millions of workers to staff our retail outlets, serve us our food, slaughter and prepare the animals that make up our diet, and pick up our trash and haul it away, predictions of radical technological revolution notwithstanding.[48] Some of these jobs, like home healthcare aides and meatpacking workers, currently offer rock-bottom pay, few if any benefits, and meager protections. Others, such as my own job of professor, are morphing into winner-take-all markets with a lucky, tenured few prevailing over legions of contingent faculty barely able to make ends meet. The bright side is that, by thinking of jobs not as inherently well or poorly paying, we can begin to imagine strategies to make the jobs of tomorrow pay like those quintessential middle-class jobs that once sustained a large and growing middle class.

Part IV explores the implications of contemporary pay-setting for some of the most pressing problems facing our country, and offers suggestions about how to reform our workplaces to ensure workers receive their fair share. Chapter 8 links current compensation practices to rising economic inequality. For years now, debates about inequality have focused on the relative contributions of three major trends: rising returns to skill, institutional shifts that privilege certain groups of workers over others, and increasingly aggressive "rent-seeking" by the powerful. Those who emphasize the role of skills point to lagging college completion rates that have left a large portion of the workforce unable to perform the high-paying jobs of the twenty-first-century economy. The result is "productivity inequality," as *New York Times* columnist David Brooks writes, with too many workers unqualified to fill the high-tech jobs that pay well.[49] Those who emphasize the role of major institutional changes point to the declining real value of the federal minimum wage and the collapse of private sector unions, which have worked in combination to leave the middle and lower end of the occupational spectrum more exposed to market forces. As has been lamented by a growing chorus of journalists, policymakers, and academics, the powerful have grown more adept at extracting "rents," or incomes above and beyond what their skills and efforts would receive in perfectly competitive markets.

But without focusing on the role of the organizations in which inequality is generated—our workplaces—and what goes on among the people within them, these debates cannot account for what's happened to the distribution of economic rewards during the past decades. The perspective that emphasizes rising returns to skill is grounded in the human capital account of pay-setting, an account this book challenges. The view that stresses institutional changes, meanwhile, too often overlooks that these result from long-term power shifts within workplaces that altered the terrain of claims-making, disadvantaging average and low-paid workers. And the rent perspective is predicated on the notion that one can subtract a worker's true earnings from the portion artificially inflated by rent-generating practices. But individual productivity is rarely objective, and often unmeasurable. Moreover, rent-generation is an integral feature of labor markets, not an anomaly. Efforts by groups of actors within organizations to restrict other groups' access to revenue while hoarding as much as possible for themselves occur in various forms in all labor markets. The challenge here is not to rid the labor market of rent. As I detail in the second half of the chapter, it's about understanding who is successful at claiming a large share of organizational resources, and who is left out.

If pay isn't some predetermined, rigid reflection of productivity or the type of work someone does, then we can imagine a different world in which a dominant trend of our current economy—ever-rising inequality, marked by stagnant pay for average workers and runaway salaries for those at the top of the distribution—is reversed. Chapter 9 explores how that transformation could happen. I argue that it's a matter of reshaping power relations within our workplaces, overcoming the employer inertia that has institutionalized poor pay in many fast-growing occupations, and instituting new high-road practices that other employers will be inspired to mimic. I focus on policy levers that can shift power dynamics within our workplaces, especially those that arm average workers with resources to negotiate greater shares. We should, for example, radically update our obsolete labor laws to promote, as opposed to inhibit, collective mobilization of workers as they confront employers in the claims-making process. I'll also explore how a new incentive structure at the federal, state, and local level could reward those pioneering firms willing to take the high road. I'll resurrect some past strategies to prevent unfair pay practices such as the much-maligned seniority pay structures and tying pay to job classifications.

Part III dispels with the notion that our wages reflect inherent characteristics of our jobs, and Part IV extends that line of thinking to argue that attaching pay to job title is one way to combat rising inequality, provided that those jobs currently underpaid get a boost while those at the top of the income distribution see their salaries reduced. Together these changes will help align our economy with what the majority of Americans think of as fair: lower incomes for those at the top, and higher pay for those at the middle and bottom.[50] Collectively, they represent a straightforward answer to the question of how to ensure the economy works for all hard-working Americans. You pay them more.

2 WHAT DO WE THINK DETERMINES OUR PAY?

IN 2018, Stephen Schwarzman netted a healthy $786.5 million as head of the private equity firm Blackstone Group.[1] Did he *earn* that much? Was he paid what he was worth? Unsurprisingly, he seemed to think so. Back in 2010, he wasn't quite as rich as today, but by any measure he was phenomenally rich. He was also outraged over an Obama Administration proposal to close the "carried interest" loophole—a provision that taxes private equity compensation at the (low) capital gains rate, instead of as ordinary income. He likened the president's idea to "war. . . . It's like when Hitler invaded Poland in 1939."[2] He needn't have worried, and probably could have kept the controversial analogy to himself: the proposal failed. The carried interest loophole carried the day, and still does, although it was slightly modified in 2017's Tax Cuts and Jobs Act.

Schwarzman's affront stemmed from what was apparently a deep-seated conviction that he *deserved* all of those millions, and that attempts to take more of his hard-earned money away were immoral acts of confiscation. He's not alone in the belief that runaway incomes at the top of the distribution are deserved. George Mason's Tyler Cowen explains rising executive pay as the natural outcome of improvements in CEO performance, writing that: "CEOs . . . really have upped their game relative to the performance of many other workers in the American economy."[3] Harvard's Greg Mankiw similarly claims that "the most natural explanation of high C.E.O. pay is that the value of a good C.E.O. is extraordinarily high."[4]

This presumption that pay reflects our performance runs through elite discourse and political debate about the bottom of the occupational spectrum. Tennessee Senator Lamar Alexander is considered a wise old sage among his colleagues, a "senator's senator," and a "bi-partisan dealmaker."[5] Yet when asked in 2013 whether he supported *abolishing* the minimum wage—stuck at the poverty level of $7.25 an hour—he didn't hesitate: "That's correct."[6] This wasn't the opinion of a young ideological upstart still in thrall to Ayn Rand. In 2013, Alexander was in his seventies, had previously served as a cabinet official, been governor of his home state, and been president of the University of Tennessee. It wasn't a one-off, misguided musing either. Alexander reiterated the stance a few years later, after Amazon announced it would support an increase in the federal minimum wage.[7] And as chair of the Senate's Labor Committee, Alexander's words mattered. They all but ensured that no federal bill to increase the minimum wage would emerge from the Senate any time soon.

Schwarzman and Alexander are united in the belief that the market, and the market alone, should determine people's pay. From this perspective, Schwarzman's vast wealth reflects the market rewarding him for his financial ingenuity. Any attempt to lower his posttax earnings only disturbs the workings of the free market. Same for those McDonald's employees earning the minimum wage: governmental interference that creates a wage floor distorts the free operation of the market, in this case leading to fewer jobs for low-skill workers. Let the market work unimpeded and, sure, some workers may toil away for $4 or $5 an hour. But that is what their work is clearly worth. Otherwise, employers wouldn't pay so little.

Cowen and Mankiw aren't the only academics who subscribe to the idea that, at a fundamental level, our pay reflects our performance. As we'll see, it's an idea firmly anchored in scholarship. So, too, is the conviction that our pay differences are driven by our different occupations. These two ideas have dominated ideas about pay, only lately to be challenged by dissenters. And these core beliefs aren't limited to the ivory tower. Most workers and pay-setters also subscribe to variations of the notion that our pay reflects our individual performance and our occupation.

WHAT SCHOLARS SAY

What passes for a unified theory of pay determination in the academic literature is grounded in the neoclassical economics framework. This human capital model holds that the price of labor is set according to the laws of supply and demand, just as prices are set for other goods and services. According to this perspective, three fundamental factors go into establishing a given worker's wage: that individual's contribution to organizational revenue; the level of market demand for the organization's products or services; and the competitiveness of the labor market. Rational workers want to maximize their wage and therefore seek out the highest bidders for their labor. Rational employers want to maximize firm profitability and will seek out productive workers who will accept the lowest wage on offer. Wages approach equilibrium as underpaid workers move to organizations that will pay them most for their contributions, and competition in the markets for products and services disciplines overly generous employers so that they either lower their wages or go out of business.[8]

Assuming adequate competition in product and labor markets (a big assumption, as we'll explore in Chapter 3), the primary factor influencing wages and salaries, then, is workers' marginal productivity. What does that mean? Only the occasional lucky worker is the scion of a wealthy business leader and reports for duty in the family trade as a matter of birthright. The vast majority of us are hired on the basis of what an employer believes we can contribute to an organization. From the human capital perspective, our contribution is the additional revenue we add to the firm, otherwise known as the marginal product of our labor. Our wage reflects the amount of money an organization would forego by not hiring us—nothing more and nothing less.[9]

Because precise measurements of a worker's marginal product are illusive (if not impossible, as we'll see in Chapter 4), researchers typically use common human capital indicators such as education and relevant experience as proxies. Scholars differentiate between general human capital, or the set of skills and expertise that can be carried from organization to organization, and firm-specific human capital, or skills that apply only to a certain place of employment. Some models suggest employers underpay workers for their firm-specific human capital, since this type of expertise isn't transferable to competitors. Others suggest that even those workers who have accumulated a great deal of firm-specific human capital receive their marginal product, especially over the long run.[10] All versions of the theory align on the idea that a worker's marginal productivity provides the baseline from which to assess his or her pay.

It's an elegant theory, and one that many scholars realize works best only in theory. Labor economists have long recognized the ways in which the neoclassical model of pay oversimplifies what happens in the real world. In *The Theory of Wages*, first published in 1932, J. R. Hicks notes the "peculiar properties" that differentiate labor markets from other markets for goods and services.[11] One of these peculiar properties is what economists refer to as nominal wage rigidity, or the well-established empirical finding that wage cuts are much rarer than you'd expect given the supply-and-demand framework.[12] As market demand recedes during a recession, the human capital model predicts employers adjust by lowering pay. In fact, that rarely happens, with many preferring to lay workers off while keeping nominal wages constant for those that remain, a textbook example of wage stickiness. Why? Cutting pay lowers morale for the remaining workers, as it violates our sense of fairness. And the unlucky workers now out of a job aren't around to complain.

Variations of efficiency wage theory, meanwhile, attempt to explain why is it that certain companies seem to pay their workers more than their productivity. The "gift exchange" version suggests that, unlike apples or aluminum tubes, humans have emotions that affect what contribution they make to production on any given day.[13] Paying them more engenders goodwill, higher morale, and a more dedicated, hardworking set of subordinates. A variant on this suggests that certain employers pay more than the market rate because of monitoring problems.[14] If the boss isn't around all the time to make sure we're on task, why not loaf on the job? A fat paycheck might lower the temptation to shirk.

Other scholars have taken power seriously and added measures of it to studies of pay-setting. Decades ago, economists David Blanchflower, Andrew Oswald, and Mario Garrett described wage determination as the "cutting of a cake into two pieces" where the "side with the greater power obtains the larger slice."[15] Workers and employers constitute the two sides, and bargaining power established by the market gives one or the other the upper hand in negotiations. By placing power dynamics at the center of pay determination, research in this mold shifts the emphasis away from a focus on autonomous workers and their skill sets. Of late, increasing numbers of academics have joined this movement, emphasizing the role of employer power in labor markets.[16] And recently, a growing body of research has investigated how firms matter in shaping pay. It seems your human capital may be worth a whole lot less at one company than at another, with the rise of superstar firms offering superstar pay packages to those lucky enough to have been hired by Facebook instead of, say, Myspace.[17]

Other researchers have noted numerous additional complications and limitations with the human capital model of wage-setting. These include difficulties in measuring marginal productivity, a topic of Chapter 4. As Bloomberg's Noah Smith writes, "it's very hard to actually know how much revenue a company would lose by firing an individual."[18] Yet many who recognize its limitations retain the human capital model as a baseline approximation and a standard against which we can measure any departure from its core tenet that workers are paid their marginal productivity. As the University of Oregon's Mark Thoma notes, the model is useful as "an idealized benchmark to evaluate actual markets."[19]

Academics find the model especially useful when analyzing market failures. In analyses of income distributions, "economic rent" does not refer to the monthly payment you hand over to your landlord in return for use of the apartment you love. Instead it describes returns on an asset, such as labor, that exceed what is necessary to keep the asset in production in a competitive market.[20] In the case of labor, any compensation beyond what it would take for an employee to keep showing up to work constitutes economic rent to that worker. A shorthand way of understanding rent in this sense is that it is the premium some workers receive due to a market failure of some sort.

The effort to analyze "rent-sharing," or how this additional money is distributed among workers in an organization, is not new.[21] Recently, however, academics studying it have highlighted the many ways in which modern labor markets fail, enabling certain groups of workers to capture rent at the expense of other workers and consumers. Between economists and other social scientists, a rising chorus blames rising rents, and their unequal distribution, for the explosion of income inequality in the United States in recent decades.[22]

Jonathan Rothwell argues that well-functioning markets that reward merit naturally result in lower inequality because the variation in individual productivity isn't that large.[23] Rent capture has distorted this process, pulling incomes apart. Nobel laureate Angus Deaton agrees, offering that "we could sharply reduce inequality itself if rent-seeking were to be somehow reduced."[24] Dismantling consolidated corporate power would increase competition throughout the economy, giving workers the chance to earn what they deserve—their marginal productivity.

Other academics are trying to patch cracks in the human capital edifice. In contrast to the growing attention to the role of market failures in our modern economy is the idea that, when it comes to determining and rewarding individual worker productivity, the market has never worked so well. Countering Noah Smith's contention that capturing marginal productivity remains exceedingly difficult, Tyler Cowen argues that improved measures of individual worker performance are an underlying driver of inequality. Cowen writes, "As we get better at measuring who produces what, the pay gap between those who make more and those who make less grows."[25] Yale Law School's Daniel Markovits echoes Cowen, lamenting a modern economy that, by increasingly rewarding merit, spurs runaway inequality and enables a self-perpetuating elite.[26] For those whose productivity lags, journalist Noam Scheiber warns: "The only safe employees are those in occupations where it's difficult to measure a worker's individual contribution to the bottom line."[27] From this perspective, methodological advances in capturing individual performance mean such safe harbors are quickly disappearing.

No one has better encapsulated than Lawrence Summers the viewpoint that the fundamental tenet of the human capital model—the idea that we're paid our marginal productivity—isn't just an "idealized benchmark," but increasingly an empirical reality. Summers's long and storied career includes stints as chief economist at the World Bank, treasury secretary in the Clinton administration, president of Harvard University, and director of the National Economic Council in the Obama administration. Early in his term in the Obama White House, Summers pinpointed what he saw as a cause of rising pay gaps in the US labor market: "One of the reasons that inequality has probably gone up in our society is that people are being treated closer to the way that they're supposed to be treated."[28]

WHAT (OTHER) SCHOLARS SAY

While many academics interested in pay-setting rely on the human capital model, at least as an idealized approximation from which to measure current deviations, other social scientists emphasize the importance of occupations in setting pay rates. In particular, closure theory argues that occupational incumbents—think here of your friendly dentist, veterinarian, or nail technician—close ranks and maintain resources for themselves by creating barriers of entry to others.[29] Chief among these are legal requirements, such as the particular licenses needed to practice law, perform surgery, and, in a growing number of states, paint customers' nails. Today, about a quarter of the US workforce requires a license to practice, a fivefold increase from the 1950s.[30] Research indicates that license holders enjoy a 15 percent wage advantage over similar workers who lack a license.[31] Licensing raises barriers to entry, reducing competition among occupational incumbents, while giving the license holders greater control over the supply of labor in their occupation.[32] In this way, scholars have linked closure theory to rent-seeking behavior—except that, in this version, the primary extractors of rent aren't powerful corporations but occupations. Rent-seeking among occupational incumbents is common in part because belonging to an occupation provides a social glue that helps overcome collective action problems. For many of us, part of our identity is wrapped up in our occupation—in the type of work we do. As a result, we share a common identity with others who work similar jobs. Occupational-based organizations, such as the American Medical Association for physicians or the American Psychological Association for psychologists, strengthen this collective identity and help coordinate action to protect the perquisites of certain jobs.

In the absence of outright licensing requirements, these professional organizations or other entities may offer certifications to qualified workers that signal a special training or skill set. Certification, even where it is not legally required, can serve the same purpose as licensing. It erects barriers between those who've completed the certification and those who haven't, decreasing competition and allowing the certified to extract more rent. Educational credentialing is another way in which occupational incumbents police their boundaries and restrict new entrants. I might have decided, many years back, that I should jump straight from my undergraduate training to become a professor. But no institution would have offered me a position or a paycheck without my having a PhD, the requisite degree to teach at a university.

This constant policing of occupational boundaries usually hums along unnoticed as background noise in our busy working lives. If you're a practicing attorney in California, you have to complete twenty-five credit hours of continuing legal education every three years. On the one hand, you can look at this requirement as crucial training to keep attorneys current on important developments in the law. On the other hand, you might recognize it as a tool to sharpen occupational boundaries ensuring that those who fulfill the requirement remain in good standing with the state bar association. The same goes for a whole host of other licensing, accreditation, and degree requirements: as much as we might doubt they're essential to our job performance, or might gripe about the time and money we spend on them, we often take them for granted as integral features of our occupations. It's only in the rare instances when fights erupt around these closure practices that their contingent nature is revealed. While most battles over occupational boundaries were settled in decades long past, some continue to smolder and erupt from time to time, reminding us of their origins as conflicts between powerful insiders and the outsiders who would like a piece of the action.

Take eye doctors. Rand Paul is the junior senator from Kentucky and a former presidential aspirant. But before all of that, he was a practicing, licensed ophthalmologist. And for a while, a self-licensed one. The American Board of Ophthalmology, founded in 1916, certifies eye doctors through a written and oral examination. While such board certification isn't required to practice (for that, you need only a general medical license), many hospitals and major insurance companies require it of their ophthalmologists. In 1992, the organization changed its rules, requiring eye doctors certified after that year to retake the test every decade to maintain their licenses. Doctors certified prior to 1992, however, were grandfathered under the old rules and exempt from new requirement. This angered Paul, who saw it as an imperious move by a powerful old guard that would raise the bar on new entrants to their field while leaving themselves licensed for life. So he started a rival licensing board, which charged less for certification and required periodic recertification of everyone, hoping to put pressure on the American Board of Ophthalmology to change its ways.[33]

Paul's National Ophthalmology Board never took off, and within a decade he shut it down. The effort was probably doomed from the start: professional bodies like the American Board of Ophthalmology gain cultural legitimacy over time as providers of widely recognized imprimaturs. These organizations usually have boards made up of esteemed members of the profession, elected by their peers and trusted to understand and advance the interests of occupational incumbents. And as a member, you benefit from being an insider in an organization whose rules and procedures make it harder for outsiders to gain access to your occupation. A big benefit is the higher pay that comes with a reduced supply of the service you offer.

Battles between occupational incumbents and would-be entrants are ubiquitous, occurring in one form or another in every field at some point in time. In recent decades, incumbents in the professions have become increasingly adept at winning them, fortifying the boundaries dividing those with the important licensing or certifications from those without. Sometimes the power struggles can be intense—and, to outsiders, downright bewildering. Consider the years-long battle in California over the certification of plastic surgeons. In the Golden State, surgeons who are certified by the American Board of Cosmetic Surgery wanted to refer to themselves in their advertising as "board certified." Ultimately, the Medical Board of California denied them that privilege, preserving it only for members of the American Board of Plastic Surgery. Why did the MBC prefer the ABPS over the ABCS? Because the ABPS was in turn certified by the ABMS—that is, the American Board of Medical Specialties, a board that certifies other specialty boards.[34]

Closure isn't the only means by which your occupation may influence your paycheck. At a fundamental level, occupations organize the division of labor, and, some contend, certain occupations are simply more important than others in terms of accomplishing organizational goals. From this perspective, employers tend to offer higher pay to the more important occupations. Occupations are aggregates of various jobs that share core features, and provide the analytical basis by which employers construct detailed job categories.[35] Many organizations, especially large ones, go to great lengths to outline the content of various jobs to determine which ones should be "priced" higher than others. This procedure "ensures that *jobs* of higher internal and external worth are paid more than *jobs* of lower internal and external worth," according to management scholars Nina Gupta, Samantha Conroy, and John Delery.[36]

Notably, employers across a wide variety of cultural and institutional contexts tend to agree about which occupations are more or less worthy. Researchers have found remarkable consistency in occupational rankings across countries.[37] While the distance in average pay between, say, a doctor and a nurse's assistant varies, in all contexts examined the doctor makes more. And once institutionalized, the boundaries that define our occupations tend to harden, becoming a "taken for granted" aspect of our working lives even in the face of technical changes in the division of labor.[38] The daily routine of a physician today looks quite different from that of a physician working in late-nineteenth-century America, but the prestige and relative earnings accorded to physicians have been constant.

WHAT WORKERS SAY

Compared to what we know of academics' thinking, we don't know much about what workers believe determines their pay. We do have a sense of their satisfaction with their pay, and of the factors that shape their attitudes toward their wages and salaries. In terms of overall satisfaction, most recent surveys suggest a workforce that is relatively content, likely reflecting increases in average wages after years of stagnation. A 2015 survey by the Society for Human Research Management of approximately six hundred US workers found that 23 percent were "very satisfied" with their pay, and another 42 percent reported being "somewhat satisfied."[39] In 2018, I surveyed 1,100 full-time workers and asked them about pay satisfaction. Consistent with those results, 29 percent reported they were very satisfied with their current wage or salary, and another 43 percent said they were somewhat satisfied. Only 17 percent, meanwhile, were either somewhat or very dissatisfied. Another recent survey of 6,600 US workers paints a less rosy picture: just over half (54 percent) of those interviewed reported being satisfied with their level of pay.[40]

The General Social Survey has been asking Americans questions on a range of issues for decades. In some survey years it includes a question about whether workers believe their pay is fair. It first introduced the question in 2002 and found that 14 percent believed their pay was much less than they deserved. A decade and a half later, that fraction had dipped slightly to 11 percent. The portion of workers who felt their pay was about what they deserved hovered at around 50 percent between 2002 and 2018. Very few of us, meanwhile, believe we're substantially overpaid: a negligible number of respondents chose this option each year the survey included the pay fairness question.[41]

What accounts for these attitudes toward pay? The scholarly consensus is pretty clear regarding the key variables. Research has consistently found that a worker's satisfaction with a given level of pay is not automatically driven by their individual human capital—their training, acquired skills, and job experience. Surely those inputs matter: nobody would be satisfied if they had spent twenty years becoming more expert at a job and were still paid like a rookie. But you'd be especially miffed if you'd spent those decades watching your colleagues' pay increase steadily. Here again, we see equity concerns playing a starring role. One recent study of German workers' attitudes toward compensation finds that worker perceptions of whether pay is fair "are embedded in workplace environments and in specific organizational contexts."[42] Multiple studies have confirmed that satisfaction with what we make is bound up with what we think our coworkers earn. This is true even after controlling statistically for our own pay.[43]

We learned in Chapter 1 how equity concerns are a driving force behind what people make. That's partly because they are a driving force behind workers' happiness with their pay—and employers, all else being equal, prefer happier workforces, if only because workers may slack off if they are unhappy. Research confirms this rather commonsense suspicion: workers do reduce their effort and engage in more "social loafing" as dissatisfaction with pay increases.[44] David Levine's analysis of manufacturing workers' attitudes and behavior in the United States and Japan found that workers who were underpaid compared to their peers were less satisfied with their pay, reduced their efforts accordingly, and were more likely to quit their jobs altogether.[45] Similar to our actual pay, then, our feelings about our pay derive from horizontal and vertical comparisons we make to workers outside and within our organizations. It turns out that the human capital model provides a rather poor account of our actual earnings—and of our attitudes toward them.

When it comes to understanding workers' views about *why* they get paid what they do, we know very little. A survey by the Society for Human Research Management conducted in 2013 provides some insight. While it did not ask workers what they thought determined their pay, surveyors did ask how important certain factors were to their overall job satisfaction, including their base rate of pay, and being paid competitively with the local labor market. The majority of respondents indicated that these two components—their base pay, and their relative pay—were important to their overall satisfaction with their job. The ability to be paid in stock options, meanwhile, was less salient, with fewer than one in five reporting that this type of pay affected their job satisfaction.[46]

No other survey I found directly asked workers why they got paid what they did. So I commissioned one. In collaboration with the survey research firm Qualtrics, I fielded the survey in the winter of 2018. I limited respondents to those working full-time, and the resulting sample of approximately 1,100 was weighted to be representative of the full-time workforce by age, race / ethnicity, gender, and educational attainment. The sample's average age was forty-four years old, and it was 47 percent female and 64 percent non-Hispanic white. Four in ten of those surveyed had at least a college degree, while 37 percent had no more than a high school degree, and the rest had spent some time in college. Nearly 44 percent of respondents had some supervisory responsibilities at work. In terms of employment sector, 70 percent of the sample worked for a for-profit firm, 16 percent for the government, and the remainder in nonprofit organizations. Unsurprisingly, respondents were spread across a wide range of industries; among the most common were construction or manufacturing (13 percent), retail (9 percent), and finance or insurance (6 percent).

The central questions of the survey had to do with perceptions of pay. For example, one asked: "There are many reasons why an employee might be paid his / her particular wage or salary. How important do you think each of the following is in explaining pay at your main job?" The list included many factors, among them your education level, your experience (years spent doing your particular job), your seniority (years worked for your particular employer), the performance of your workplace or organization, the cost of living in your particular area, your own individual performance, and your occupation. Respondents rated each on a four-point scale ranging from "not at all important" to "very important."

In general, workers believed all the factors listed above to be at least somewhat important in pay determination, suggesting that workers conceive of pay-setting as a multifaceted process, not reducible to just a variable or two. Education is a good example: just over a third said this factor was very important in determining their pay; another third responded that it was somewhat important. Seniority and experience also stood out for the high fractions of workers indicating these were important to pay. Fully 55 percent said experience was very important; another third said it was somewhat important. Only 11 percent said seniority was unrelated to their pay. Organizational performance likewise garnered a lot of support: half the sample saw it as a very important factor in deciding their pay. Four out of five believed it was at least somewhat important.

Yet no factor received as much support as "your own individual performance." Figure 2.1 presents the breakdown of answers.[47] As displayed, two-thirds of the sample said it was a very important determinant of workers' pay—a far higher percentage than for any other factor. Another 19 percent said it was somewhat important. Combined, 85 percent of full-time workers believed their individual performance was an important basis of their pay. These high percentages do not differ appreciably between men and women or white workers and racial / ethnic minorities. There are difference by educational level: interestingly, workers with a college degree or more were slightly less likely than workers with a high school degree or less to say individual performance was very important (62 percent versus 70 percent). Compared to government employees, workers in private sector, for-profit firms were also more likely to think individual performance was very important to their pay. Still, six in ten government employees indicated that individual performance was very important.

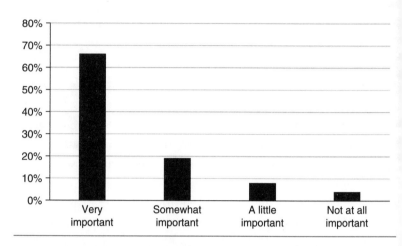

Figure 2.1   Importance of "own individual performance" to pay

Overall, then, US full-time workers believe their own individual performance is a key determinant of the number on their paycheck. Here we see congruence with the human capital model and its emphasis on individual worker's contributions to organizational revenue. What about the role of occupations in structuring pay? Compared to individual importance, a smaller fraction indicated occupation was a very important factor in determining wages and salaries. But it was still substantial: just over half the sample said occupation was a key determinant of earnings, and another third said it was somewhat important. Indeed, it ranked in the top three factors included in the survey in terms of the percentage indicating it was a very important factor determining their pay.

In Figure 2.2, factors are presented in ranked order according to the percentages of respondents who called each a very important pay influencer. As shown, no factor ranks as high as individual performance. Experience and occupation follow. None of the other potential drivers were considered very important by a majority of respondents. And

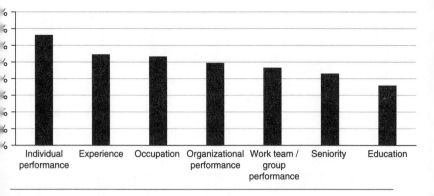

Figure 2.2   Percent saying factor is "very important" to pay

neither do any factors listed on the survey and not shown here, such as "individual negotiations" and "cost of living," exceed 50 percent.[48]

While individual performance and occupation are two popular explanations for workers' pay, Figure 2.2 also makes clear that they aren't the only things workers believe are important. Most of us, at least when pressed by a questionnaire, see pay determination as multidimensional. To probe further into other issues workers think affect their paychecks, I included an open-ended question asking respondents to name other factors influencing pay. Some pointed to fixed rates determined elsewhere, such as public sector workers who replied that their salary was set by the state legislature. Others mentioned a "standard rate for the job," indicative of how wages get attached to particular jobs, inertia sets in, and soon jobs are seen as having a natural pay range. One worker highlighted another aspect of inertia: the importance of your starting wage. "Initial salary offer followed by small or nonexistent annual increases," this respondent noted, reinforcing the message of various studies documenting the long-term effects of starting pay points, such as the years-long penalties that accrue to those who enter the labor market during a recession.[49] Finally, two workers hinted at a key theme of this book—namely, the importance of power when it comes to pay-setting. Asked about factors determining pay not already listed, they mentioned the role of the boss. "Our raises come out of the bonus our boss gets each year," wrote one, "so he decides on how much of his bonus he wants to give up." The other added the importance of "who you know," succinctly noting the role of powerful actors within networks in structuring pay.

Prior to this survey, not only did we not know much about the factors workers think *do* influence their pay, we also didn't know what factors workers think *should* influence their pay. In another question in my 2018 survey, I presented the same set of factors and four-point scale and asked respondents: "How important do you think each of the following should be in determining your pay at your main job?" Figure 2.3 displays the responses to this question in detail.

In general, the responses on the "do influence" and "should influence" questions aligned; workers felt the reasons they were paid were the right ones. A high percentage indicated, for example, that seniority should be a very important determinant of their pay, and comparatively few believed that individual negotiations with their employer should matter. A slight difference showed up in their rankings of experience as a determinant of their wage or salary: fully 61 percent said experience should be very important, whereas 55 percent had said they believed it actually was very important. Once again, no factor garnered as much support as individual performance. Workers actually indicated the factor should be more important to their pay than they think it is: fully 92 percent ranked it as very important or somewhat important on the "should" list, and almost nobody believed it rated no importance at all.

While strong majorities of workers across sectors, education levels, races, and genders concur with the idea that individual performance

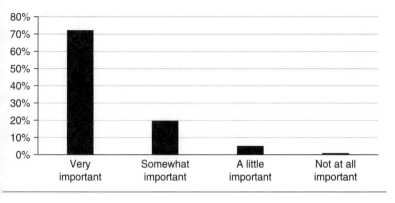

Figure 2.3　How important should "own individual performance" be to pay?

should be a very important factor in structuring pay, there are some notable differences between groups. Three-quarters of those working in private sector, for-profit firms believe this compared with two-thirds of government employees and employees of private sector non-profits. Meanwhile, workers with the lowest formal education were most likely to believe that individual performance should be very important in deciding pay: fully 80 percent of workers without a high school degree subscribe to this notion. And women were slightly more likely than men (74 percent to 71 percent) to express this belief.

Figure 2.4 displays the percentages of workers who believe various factors should be very important in determining their pay. The relative rankings of choices mirrors those shown in Figure 2.2, with the exception of experience. Given the high percentages for multiple characteristics, it's clear that many full-time workers today not only think their pay is based on a number of factors, but also think it should be.

Open-ended responses to the question about what should influence workers' pay provided a few suggestions beyond the ten characteristics specifically listed. One worker felt loyalty to the organization

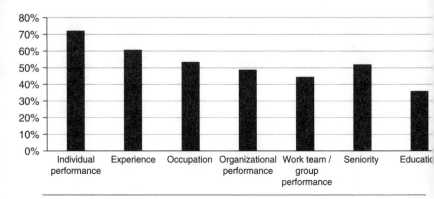

Figure 2.4   Percent saying factor should be "very important" to pay

should be rewarded; another took the prize for unorthodox ideas by suggesting pay should be pegged to a worker's family composition.[50] A couple of respondents suggested that attendance should be a key factor.

Finally, one respondent wrote: "I think that the wages of those doing similar jobs should be played into it. I understand certain factors relating to performance and skill that may influence pay, but within reason for those that do a similar job at a similar level, the pay of one person should be similar to another's." By proposing "equal pay for equal work," this worker was invoking a notion often heard in contemporary gender discrimination discussions. It is a principle that guides pay-setting at many organizations. What's interesting is how rarely this standard emerges in academic or lay discussions about pay-setting, aside from debates about gender pay gaps. On a superficial level, it's an idea consistent with the occupational model of pay determination. But that model ties pay to features inherent in the occupation itself, not to a notion that maintains, as the worker quoted above does, that paying people similarly for doing similar work is a fair way to distribute organizational resources.

WHAT PAY-SETTERS SAY

Only rarely have researchers asked those actually in charge of setting pay how they do it. For many, the dominance of the human capital model obviates any need to question employers about their behavior. It doesn't help that interview research is uncommon in modern labor economics, the field in which questions about who makes how much money and why are so central. But a few researchers have done just that: they've actually talked to pay-setters about their approaches to setting wages and salaries.

One is Truman Bewley, whose work I briefly noted in Chapter 1. Bewley was puzzled about the stickiness of wages, and the related pattern of employers' being more likely to cut workers during a recession than to cut pay. During the economic downturn of the early 1990s, Bewley went out and talked to hundreds of managers, labor leaders, and business consultants. One overall impression he took away from these conversations was that any monocausal understanding of pay couldn't capture the messy, complex, real world of wage determination: "Fieldwork makes obvious the enormous variety in the economic world."[51] That truth will prove to be a background theme of this book. He also discovered just how crucial equity concerns are to pay-setting, finding that it often makes more business sense to let some workers go than to reduce workers' pay. As he writes, "the advantage of layoffs over pay reduction is that they 'get the misery out the door,'" rather than leaving a company with a workforce aggrieved by wage cuts.[52]

Another investigation into wage rigidity, conducted at about the same time as Bewley's interviews, broadly echoes his findings. Carl Campbell III and Kunal Kamlani surveyed nearly two hundred firms to discover why employers so rarely reduced workers' pay. Internal equity issues proved paramount. As they conclude, "Most firms appear to keep wage differentials between workers smaller than productivity differentials because they are concerned that large wage differentials for similar workers would be harmful to morale."[53]

PayScale is an internet business that collects compensation information from workers. Periodically it also surveys employers about their compensation practices, asking, among other questions, what factors led firms to issue raises to their employees in the prior year, whether they offer performance-based pay, and if so, what levels of performance—organizational, team, or individual—they reward. PayScale's 2017 survey of over seven thousand organizations in the United States and Canada indicated that the top reasons employers handed out bonuses were for performance, market adjustments, rises in the cost of living, retention of certain employees, and adjustments to rectify internal pay inequities.[54] While the emphasis on performance (broadly defined) is generally consistent with a human capital theory of pay determination, other reasons on the list are not. Market adjustments and retention offers speak to organizations mimicking one another. Maintaining internal equity and keeping up with workers' rising cost of living reflect employers' sensitivity to workers' understandings about what's fair.

Bewley's advice was that "it is well worth the effort to get out of the office and face economic reality rather than invent it."[55] Building off his and others' work, I decided to ask people involved in setting wages and salaries how they went about this crucial task (although, to be honest, I rarely had to leave the office to accomplish this). In the spring of 2019, again in collaboration with the Qualtrics survey research firm, I conducted a survey of pay-setters. To generate a sample limited to those in positions in which a core function was determining the pay of other employees, I asked the following question of full-time workers: "As part of your job, do you make decisions about compensation at your workplace?" I screened out anyone who did not. I further limited the sample to those who indicated that their job title was one of the following: human resources manager, human resources associate or assistant, business executive, mid-level manager, or business owner.

The resulting sample of 161 respondents worked full-time in a variety of managerial and executive positions and included a number of human resources executives and directors, a chief financial officer, a chief information officer, a handful of CEOs, and numerous other top-level managers. The sample was 55 percent male, indicative of gender imbalance at the top of many corporate ladders. Three-quarters of the sample were white non-Hispanic, with an average age of forty-one. Unsurprisingly, given the choice of job titles, the overwhelming majority of respondents had at least a bachelor's degree, and a third held advanced degrees. Over 80 percent of respondents worked for private, for-profit firms, with the rest almost evenly split between nonprofit and public sector organizations. A number of industries were represented. About 10 percent of the sample worked in health-care, 9 percent in manufacturing, and 14 percent in professional or business services. A majority of respondents worked in firms with a hundred or more workers, and over a third worked in organizations with five hundred or more employees.[56]

The survey included a number of items related to pay-setting. One asked: "How important is starting pay in determining long-term compensation at your work?" Nearly two-thirds of the sample responded that it was very important; another third said that it was important. Whatever initial salary you do or don't negotiate upon hire has long-term ramifications.

The core question about pay determination echoed one from the worker survey discussed previously: it asked respondents to reflect on

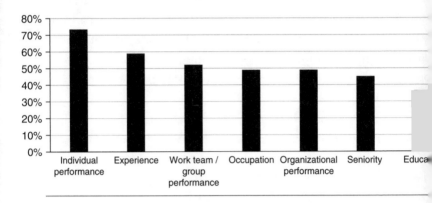

Figure 2.5   Percent saying factor is "very important" to pay

what factors they considered important when setting compensation
levels for employees. Specifically, the item reads: "There are many
reasons why an employee might be paid his / her particular wage or
salary. How important do you consider each of the following when
you determine other employees' compensation at your job?" Essentially the same factors included in the employee survey were listed.
Figure 2.5 displays results for those categories that received high percentages of "very important" responses, in descending order. (Not
shown are some factors selected by less than 50 percent of respondents, including employees' own negotiations with the employer,
and the current cost of living.) It is striking how closely the results
mirror those from the employee survey, not only in terms of the
ranking of the categories, but in the percentages choosing "very
important." About half the sample indicates that occupation, the
performance of the work team or group, and organizational performance are very important factors used to establish pay. Nearly
60 percent say that experience is very important. And, as with the
worker survey, no characteristic ranks higher than individual per-

formance. Nearly three-quarters of this group of pay-setters list it as a very important determinant of their colleagues' compensation. The small survey sample prevents much fine-grain analysis, but it is possible to see a gender breakdown in the results. Compared to men, women pay-setters were more likely to say individual performance was a very important factor in pay determination.

The survey provided pay-setters with the opportunity to write in factors they believed to be important in setting pay that were not listed. The vast majority indicated that the survey had sufficiently covered the reasons. But a few responded to this open-ended question. One simply highlighted the multifaceted nature of pay determination, saying "It has so many factors." Another wrote in "Internal equity" as a key consideration. A particularly honest respondent pointed to something no textbook mentions as an explanation for why we get paid what we do: "My gut feeling." Pay-setters have power over those whose pay they determine, and sometimes they exercise that power arbitrarily.

An additional question asked: "Of the factors listed, which one do you think is the most important when you determine other employees' compensation?" Figure 2.6 presents the answers, with the factors arranged in the same order as in Figure 2.5. Once again, there is a clear-cut winner: employee's individual performance (nearly 40 percent), followed by employee's experience (26 percent). Three other determinants garnered just under 10 percent, and only 4 percent of the sample selected occupation. Here, too, women were more likely to say individual performance is the most important determinant of pay; nearly half of women respondents called individual performance most important, compared to a third of men.

Some caution should be taken in interpreting the small percentage choosing occupation as most important: many of these respondents

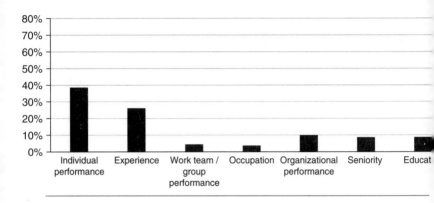

Figure 2.6   Percent saying factor is the "most important" to pay

set wages and salaries for particular jobs or groups of similar jobs. Most organizations, moreover, include a limited number of occupations within them. A private school doesn't employ coal miners or sheet metal workers, and a car manufacturer isn't likely to have English teachers or social workers in its ranks. As will be discussed in a later chapter, many organizations rely on subcontractors to do the work of all but their "core workers," meaning that if, for example, you recently stayed at a Holiday Inn, you likely encountered few actual Holiday Inn employees. Major hotel chains partner with staffing firms to provide labor to work the front desk and tidy up guest rooms. As a result, a typical pay-setter at a firm sets pay for only one occupation, or no more than a handful, lowering the importance of occupation as a driver of different pay levels at that organization.

As with the worker survey, the pay-setter questionnaire also asked respondents to reflect on what they thought *should* factor into pay decisions. The key question was: "How important do you think each of the following should be in determining employees' compensation at your main job?" Figure 2.7 presents the factors in the same order

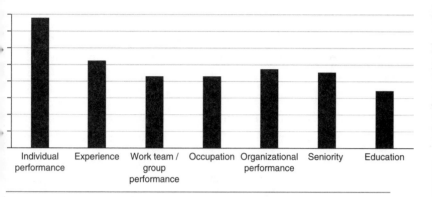

Figure 2.7   Percent saying factor should be "very important" to pay

as Figure 2.5. As shown, experience ranks relatively highly—but, once again, no characteristic proves as popular among this group of pay-setters as individual performance (78 percent). Nine in ten women believe individual performance should be very important in deciding pay, along with two-thirds of men. No other factor aside from experience was deemed very important by more than 50 percent of the respondents.

Few respondents provided open-ended answers to the question about factors that should help determine pay, but one did point to the importance of internal equity, and another noted that whether a worker was a "team player" should be considered. Another believed it made sense to look at what similar jobs in the same city paid when setting wages and salaries for her own employees.

Workers, managers, and human resource directors all seem to agree. They believe that experience, work team or group perfor-mance, and organizational performance are important factors when it comes to setting pay. So, too, are seniority levels and occupation. And my surveys suggest that many Americans—whether they have a role in setting pay or simply receive it—believe that these five factors *should* be crucial in determining what we take home. But one factor stands above all the rest in terms of both how important respondents believe it to be and how important they think it should be: individual performance. Americans' belief in the importance of their individual performance to their pay reflects both the deep-seated cultural sentiment of individualism and the longstanding, dominant tradition within the academy that likewise views a worker's individual performance as the core determinant of pay. This academic understanding reinforces a general tendency among ordinary Americans to locate individual economic success or failure within the self, rather than in broader political or economic structures.[57] Of all the reasons why we get paid what we do, many academics, workers, and pay-setters in the United States think that individual performance is the crucial one, and also think that's exactly as it should be. The question is, are they right?

In a word, no. In Part II, I explain why.

PART II

PAYING FOR PERFORMANCE?

3 EMPLOYERS AGAINST THE FREE MARKET

THE NORTH KOREAN REGIME is known for many things. Reducing gender pay disparities in the United States is not one of them. But reduce them it did, albeit unintentionally, among a handful of actresses who discovered they were being paid significantly less than their male costars after the regime hacked and released confidential information from Sony Pictures in the fall of 2014. One of the leaked documents was a spreadsheet outlining salaries for various company employees, including performers in Sony movies. Actress Charlize Theron used the information to negotiate a $10 million dollar raise that put her salary on par with her male costar in the 2016 fantasy film *The Huntsman*.[1]

Why didn't Ms. Theron know of the discrepancy prior to the hack? Because salary information at Sony was—and remains, as at many companies today, a closely guarded secret. That allowed the firm to pay A-list actresses like Theron less than their male counterparts without risking the outcry that would come from disclosure. And Theron wasn't alone. For their work on *American Hustle,* Amy Adams and Jennifer Lawrence each earned an Oscar nomination. What they didn't earn was pay equal to what the men in the film took home.

Pay secrecy policies—workplace rules, formal or informal, that ban or discourage workers from discussing their pay with one another—are the norm in private sector workplaces in the United States today.[2] In the perfectly competitive labor market assumed by the human capital model, both the employee and the employer are price *takers:* they respond to the market-determined wage. In the real world, employers use available resources to gain power in pay negotiations. One resource is information, such as information about pay. Shielding company pay information from workers introduces an information asymmetry into wage bargaining that disadvantages those, like Amy Adams and Jennifer Lawrence, who are left in the dark. Obscuring company financial information from employees is another tried-and-true tactic. When negotiating over a portion of your organization's revenue, it's important to know the size of the available pie; otherwise, you are left to bargain over the crumbs your employer claims are all that remain. Alan Manning describes worker ignorance as one of the key sources of "monopsony" in labor markets, or employer power stemming from labor market frictions.[3] Ignorance about your own firm's finances and pay scale, and how its competitors compare, keeps you from knowing whether you're getting your fair share and removes your negotiating leverage.

Maintaining this type of information asymmetry is but one common approach to obfuscate workers' worth, impede their mobility, and otherwise stifle competition in labor markets.[4] Others include noncompete clauses, which bar workers from leaving for a competitor for a specified period of time, and no-poaching agreements, which bar employers from hiring from other firms in the industry. Despite rhetoric championing the unimpeded free market, we often find employers working overtime to ensure no such thing operates in the market for labor. Employers rely on these tools in organizational claims-making for one key reason: they work, helping to shift power away from employees staking claims over their share of organizational revenue.

KEEPING SECRETS

"Information is power," Jeffrey Pfeffer writes, "and sharing information diffuses that power."[5]

Lilly Ledbetter was a longtime manager at an Alabama Goodyear Tire & Rubber plant, giving the manufacturer nearly two decades of her career. What the company didn't give her was equal pay for equal work. Years into her tenure at Goodyear, an anonymous colleague slipped a note into her mailbox including a listing. On it, her pay was shown next to the pay of others occupying her same position at the plant. The others listed were all men. Her pay was lower, substantially so.[6] Ledbetter filed a sex discrimination suit, and the case eventually landed before the Supreme Court. In the spring of 2007, five justices ruled against her, arguing that she had failed to bring her claim in a timely manner. Existing law maintained that one had to file suit within 180 days of the discriminatory action. It took Ledbetter much longer for an obvious reason: she had no idea she was being discriminated against. Goodyear maintained a strict pay secrecy policy and, were it not for that sympathetic colleague, she might never have found out about the pay disparity. After the Supreme Court ruling, Congress took action, passing the Lilly Ledbetter Fair Pay Act in early 2009. The law was the first piece of legislation signed by President Obama, who announced at the signing ceremony, "I intend to send a clear message: That making our economy work means making sure it works for everyone."[7] Case closed and message sent, right?

Not exactly. The act extended the statute of limitations for a plaintiff to file a pay discrimination lawsuit. It did nothing, however, to foster transparency in the workplace. A survey of approximately 1,100 US workers conducted in 2010 by the Institute for Women's

Policy Research (IWPR) revealed that whatever message the president intended to send, employers did not interpret it as a reason to scrap pay secrecy policies. The survey asked respondents which of these things was true about wages and salaries in their workplace: discussions of them were formally prohibited, discussions of them were actively discouraged, discussions of them were allowed, or pay information was publicly available. Nearly a third said that management discouraged discussion of wages. Another 18 percent reported that talking about your pay or inquiring about the pay of others was formally barred at work. For roughly a quarter of respondents, wage and salary information was publicly available, and 17 percent reported they were allowed to discuss such matters. The remaining workers didn't know what their workplace's policy was.[8]

In the fall of 2010, then, roughly half of the US labor force worked under a pay secrecy policy of some kind. What's so strange about that finding is that workplace restrictions on this type of speech are illegal, and have been for a long time. Courts have consistently ruled that discussion about wages is considered concerted activity, and protected under the National Labor Relations Act (NLRA), a law passed in 1935.[9] But as we'll explore in greater detail in Chapters 6 and 7, just because something is declared illegal under the NLRA doesn't mean employers comply. One reason for this is that punishments for violating the NLRA are pitifully small. Maximum penalties for violating certain NLRA statutes amount to little more than offering back pay to the aggrieved worker and rehiring her if you fired her for protected conduct, such as asking her coworkers about their pay. As a result, as one legal scholar puts it, "Ignoring the law is easier and more efficient for employers because the NLRA does not adequately incentivize compliance."[10] In 2010, employers of half of all workers took the easier, more efficient route.

The NLRA is also so inadequately publicized and policed that it's actually unclear whether employers with pay secrecy policies know they are in violation of the law. We know that many workers do not know that they have a right to discuss their pay.[11] No survey assesses employers' legal knowledge on the issue. But in the 2019 survey of pay-setters described in the Chapter 2, I included a question about whether the respondent's firm had a pay secrecy policy. These respondents were in positions that gave them authority to set pay in their workplace, including dozens of managers, and some at the very top of their organization's pyramid. And yet, much like the IWPR survey of workers, roughly half of those sampled said their firm had a pay secrecy policy of some kind: 38 percent reported their organization discouraged discussions of wages and salaries; another 8 percent had a formal ban in place. If they were knowingly breaking the law, we'd expect that percentage to be lower—anonymous survey or not, many people aren't so eager to own up to illegal activity.

WHILE THE ACT NAMED after her didn't address pay secrecy, Lilly Ledbetter's travails along with the Sony disclosure motivated lawmakers to strengthen existing laws against these common workplace restrictions. In 2014, over fifty Senators cosponsored the Paycheck Fairness Act. Among other aims, the legislation would stiffen penalties against employers that maintained pay secrecy policies by subjecting guilty employers to compensatory damages. Despite majority support, the act fell victim to a Senate filibuster, joining similar bills that went down to defeat in 2010 and 2012.[12]

Attempts to make what is technically illegal really illegal continue at the congressional level, but with divided government, the likelihood of any current effort becoming federal law is extremely

Figure 3.1   States with pay transparency laws

low.[13] President Obama circumvented Congress in 2014 by signing an executive order prohibiting federal contractors from maintaining pay secrecy policies—in effect, putting some teeth behind the existing legal prohibition against pay secrecy, at least for those firms that do business with the federal government. When signing the order, President Obama declared, "Pay secrecy fosters discrimination and we should not tolerate it."[14] A number of states have stopped tolerating it too, with ten of them, plus the District of Columbia, having passed legislation banning pay secrecy rules since 2010. Figure 3.1 shows the states that had laws in effect as of 2020 that prohibited the policy.[15] Lightly shaded states denote those that had laws on the books prior to 2010; states shaded darker passed more recent legislation. Connecticut, Delaware, Maryland, Massachusetts, New York, and New Jersey are among the states that now have formal laws proscribing employers from sanctioning workers who discuss their own pay or inquire about the pay of others.[16]

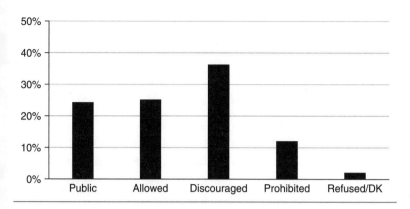

Figure 3.2   Pay secrecy in US workplaces, 2017

Nobody had surveyed the American workforce since the IWPR had back in 2010—before much of the contemporary national attention and state legislation on the issue. A team of us decided to field a new survey in the fall of 2017, in partnership with the survey research firm GfK (now Ipsos). We limited our sample of approximately 2,600 workers to full-time workers and weighted it to be representative of the full-time national labor force by gender, race, ethnicity, region, education, and household income. Among other items in our questionnaire, we replicated the IWPR's question about pay secrecy to see if employers had responded to recent national attention and flurry of state-level action. Turns out, many hadn't. Figure 3.2 displays the results.[17]

The figure displays the percentage of respondents who reported that their organization made wages and salaries public, allowed discussion of wages and salaries, discouraged such discussions, or prohibited them outright. As shown, the modal answer—the category with the highest percentage of respondents—was that such discussions were discouraged. Over a third of our sample indicated that their employers discouraged talking about wages and salaries at work, slightly higher than in IWPR's 2010 survey. Another 12 percent said there were formal prohibitions in place barring talk about pay, down from 2011. Approximately a quarter of the sample reported that discussions about wages and salaries were allowed, and another quarter said that pay was made public. The remaining 2 percent either didn't know their company's policy on pay secrecy, or did not answer the question. Respondents in states that had recently passed laws against the practice were only slightly more likely to work in transparent workplaces than respondents in states that hadn't taken any action.

Similar to 2010, then, roughly half of the American workforce believes it is discouraged or outright banned from discussing wages and salaries. This is despite the attention to the issue brought by the high-profile exposés of blatant discrimination at Sony, Goodyear, and some other companies with pay secrecy policies—and despite all the federal and state-level actions meant to strengthen the rights we already had as workers to talk about our pay or inquire about the pay of colleagues.[18] My past research identifies two organizational characteristics that are strongly associated with whether or not a workplace has a pay secrecy policy: unionization and sector. As I've written, "unions fight to publicize company pay and financial information in order to gain leverage in contract negotiations," while public sector employers are often subject to stringent rules requiring that they provide key workplace information (including pay information) to employees.[19] On the other hand, among workers in nonunion, private sector workplaces, pay secrecy is the norm. And most US workers today don't belong to a union, and don't work for the government.

Why the lack of significant movement on the issue? The answer is not wholly clear, but our existing legal framework provides one clue. The country's labor laws are outdated, the penalties for violating them insufficient to ensure compliance, and the tools in place to enforce them limited. A second clue emerges from another question we included on our survey. We asked those workers subject to a pay secrecy policy of some sort whether they agreed or disagreed with their bosses' prohibition on discussing wages and salaries. The results were clear: nearly 70 percent of respondents working under a pay secrecy policy supported it. And while men were slightly more likely to support these workplace speech restrictions than women, two-thirds of women respondents reported that they agreed with their firm's policy.[20] Without a groundswell of workers agitating against their companies' stance, many firms appear content to violate the law, to the extent they recognize they're in violation of it.

As a result, pay secrecy policies remain illegal and common. Again, this matters to worker pay because pay secrecy policies, whether formal or informal, introduce information asymmetries into organizations. Certain actors possess key information; others don't. Some types of information, such as whether your company's annual retreat will be held at a ski or beach resort this year (should you be so lucky), are largely immaterial to your annual salary. Other types, such as how much the colleague in the cubicle next to you is making, are germane to your pay. As Cynthia Estlund puts it, "information asymmetries confer a bargaining advantage on the more informed party."[21] This advantage shifts power toward the informed in a few key ways. Edward Lawler outlines a process of how power plays out in workplaces consisting of three observable "moments": power capability, power use, and actual, realized power.[22] Briefly, power capability refers to the potential one party in a bargaining framework has to extract a resource (such as money, in the form of pay). Power use refers to how the party employs tactics to extract that resource. Actual or realized power refers to the benefit to the party realized as an outcome. All three prove important to pay determination in various ways. For example, knowledge of your workplace's pay scales increases your capability by legitimating potential demands for higher pay. This information might also raise your likelihood of using power to ask for that raise, as it motivated Charlize Theron to do after the Sony hack. It might also contribute to your success in winning that raise, and with that outcome, yield actual power. In short, having the data to support a claim that you're being underpaid arms you with a powerful, legitimating resource. Lacking that information, you're left either completely in the dark about wage discrepancies or simply reliant on what your manager or human resources department does or does not tell you.

Of course, workers have some latitude as to how strictly they comply with policies. We know that employers are all too willing to overlook the legal restrictions on this type of speech ban, but what if workers are just as willing to ignore their employers' desire for secrecy? In our survey we asked workers whether they knew the wages or salaries of at least some of their coworkers. Nearly two-thirds said they did. Of those respondents who reported working in transparent workplaces, 75 percent said they knew what some colleagues made. Among those in workplaces with pay secrecy policies, that fraction dropped to around half. While it's clear that instituting a pay secrecy policy is no guarantee that your workers won't discuss their pay, it's more effective than having no policy at all.

While the anecdotal cases continue to pile up, only a few studies exist that systematically explore the relationship between pay secrecy and workers' wages. One recent investigation capitalizes on the variation in state laws to assess whether workers earn more in states that are less tolerant of pay secrecy policies. Findings indicate that, controlling for other factors, highly educated women working in states with strong bans on pay secrecy earn more than highly educated women in states without such restrictions. As a result, gender pay gaps among the college-educated are also smaller in states that have taken action on the issue.[23]

Another recent study explores a unique aspect of contemporary Norway: total transparency regarding tax information. That's right: in Norway, any citizen can look up the tax returns of any fellow Norwegian, from the upper reaches of the economic and political elite right down to their butlers and chauffeurs. Norwegians' right to transparency didn't emerge after some recent political scandal—say, their head of state refusing to release his tax returns. It extends all the way back to 1863.[24] But this information wasn't always so easy to access. Prior to 2001, the information was available only in printed book form. Looking up your neighbor's tax returns required trudging down to your local library or townhall, hoping your neighbor hadn't pulled the relevant page from the massive book first.

Starting in 2001, the government decided to put the information online. Several newspapers partnered with it to create easily searchable online databases listing each taxpayer's income, net assets, and the amount of taxes paid for any particular year.[25] Just like that, everyone in the country had access to this information from the comfort of their own home. Hits on the websites skyrocketed, leading to server breakdowns at several newspapers.[26] A pair of economists took advantage of the information shock to study what happened to the behavior of workers in the aftermath of the online disclosure. They looked at workers similar in education and age, and found that after the news sites' publication, those who earned comparatively less were more likely to quit their jobs. These workers ended up earning 5 percent more in new jobs, "suggesting that the information shock motivated the low relative earners to find better paying jobs."[27]

A third study focused on professors' salaries in Canada. Provinces introduced rules requiring disclosure if a professor's salary exceeded a certain amount. The disclosure rules went into effect at different times in different places, allowing the team of researchers to track pay trends over time across a range of transparency or secrecy contexts. What they found was that publicizing this information narrowed gender pay disparities, largely through the reduction in male professor salaries, and especially in those university settings in which faculty belonged to unions.[28]

Pay information isn't the only valuable source of knowledge in our workplaces. Knowing the company's finances—profit levels, revenue streams, operating costs—can also prove vital in both motivating you to make a claim for a higher raise, and in legitimating that claim once made. That's the conclusion of a series of investigations into the dissemination of workplace financial information. One of these was published in 1988, and based on a survey of approximately one hundred US manufacturing employers.[29] Another, in 1991, used the same data.[30] The authors found substantial variation in terms of the company information employers were willing to share with their workers. About half distributed annual financial statements; just 13 percent shared budgeted income statements. Nearly 60 percent were transparent about company productivity measures, including output per employee. Information about salaries offered to recruit workers from other firms was largely off-limits, as only a quarter shared it.[31]

What differentiated firms that disclosed financial information from those that didn't? The more transparent employers believed that sharing it would engender goodwill and spur higher productivity; their workers would be more loyal and work harder in exchange for their bosses' trust.[32] This managerial belief wasn't borne out in the data: measured productivity was not related to managerial disclosure of financial information.[33] Pay, however, was. Workers employed by firms that shared financial statements earned 5 percent more than those in organizations where financial statements weren't provided. And in companies that shared information on salaries offered to competitors' employees, workers earned 9 percent more than their equivalents not privy to such data.[34]

In 2015, a colleague and I published a follow-up study using data from tens of thousands of workers spread across some three thousand firms in Great Britain. Our results largely confirmed what was found by those pioneering studies decades ago: workers who had access to company financial information earned more than those who didn't. Specifically, we found that workers who said their managers were very good at sharing organizational financial information earned 8–12 percent more than those who said their managers were very poor at disclosing such information. These results held even after we compared workers in companies with similar profit levels and compared workers with similar experience levels and feelings of loyalty toward their employers.[35] As we concluded, "learning the size of the potential pie (1) provides an important resource for a worker or group of workers to bargain with, (2) increases the likelihood of bargaining, and (3) increases the chance of success."[36]

It's no wonder, then, that many employers choose the secrecy route when it comes to pay and company finances. Disclosure shifts power to workers, legitimizing claims to higher wages and salaries. But there is another reason employers are reluctant to release potentially sensitive information to their employees, and it has to do with equity. From the employer's perspective, disclosures about pay or company finances can raise serious equity concerns among workers who discover that some peers are making more than they are, or that they are taking home a very thin slice of the available pie. Research coauthored by George Akerlof with the past chair of the Federal

Reserve, Janet Yellen, helps us understand why transparency may lead to feelings of unfairness.[37] Drawing on a range of historical examples from sociology and economics, they highlight how productivity dips when workers perceive their pay to be unfair. Workers carry an idea about what constitutes a fair wage, and when their actual pay falls below that level, they withdraw effort. Overall organizational productivity declines as a result. How do workers decide what's fair? Often, as we learned in Chapter 1, they do so by referencing what others are making, or by comparing their pay to their notion of what the company could afford to pay them. We can only perceive our pay to be unfair if we have something to compare it to—such as to the enormous amount budgeted for the boss's office renovations despite a years-long general salary freeze, or to what our colleague down the hall makes.

The two-tiered pay system is an example of a compensation scheme many feel is unfair. In these systems, starting pay for new hires is substantially less than it was for workers who arrived at the firm years prior. Among recent arrivals this often leads to feelings of unfairness, if they're aware of the inequity. When the *New York Times* reported in the 1980s on its widespread use to reduce labor costs and weaken unions, it noted that many employers were finding it "produced a resentful class of workers. . . . At some companies, it has caused turnover to soar and made recruitment more difficult."[38] Workers see themselves performing the same job as the person next to them, and know they make substantially less for their efforts.

In early 2008, the *Sacramento Bee* created a website publicizing the pay of state employees, creating another environment in which researchers could explore the consequences of horizontal inequities. A team of economists took advantage of the sudden disclosure to track how employees reacted at three branches of the University of California system.[39] The researchers contacted a random sample of faculty and staff to notify them about the website, and measured their reactions over time. Findings were a mixture of the predictable and the rather unexpected. Workers who received the treatment were more likely to look up their coworkers' pay on the website. Predictable enough. Those who did and discovered they were underpaid compared to similarly situated peers expressed anger and an uptick in job searching. Also a foreseeable finding.

Workers who discovered they were overpaid, however, experienced no symmetrical emotional response. They weren't suddenly more loyal to their bosses or more satisfied in their workplaces. In fact, their behavior didn't change at all. They just went about their business as if the information disclosure hadn't even registered. Why? It turns out that most of us think we're pretty good at our jobs. And most of us think we're better than the majority of our colleagues. It's a real-life version of the fantasy Lake Wobegon town of *Prairie Home Companion* fame, a place "where all the children are above average."[40] Our overestimation of ourselves goes way back. One survey from the 1960s asked professionals and managers how their performance measured up against their peers. The average self-rating was the seventy-seventh percentile, meaning that, on average, respondents rated their performance as better than three-quarters of their coworkers' performance. Only two of the hundred or so respondents said their performance was below average.[41] That's a mathematical impossibility, and one that poses a conundrum for employers who would like to be, or are being forced to be, more transparent about pay. Employers' worries about the subsequent equity issues that arise after disclosure have led to an organizational landscape where few private sector companies willingly share salary or organizational financial information with employees.

But some do. Starting in the mid-1980s, Whole Foods founder and CEO John Mackey publicized pay and company financial data to all of his workers.[42] It didn't hurt the company's growth, or its ability to attract applicants. If anything, the openness contributed to an environment in which workers felt trusted and empowered—and reciprocated with loyalty to the firm. For two decades, Whole Foods ranked as one of the top hundred US companies to work for, although morale seems to have dipped since Amazon's purchase of the grocery chain.[43] Another example is Buffer, a social media management firm founded in San Francisco in 2010. The firm stands out for a few reasons, one of which is its appointment of a "Chief Happiness Officer" and another of which is its radical pay transparency. Not only does the company provide pay information for employees, it provides a salary calculator for all potential employees to estimate what they would make should they come to work for the firm.[44]

In many firms, as Matthew Edwards has noted, "money talk" may well be the "last conversational taboo."[45] But these examples show that it need not be. Buffer's story may be better known thanks to wide coverage by the business press (just Dan Price's announcement of his firm's $70,000 minimum annual salary was the subject of many articles) but there are thousands of organizations employing millions of us that disclose pay with little or no fanfare. I used to work at one. The University of Washington, like the vast majority of public universities, must make information about employee salaries publicly available. This is true of most public sector organizations. When I discuss Norway's approach to pay transparency to various groups invariably there are gasps in the audience. Many Americans react viscerally against such radical openness. But there is an entire sector of our workforce that already operates according to rules of disclosure closer to those that prevail in Norway than in most private sector businesses in the United States. In the public sector, research finds that wage disparities of various kinds tend to be lower. This is true of gaps between those at the top and bottom of the organizational hierarchy.[46] It is true of disparities between men and women.[47] And it is true of wage differences between white workers and racial and ethnic minorities.[48] One possible reason is that equity concerns arise when workers are aware of colleagues' pay, and adjustments are made as a result.

While this point is often elided, the real issue in debates about pay secrecy isn't the disclosure—it's what's being disclosed. Feelings of unfairness among workers aren't the inevitable outcome of sharing pay information. They stem from learning of pay differences that workers consider unjustified. The social psychology described above does present thorny issues for employers who want to be transparent, but the challenges shouldn't be seen as insurmountable. We have evidence to support this claim. Roughly a quarter of respondents to our 2017 worker survey indicated that pay is public at their workplaces. Just as we asked those employees who worked under a pay secrecy policy whether they were in favor of it, we asked those in transparent workplaces whether or not they support their organization's policy about wage and salary openness. Nearly 80 percent said they did.[49] Surveys continue to show that most of us are reluctant to disclose our pay to colleagues.[50] Yet people seem to be very supportive of policies that handle the disclosure for them.

Personal privacy preferences aside, when employers keep pay and firm finances secret, it deprives workers of key information useful for wage bargaining. It also reveals another way in which the human capital model is inadequate for understanding contemporary labor markets. That model rests on an assumption of at least some semblance of perfect information, with all sides to a transaction armed with the same relevant data for bargaining. Employees can't know if they are being paid appropriately if they don't know the going rate and are prevented from finding it out. When workers can discover their value, power shifts in claims-making. If you're an employer trying to keep that from happening, you block your worker's access to information. And that's not the only tactic that can be effective. Limiting their job options can be, as well.

(IM)PERFECT COMPETITION

For years, Jimmy John's, the sandwich shop chain, included in its employment contracts a clause forbidding employees from working for any competitor that sold "submarine, hero-type, deli-style, pita, and / or wrapped or rolled sandwiches" within three miles of one of its establishments. The prohibition lasted for two years after the worker left the company.[51] Such clauses, known as noncompetes, have classically been used to restrict an employee from using current knowledge or information gained through employment at a firm to compete against that firm, whether by going to work for an existing rival or starting up a new business. They were once largely limited to technology and other sectors where workers were exposed to trade secrets. Not so anymore, unless you count the makings of a Big John roast beef sandwich as a valuable secret (the ingredients of which are listed on the Jimmy John's menu).

The spread of noncompetes through one occupation in particular has provided us with a front-row seat into their effect on claimsmaking in organizations. Journalists make a living unearthing the previously undisclosed, and in journalism noncompetes are increasingly the norm. In 2017, the conservative news website the *Independent Journal Review,* or *IJR,* asked all its employees to sign an agreement not to take a job with a competitor for at least six months after leaving.[52] There was no geographic restriction on the noncompete: it applied to news outlets "anywhere in the world." But noncompetes are a nonpartisan affair. An extensive noncompete at liberal *NowThis* prohibited its journalists from leaving for a long list of other news organizations, among them *Vox, Vice, CNN,* and *Conde Nast.*[53] The restriction applied for a full two years following exit from the organization.

While *IJR* and *NowThis* may not be household names, many holdings of Sinclair Broadcast Group are. The media giant is the largest owner of television stations in the United States, operating Fox, ABC, NBC, CBS, and Univision affiliates on a local basis. In all, Sinclair operates 173 stations in 81 markets, reaching 40 percent of the US population.[54] The company is number one in terms of size, and may also top its industry in anticompetitive fervor. Beyond featuring the industry-standard six-month noncompete clause, its employment contracts with on-air talent and reportedly other journalists include a liquidated damages clause. This means that an employee who has signed a contract with such a clause, but then chooses to leave the company before its expiration, may have to pay breach-of-contract damages to Sinclair amounting to as much as 40 percent of annual compensation. For a news anchor, this is a double whammy: not only are you barred from working for a rival station for half a year, you'll also be subject to a clawback of some of your pay.

Most employees subject to noncompete and liquidated damages clauses never test their enforceability. And in most instances, firms decline to pursue legal action when workers who have signed such contracts go to work for competitors. That doesn't mean the clauses are ineffective. As Barrett Bloom, an employment lawyer in Seattle, commented about Sinclair's noncompetes, "If reporters aren't willing to test them, then they are effective."[55] Even a small threat of legal action can cause a worker to think twice about reaching out to a competing firm for a better job offer. And should a competitor offer better pay, the presence of a noncompete hinders the worker from taking the counteroffer. Noncompetes shift dynamics in organizational claims-making by removing an important source of worker power: the ability to seek a better deal.

And just because employers don't usually enforce noncompetes doesn't mean they never do. Stephanie Russell-Kraft found this out the hard way. Her contract with *Law360*, an outlet for legal news, contained a noncompete clause to keep her from moving to any competing legal journalism site. But she watched as colleagues departed for competitors without retribution during her two years at *Law360*; further, as a journalist covering the law, she knew the refrain from many lawyers that these clauses were often unenforceable in court. So when an opportunity opened up at Reuters, she didn't give the clause in her contract much thought. Unfortunately, *Law360* did, giving notice to Reuters' general counsel that she was in violation of her noncompete. Reuters fired her two days later for not having disclosed it when asked. Could she have won a case to have the contract declared illegal? Probably, but as she has written, she lacked the "$50,000 to cover the cost of proving it in court."[56]

As of 2014, nearly 20 percent of the American workforce was subject to a noncompete of some kind.[57] Research shows Stephanie Russell-Craft isn't the only one hurt by their spread. Matt Marx's in-depth interviews with over fifty workers in one high-tech industry—automatic speech recognition—found that those bound by noncompetes who changed jobs were much more likely to take an unwilling "career detour" out of that industry. About a quarter of interviewees said they made these costly detours because of their noncompetes, even in the absence of threatened lawsuits—evidence of the chilling effect these clauses have.[58] Marx's related survey of 1,029 electrical engineers working in a variety of industries found that 43 percent had signed noncompetes. Of the ones who signed and later changed jobs, about a third left the industry in which they had been working.[59]

From the employer's perspective, noncompetes solve a dilemma arising from the decline of the internal labor markets that used to be so prominent. In the post–World War II era, pay and promotion practices were based on certain assumptions: internal career ladders, the development of firm-specific skills, long-term commitment to the employee, and pay tied to positions rather than to people's individual traits. Anytime you hear of someone who "rose through the ranks" of an organization over many years, you're hearing about a setting where people competed for pay and promotions within some sort of internal labor market structure.

Many firms have shed their internal labor markets, trading them in for greater flexibility in hiring and firing and the nimbleness needed to respond to market shifts and waves of technological change. As a result, US workers' average tenures with employers have fallen.[60] The "company man" of yesteryear (when it was mostly men who competed in internal labor markets) has been replaced by the free agent who arrives at an organization without the expectation of a long-term commitment. But this new system can provide workers with leverage, especially those with in-demand skill sets. They can readily pick up and leave for other jobs—or threaten to, anyway. Noncompetes neutralize this advantage, disempowering workers and leaving them unable to take advantage of a free market for their labor.

While research finds that these clauses are more common in high-paying professions such as electrical engineering, they've crept down the occupational spectrum, and not just at Jimmy John's. From fast food and camp counseling, to yoga instructing and Amazon warehouse work, noncompetes have proliferated across the US jobs landscape.[61] Approximately one in six sales workers have signed them. Over 10 percent of construction workers have.[62] Noncompetes are even more common in hair salons, where 20 percent of stylists are subject to them. Monica Baugh left her station at a salon in Joplin, Missouri, after a disagreement with her employer. She soon found work at a nearby establishment. With that move came legal trouble, as her ex-employer decided to enforce the noncompete she had signed, and sued the twenty-year-old stylist. Baugh couldn't afford a lawyer to try her case, and eventually settled with her ex-employer out of court. Looking back on the inclusion of noncompetes in so many stylists' contracts, she concluded: "It just traps people, and it's not fair."[63]

Missouri is a state that's relatively friendly to the enforcement of noncompetes. The Show Me State allows noncompetes that cover not only trade secrets, but also "customer lists and customer relationships"—the valuable assets salon owners are trying to protect with the clauses.[64] California, on the other hand, bans the enforcement of all nearly all noncompetes. That doesn't stop employers in the Golden State from slipping them into their employment contracts: over a fifth of workers in California report having signed one at their current job. A recent White House report notes that in jurisdictions like this, "firms may be relying on a lack of worker knowledge" of enforceability.[65]

Firms may also be relying on lenient penalties for requiring employees to sign overly broad or otherwise legally unenforceable noncompete agreements. Here, too, we see considerable variation across states. In most states, the penalty is simply an order to rewrite the agreement in accordance with state law. A handful of states take a more proactive approach, declaring that if an employer includes any provision in a noncompete clause that is unenforceable under state law, the entirety of the clause will be considered null and void.[66] As the persistence of noncompetes in California makes clear, neither of these approaches is sufficient to eliminate employers' incentive to include them in employment contracts.

But states' stances toward the enforceability of noncompetes do seem to affect the pay of workers subject to them. Related studies find that workers earn more in states that do not enforce noncompetes. Hawaii, for example, banned all noncompetes for employees in technology businesses in 2015. A team of researchers tracked the starting pay of technology workers in the state in the two years before and after the prohibition took effect, finding that the ban led to significantly higher starting wages for technology workers.[67] The same researchers found that technology workers working in an "average" enforcement state had 5 percent lower cumulative wages after eight years than equivalent workers in Hawaii, California and other nonenforcing states.[68]

Why do people sign noncompetes in the first place? Or why don't they negotiate for benefits in return for signing them? The general power imbalance between employers and employees provides one answer: individual workers might not have alternative job choices, or might reason that the clauses are ubiquitous in their industry. Only a tenth of workers who have signed a noncompete say they negotiated over its terms or asked for something—such as higher compensation—in return for signing it. Another key reason worker don't negotiate? Because employers frequently present the noncompete after the negotiations are over. In his survey of electrical engineers, Marx found that only a third of those who signed a noncompete were presented with it at the time of the job offer. Nearly half didn't receive the noncompete until they had started the job. One survey respondent's experience was typical: "I never received any information ahead of time before showing up. And then it was the first day when I had all the paperwork in front of me: health insurance, 401(k), and the noncompete. It was either 'sign it and work here or don't sign it and don't work here.'"[69]

That's power for you.

ORGANIZED MIMICRY

In 2005, Apple CEO Steve Jobs learned that fast-growing Google was trying to lure away a team of Apple software developers working on a highly strategic project. He wasn't pleased. As recalled by Google cofounder Sergey Brin, Jobs called Brin and vowed, "If you hire a single one of these people, that means war."[70] Brin backed down. Soon, the two technology titans came to an agreement not to poach talent from one another, and both then pursued similar agreements with other Silicon Valley firms. The executives policed the arrangement vigorously: in 2007, a Google recruiter, perhaps unaware of this new form of collusion in the industry, approached an Apple engineer. Jobs found out about the transgression and quickly complained. Google fired the recruiter within days.[71]

When word leaked of the agreement, a group of engineers filed a class action suit. It alleged that Apple, Google, Intel, and Adobe had established multiyear no-poaching agreements that barred the participating firms from recruiting each other's talent. Why did the engineers care? Because, like noncompetes, no-poaching agreements hinder the claims-making power of in-demand workers: the suppression of outside job offers means less opportunity to bid up pay. A rising Apple engineer making, say, $135,000 annually has a pretty powerful claim at his disposal if Google offers him $165,000 to jump ship. Apple might counter the outside offer by increasing his pay, or the worker might accept Google's higher annual salary. Placing employers in competition like this is a tried-and-true way for workers to shift power dynamics in their favor. But it can't work if the firms have already agreed it is not in their interests to compete for labor.

The class action lawsuit dragged on for years. The tens of thousands of engineers represented in the suit demanded $3 billion, but a decade after the collusion began, they settled for $415 million, and each engineer received just under $6,500.[72] Certainly, $415 million is a lot of money, and the settlement represented a victory for the aggrieved workers. But these were highly paid professionals who could have negotiated raises worth many multiples of the court case's spoils if they had received the right calls from executive recruiters. That is, if they hadn't been working for firms who were mimicking other firms' no-poaching policies.

Perhaps it's hard to conjure much sympathy for the already well-remunerated set of software engineers who have driven up housing costs in the technology corridors of San Francisco, Seattle, and other cities (and who won at least some of their lost compensation back). In that case, consider that such anticompetitive arrangements, sometimes tacit and sometimes explicit, have also been found in many other industries, including fast food.[73] That's right: *fast food.* Alan Krueger, a past chairman of the President's Council of Economic Advisors, found that no-poaching rules are "ubiquitous" in fast food franchising agreements. More likely than not, if you are the operator of a local Pizza Hut, one of the documents you signed as the franchisee prevents you from hiring from other Pizza Huts. The same is true of Burger King. In 2017, of the major fast food chains, nearly 80 percent contained this sort of "no hire" rule.[74] Some agreed to drop them after Krueger and fellow labor economist Orley Ashenfelter publicized the practice.[75]

Fast food isn't the only low-paying industry in which no-poaching agreements are common. Franchisees of many of the major fitness chains, including Curves, routinely sign contracts with such clauses. The same is true of some businesses where you have your car serviced, such as Jiffy Lube. Business owners have argued that the costs of training new hires justify such protection from poaching.[76] Yet it takes very little time to train an entry-level employee at, say, Burger

King. And of course, a non-collusive way to hold on to productive workers would be to pay them a higher wage. It is often when employers are reluctant to do so that they instead search for such workarounds as noncompetes and no-hire rules. Indeed, Krueger and Ashenfelter conclude that the presence of these rules among many low-wage employers helps "explain a recent puzzle in the labor market: unemployment has reached a sixteen-year low and job openings are high, yet wage growth has remained surprisingly sluggish."[77]

Mimicry becomes outright collusion when it is organized, secretive, and intended to deprive workers of a vital tool to negotiate higher pay. It's often illegal, as the Silicon Valley settlement demonstrated. It's also commonplace in today's labor markets.

THE POWER OF CONCENTRATION

In the late nineteenth century, five major tobacco companies competed for the business of the nation's growing number of cigarette smokers. Realizing the fortunes to be gained from combination, they joined forces in 1890 under the bland moniker of the American Tobacco Company, and proceeded to buy up over a dozen more competitors in short order. By the dawn of the twentieth century, the conglomerate manufactured 86 percent of all cigarettes sold in the United States.[78] Not content to monopolize the cigarette industry, American Tobacco Company, led by James Buchanan Duke, also acquired hundreds of other tobacco product manufacturers. For example, following a fierce price war between leading producers of snuff (smokeless tobacco), Duke and his fellow tobacco tycoons stepped in and engineered a cease-fire in the form of the American Snuff Company, a combination of the leading snuff sellers of the day, which Duke and his allies controlled.[79] What these tobacco industrialists lacked in creative branding they made up for in market dominance. By 1910, they had cornered four-fifths of the non-cigar tobacco market.[80]

The American Tobacco Company was the quintessential monopoly of its day, a firm that successfully eradicated nearly all competition for its products, effectively becoming the sole seller of manufactured cigarettes, snuff, and other once-popular tobacco products. It quickly attracted scrutiny from the federal government, and became one of the first test cases for the country's anti-monopoly legal regime. In 1890, Congress passed and President Harrison signed the Sherman Antitrust Act, a broadly written law meant to preserve market competition. In 1911, the Supreme Court ruled that American Tobacco Company violated the law, and ordered the conglomerate split into four competitors. Smokers now had some meaningful choices with market competition restored. The law worked as intended.[81]

The story of the American Tobacco Company encapsulates the country's approach to corporate consolidation. Allowing consumers to have meaningful product choices at prices that aren't artificially inflated is what matters. Other problems that arise as a consequence of corporate consolidation are not the focus. As Marshall Steinbaum has noted, "We have confined antitrust policy . . . to a small subset of the issue: 'What's the price of detergent and how many options do consumers have?'"[82]

Studies by Steinbaum and others are increasingly directing attention to another area where consolidation has consequences: worker pay. Ensuring that people don't overpay for goods is important, but so is ensuring they aren't underpaid for their labor. Whereas monopoly power allows a firm to fix prices for its goods or services, this particular type of monopsony power allows a firm to fix pay for workers. Corporate consolidation, as one journalist explains, allows a "powerful, concentrated company to fix wages for employees, driving them lower than they would be if workers could bargain more effectively or leave for higher pay at other employers."[83] Research finds the number of US labor markets in which workers have few employment options has grown in recent decades, and this growth may play a role in suppressing worker wages.[84]

Thus, even if we could curtail employers' abilities to collude, keep pay secret, and include noncompete clauses in their labor contracts, that wouldn't eliminate all employer power. Anti-competitive practices such as no-poaching agreements and the spread of noncompete clauses limit employee mobility and along with it workers' ability to bid up their pay through outside offers. But there is evidence, too, that in many labor markets, increasing employer concentration has left workers without enough job options. If you own the only factory in town, you don't need noncompete clauses or no-poaching agreements because there are no competitors to compete with or poach from. Employer concentration is what's happened in many US labor markets from the late 1970s on. Especially in areas lacking labor unions—workers' major countervailing power source—growing employer concentration has driven down wages.[85] A recent investigation using data from the employment search site careerbuilder.com finds that more concentrated local labor markets are associated with lower starting pay, net of other core factors that help determine starting wages. Firms in highly concentrated markets post wages on the site 17 percent lower than firms in less-concentrated areas.[86] Once a market for labor has been dominated by a powerful employer, inertia sets in, leading to wages persistently below what they would be in more competitive labor markets.

Corporate consolidation can reduce wages directly, as we've just learned, or indirectly through the actions of supplier firms. Imagine you're a shirt manufacturer. Your shirts, which combine the latest in sweat-wicking materials with a slick design suitable for a strenuous workout or a casual dinner, put you at the forefront of the growing "athleisure" market. A dozen retail chains would like to offer their customers exclusive collections of your product, and you're able to leverage various offers to bid your price upward. The contract you eventually sign with the winner of the bidding war provides a revenue stream sufficiently large to offer your workforce generous salaries. Now imagine that your innovative product is launched some years down the road, at a point when the dozen retail competitors have all been wiped out by an industry giant—we'll call it Malwart. Now, instead of numerous businesses competing for your product, there is only one. Your leverage is nonexistent. Either accept the terms of its offer, or start selling shirts out of the trunk of your car.

Research offers a clear picture that corporate consolidation in recent decades led directly to the squeezing of suppliers, who subsequently cut labor costs to maintain their contracts with powerful lead firms. Nathan Wilmers of MIT finds that since the 1970s publicly traded firms in a few key industries, including manufacturing, have become more dependent for their sales on large buyers.[87] And as a firm's revenue comes increasingly from sales to dominant buyers in concentrated markets, wages typically go down. When the Walmarts and Amazons of the world are essential customers, they gain power to dictate how much they'll pay for your goods or services.

WRITING IN THE LATE 1940s about the nation's efforts to rein in monopolies, lawyer Wallace Murchison noted, "Certainly efforts to eliminate competition have been at least as characteristic of the American economy as competition itself."[88] True then, and true today.

Anti-competitive practices among employers are pervasive, have expanded in scope, and have constrained worker pay since the 1970s, when average wages for workers began to stagnate. In 2015, Thomas Donohue, president of the US Chamber of Commerce, decried the growing hostility to free enterprise, the vibrant entrepreneurship that "made the United States the land of opportunity and created the American Dream."[89] His ire was directed at "big government," but another big target was closer at hand: the major corporations the Chamber lobbies on behalf of, who, by lowering competition through illegal, semi-legal, and perfectly legal means, have produced today's "rigged labor market."[90] Despite all the rhetorical support for free markets, it turns out that employers would rather corner their market, not free it, especially their market for labor.

4 MISMEASURING PERFORMANCE AND THE PITFALLS OF PAYING FOR MERIT

FOR DECADES, investing in Countrywide Financial Corporation proved a safe and incredibly remunerative bet. A $1,000 Countrywide share purchase in 1982 was worth $130,000 in 2002.[1] Profits in 2003 exceeded those of Walt Disney and McDonald's. By then, Countrywide was the nation's largest mortgage lender. The CEO and cofounder of the firm, John Mozilo, received over $32 million in 2003. Just three years later, his package had more than doubled, to just under $69 million—qualifying him as one of the top-ten highest paid CEOs in 2006.[2] An innovation-focused student networking group at UCLA awarded him its Award for Executive Leadership in 2002.[3] Harvard invited him to deliver its prestigious John T. Dunlop lecture in 2003.[4] Not bad for the son of a Bronx butcher.

It turns out that 2007 is when you'd want to have sold that Countrywide stock. That's the year the price peaked, and the beginning of what would be a swift end to the firm. In early 2008, massive losses stemming from the collapse of the housing market led to a takeover by Bank of America. In 2009, the Security and Exchange Commission charged Mozilo and other top executives with fraud. The parties settled for a record $22.5 million fine, and the government barred Mozilo from ever again serving as a director or officer of a publicly traded firm.[5]

What accounted for the rapid rise and even quicker descent of Countrywide? Various factors played a role, including an overheated housing market, faulty forecasting tools that underestimated the likelihood of a market correction, and the rise of mortgage vehicles that deliberately obscured the risk involved. But turbocharging the effects of these was a change in how Countrywide defined performance for its legions of mortgage lenders. For decades, Countrywide stood out from its peers by not paying its salespeople by commission. Mozilo felt that tying pay to sales encouraged unscrupulous behavior by workers willing to do anything to make a deal.[6] By the turn of the century, that feeling had changed, and Countrywide began paying its salesforce by commission. Critically, the commissions varied according to the type of mortgage sold. Riskier, subprime loans were more lucrative, and so the company offered more in commissions for originating them. Loans that had higher prepayment penalties offered higher commissions. Commissions for loans with variable interest rates increased if the interest rate charged to the borrower did. Not surprisingly, as one former salesperson told the *New York Times,* the commission structure "was designed to reward salespeople for pushing whatever programs Countrywide made the most money on."[7] Those programs tended to be the costliest for the borrowers, and, as a result, Countrywide brokers pressured borrowers whose credit scores might have qualified them for conventional prime mortgages on modest homes to instead take out more expensive subprime mortgages and buy larger properties. The logic was that housing prices would only continue to rise, and the borrower would still come out ahead. These were the loans that millions of Americans found impossible to pay back as the housing market cooled and then cratered, taking the economy down with it—and Countrywide, too.

For Countrywide salespeople, performance came to be defined as the volume of loans originated, and the more leveraged the loan, the better—especially since the bank could offload the risk by selling the mortgages to the eager buyers at government-backed Fannie Mae and Freddie Mac. Yes, this way of measuring and rewarding performance had its internal critics (company whistleblowers had warned of the potential consequences), and it spurred disastrously exploitative and fraudulent practices.[8] But it did have the virtue of being easy to measure: each loan had a value attached to it, and workers received a predetermined fraction of that value for selling it. Sales is unique in this regard. In many other occupations, determining the value various types of workers add to the organization isn't so straightforward.

That hasn't stopped managers from trying to put a fine, numerical point on performance—even in a far less measurable role like my own. In 2010, for example, an administrator at Texas A&M came up with a way to assess the cost-effectiveness of the Aggie faculty. The simple calculation he used assessed professors according to two variables: the numbers of students in their classes, and amounts of grant money they generated. Students bring in a certain average amount of tuition per class, and grants, of course, have clearly specified values. Any professors whose tuition and grant dollars added up to more than their salaries were in the black—paying off for the university. But forty-five of the university's fifty top-earning faculty landed in the red.[9] That result instantly raised objections: What about the value to the school's reputation, and to society, of publishing pathbreaking research? What about time spent mentoring struggling students to ensure they graduate? Not part of the formula. The unintended release of the spreadsheet triggered widespread outcry among the faculty. Some faculty felt the simplistic equation was the problem—that more considerations should be factored into it. Others questioned whether a professor's performance could be measured at all.[10]

In Chapter 3 we learned of many ways employers restrict competition in contemporary labor markets, preventing workers from pursuing other opportunities or accessing the information they need to bargain effectively. If we want to restore competition in labor markets and allow workers to be paid for their marginal productivity, we should rid these markets of distorting mechanisms like non-competes and pay secrecy policies. Would doing just that be sufficient? It would be from the perspective of the classic human capital model of pay determination—a model that presumes a frictionless labor market in which we are paid solely on our individual contributions to our organizations. Proponents of this model might concede that this is not a current reality in most industries, but nonetheless believe in both its possibility and its desirability. It's also a perspective aligned with what many workers and pay-setters think determines pay, as documented in Chapter 2. We believe that we get paid based on our individual contributions to our organizational revenue. To the extent we don't, we certainly think we should.

This model rests on three wrong assumptions: that there is such a thing as a worker's marginal product; that such a thing can be calculated, and that paying workers based on it is a good idea. In this chapter, we'll see these three assumptions fall apart in the messy real-world of pay-setting. We'll start by exploring an incredibly common feature of many jobs: a lack of consensus over what constitutes productivity. As with the case of professors, definitions of productivity vary, and are frequently the sites of power struggles involving actors making claims about how to define performance in their jobs. Faculty at Texas A&M did not agree with their chancellor's calculation of performance, and argued forcefully against it. We tend to see competing visions of organizational performance in sectors, such as higher education, where organizations have a range of missions. Some prioritize teaching, while others believe a university rises or falls on its research. In other words, definitional disputes often stem from disagreements about what an organization's "product" should be. If we disagree about our organization's product, we'll disagree about each worker's marginal contribution to it.

Second, we'll explore the issue of measurement. The marginal product perspective and its variants assume that there is an objective measure of productivity that captures just how much of a contribution an individual worker is making to her organization. To the extent that the measure doesn't currently exist, or is only a crude proxy for true productivity, it's simply a matter of perfecting the measurement. Management at Countrywide no doubt believed they had an objective measure of broker productivity. After all, it was about selling more of the most profitable offerings in a for-profit enterprise. But it also encouraged workers to push customers toward taking on risks they could not personally assess, pushed the firm toward its downfall, and contributed to the subprime mortgage crisis that precipitated a global recession. There were other options—there always are. The definition of productivity in any job involves choices and trade-offs, so there is no such thing as a single, objective measure awaiting discovery.

Problems with measurement go beyond the numerous choices involved in crafting an appropriate metric. For many jobs today, the whole effort to measure marginal productivity is misguided—not because the right tools haven't been developed, but because there is no way to disentangle the productivity of one worker from that of others in the organization. For these jobs, productivity should be understood as a collective endeavor, a social achievement, not the sum of atomized employees working individually to accomplish the organization's goals.

Third, we'll examine how proponents of the human capital model tend to ignore or downplay the workplace consequences of pegging pay to productivity. As the growing scholarship on performance pay in workplaces demonstrates, there are clear pitfalls to paying workers strictly according to their individual performance, however defined. That's due to a range of factors, including the equity issues that arise under these pay allocation systems, and the fact that there's rarely a consensus around what performance actually is and how it should be measured. There is another reason, as well. Productivity has a social aspect to it even in those jobs, such as sales, that do lend themselves to measures of individual performance tied to organizational outcomes. Rare is the job in which someone toils in total isolation, depositing the fruits of their labor in some kind of organizational bin at the end of each working day. In well-functioning workplaces, we learn from, cooperate with, and assist those around us, and these interactions affect our own performance. When an organization allocates pay simply based on individual productivity, what should be a cooperative workplaces can turn competitive, which can lower overall productivity.

As we learned in Chapter 2, nearly every worker wants to be paid for her performance. Nearly all pay-setters want to allocate pay according to individual performance, as well. In theory, it's an intuitive, no-brainer idea. In practice, it's incredibly complicated, in many cases downright impossible, and, as it turns out, pretty rarely done. Researchers did document a sharp jump in pay-for-performance plans beginning in the brutal early-1980s recession, when firms were desperate for new ways to boost efficiency.[11] Using a broad definition of performance pay, Maury Gittleman and Brooks Pierce found that, in terms of total hours worked in jobs with performance-related pay, such compensation plans peaked in the early 2000s. They subsequently declined.[12] Between the mid-1970s and the end of the 1990s, just over one-third of jobs had been found to have some component of performance pay attached to them; the majority did not.[13] General Social Survey 2018 data reveal that about a third of workers say that at their jobs they are eligible for some type of performance-based pay, whether in the form of individual or group bonuses or any form of profit-sharing.[14] While many surveys fail to distinguish between workplace, group, and individual performance-pay plans, the 2017 survey of pay secrecy I collaborated on included a question about whether respondents received payments based on individual performance. Only one in ten workers replied yes; most said they received only a basic, fixed salary or wage.[15] And in a 2009 review of a variety of incentive pay practices, a team of researchers found that "relatively few workers have pay that varies in a direct formulaic way with their productivity, and that the share of such workers is probably declining."[16] Moreover, even among those workers whose pay is partly tied to measures of individual productivity, that share is usually a small portion of total compensation.[17]

DEFINITIONAL DISPUTES

In 2014, Time Inc., which then owned over ninety publications, included in its employee rating system a measure of its journalists' performance at producing content that was "beneficial to advertiser relationship." Alongside more expected criteria like the quality of their writing and the newsworthiness of their stories, this was factored into the decision of who would be laid off."[18] The reaction, not only among Time Inc. employees but across the industry, was dismay— understandably, since this ignored the strict separation of editorial and profit concerns that has long been a proud tradition of newsrooms.

But how *should* one measure journalistic productivity? Stories filed per week? Words per hour? What about the doggedness of investigation and cultivation of sources required for deep reporting on, say, corruption among the political elite or mass suffering in distant locales? In 2019, the Pulitzer committee awarded its prize for international reporting to the Associated Press's Maggie Michael, Maad al-Zikry, and Nariman El-Mofty. The trio's winning series documented ongoing atrocities in Yemen, detailing the everyday struggles of Yemenis suffering under a brutal war that wasn't being covered extensively in the Western press. It wasn't the type of work that would score high on the "beneficial to advertiser relationship" metric. Nonetheless it was influential in the world and boosted the organization's reputation by winning journalism's highest honor.

How would you translate all the value of a good journalist's work into a properly weighted productivity metric? Debates on this question are ongoing—with serious economic consequences for the writers that comprise our Fourth Estate. On one side tend to be newsroom employees fighting efforts "to quantify the unquantifiable."[19] On the other side tend to be executives responsible for ensuring that revenues tally up to more than its cost. The unresolved question in publishing organizations around the world is: What forms of journalistic effort and talent should be valued, and how much weight should be given to each form? For critics of Time Inc.'s spreadsheet, the appearance of putting as much weight on content "beneficial to advertiser relationships" as on impact of stories and productivity violated what the goal of journalistic enterprises should be.

Another category in the spreadsheet touched a related nerve for journalists, given the new view into one measure of productivity that came with online publishing: "Audience / Traffic." Gawker.com, once a disruptive upstart in the digital media landscape, was an early pioneer of the "clickbait" approach in online media: publishing salacious, outrageous, and otherwise contagious headlines in a bid to generate "clicks," and, as a result, reap more advertiser dollars.[20] The company allocated bonuses according to the number of clicks a writer's articles generated, explicitly tying pay to this particular measure of journalistic achievement. The type of output that maximizes clicks tends not to be the type that earns critical press. The tension between rewarding content that racks up page views versus rewarding content that yields Pulitzers is one every journalistic endeavor with an online presence must manage. Gawker's hard-charging founder, Nick Denton, eventually admitted that "A lot of our traffic last year came from stories that we weren't ultimately proud of."[21] He decided to replace his company's incentive scheme with one that set its sights higher. A widely respected journalist, Tommy Craggs, was brought in to oversee the news content division, and one of Craggs's first moves was to shelve the old bonus structure and design a new one that rewarded quality.

Of course, judging "quality" is a subjective endeavor and far more time-consuming than checking website data. As a result, organizations across many fields rely on various equivalents to counting clicks to gauge performance, and some of them tie pay to such easily measured results. The problem is, as the historian Jerry Muller has written, "what can be measured is not always what is worth measuring; what gets measured may have no relationship to what we really want to know."[22] Such a situation leads to "The Folly of Rewarding A, While Hoping for B," as the title of a widely cited article on the topic puts it.[23] Such folly is basically guaranteed in workplaces where there are competing ideas about the organization's goals—where different people are hoping for different Bs.

Often, "rewarding A" leads people to ignore some rather important Bs. In 2009, an average of 360 million people worldwide were active on Facebook. That was 359 million more users than five years prior. By a decade later that number had skyrocketed to 2.4 billion.[24] Facebook is "close to saturated in developed countries," a news report announced in late 2018, having signed up huge majorities of its targeted demographics as users.[25] The company's old motto was "Move fast and break things," and this wasn't just marketing bravado. The firm's organizational culture didn't prioritize thorough pretesting or careful avoidance of potential unintended outcomes as it launched innovations in pursuit of exponential growth. As the company's reach became enormous, its relative inattention to user data privacy and security in particular had serious effects, from misuses of user data by political consultants to outright breaches by hackers. Investigations into rampant disinformation and manipulation by foreign entities in elections here and abroad sparked public outcry and governmental scrutiny, especially in the aftermath of the 2016 US presidential election. The swirling controversies caused Facebook to revamp the structure of its performance-based pay. In the past, the company had given everyone annual bonuses largely determined by whether the whole company had met that year's aggressive growth target. After the controversies erupted, and lawmakers had marched the company's founder to testify on Capitol Hill, Facebook decided to change its bonus policy, and start basing bonuses in part on "how well the company achieves its goals on a metric of social good."[26] Compared to measuring growth in the number of monthly users, there would be no easy formula for figuring out progress on the new goals, Facebook's chief technology officer acknowledged to a *Fortune* reporter.[27] Nonetheless, the company decided its past measures of performance, while easily quantifiable, were not focusing its people on what mattered most. That says a lot coming from a Silicon Valley tech giant run by coders and engineers more comfortable with "objective," quantitative metrics like user growth rather than with fuzzier, more subjective assessments of "doing good."

Defining "performance" gets no easier in the public sector, where generating profits isn't a concern. As a sector reliant on taxpayer dollars, government demands of its workers that they perform public service sufficient to justify those taxes. Often these public sector organizations have multiple missions, making it difficult to peg pay to one simple indicator of performance. Back in the 1930s, when Herbert Simon, who would later win the Nobel Memorial Prize in

Economics, was a student at the University of Chicago, he assisted the director of the International City Managers' Association on a study of how best to evaluate municipal administration. Their conclusion? Do not rely on any single measure of performance. Many public services have multiple purposes.[28] Deciding which one to prioritize inevitably involves trade-offs—not to mention power struggles between parties with competing ideas about which should take priority.

Take the police. Their duty is "to protect and to serve." These broad imperatives speak to the multiple missions of every police department. Solving crimes is important, and so is preventing them. Officers and their superiors often disagree about which of these to prioritize, and how to gauge individuals' contributions toward accomplishing organizational goals. What measures capture best how well a cop is protecting and serving? An outcome measure like a drop in crime on her beat? The problem is that it might have been more due to other factors, or the greater efforts of her partner and others responsible for responding to calls in that area. What about an activity measure such as number of arrests made or citations issued per month? The potential to create perverse incentives is obvious, but nonetheless variants of these measures are widespread in pay-for-performance systems. Some cash-strapped municipalities even nudge their officers toward more revenue-enhancing activities—levying fines and fees for minor infractions—because their main objective is to shore up budgets depleted by programs that have nothing to do with policing. One result is lower clearance rates for serious crimes, as officers' attention is diverted to other tasks.[29]

In 2015, in the aftermath of widespread protests over police-involved shootings in a number of cities, the Obama administration appointed a President's Task Force on 21st Century Policing.[30] One of its recommendations was that police departments should increase the number of college-educated officers in their ranks.[31] Task force members presumed that more highly educated officers would police more in the spirit of problem solving, community engagement, procedural justice, and other priorities the task force was calling for. A recent investigation into the role of a college education on policing practices, however, finds no evidence this is true. First, the authors note that "Stops, searches, and arrests remain among the most important enforcement metrics for determining who gets rewarded and promoted in US police departments."[32] Second, analyzing data on over sixty thousand traffic stops, the authors find that college-educated officers are *more* likely than their less-educated peers to pull over drivers for less serious violations, perform searches, and make arrests.[33] College-educated officers, it would appear, are especially responsive to the incentive systems of their departments. The good news is that, by recruiting more officers with a college degree, a department could see faster uptake of any new way of measuring performance. "The challenge, then," the authors conclude, "is to change the reward structure of policing."[34] Indeed.

For many jobs, definitional disputes center on whether individual performance can be defined at all. In 2004, the Bush administration attempted to change the performance management system for Defense Department employees. In place of what it viewed as the overly cumbersome human resources procedures in use for decades, officials installed a new set of practices called the National Security Personnel System, or NSPS. The new system's goals included increasing managerial flexibility in hiring, compensating, suspending, and firing employees. With this in mind, the Defense Department implemented an individual performance measurement system. Each worker would be rated annually on a five-point scale (unacceptable, 1; fair, 2; valued performer, 3; exceeds expectations, 4; and role model, 5). If your supervisor found you to be a role model, to exceed expectations, or at least to be a valued performer in your role, you were eligible for a performance-based pay increase. If your supervisor deemed your performance just fair, your salary would only benefit from a cost-of-living adjustment. If your performance was rated unacceptable, you were allowed to keep your job, but your pay would not be increased that year.[35]

Union representatives and most employees despised the new system. Their complaints and other problems with implementation and system design ultimately motivated the government to scrap the whole project. In the fall of 2009, NSPS died after a new Congress repealed the legislation that had birthed the system after just two performance appraisal cycles (for 2006 and 2007).

Looking back on the failure of the NSPS at the Department of Defense, observers debated what core issue caused its demise. Some blamed poor implementation, citing problems with communications and roll-out, and others pointed to design flaws such as an overly complex set of rules and procedures. Certainly none of these issues engendered goodwill among the workers subject to the change. But some critics question whether it's even possible to link pay to performance for federal government workers. Journalist John Stein Monroe has covered the public sector beat for decades, focusing especially on technology workers within government. Attempting to glean insights from the NSPS failure for other federal attempts at pay for performance, he notes that "Such systems depend on having clear and measurable job objectives. The problem is that the nature of government often defies simple metrics." He quotes Laura Langbein, a professor of public policy at American University, saying that in a large federal project, teamwork is the most important driver of performance, and "the contribution of my skill to the total output is not clear."[36] This difficulty in disentangling one's individual contribution from others' is especially acute in the collaborative, knowledge worker jobs that have expanded over the past decades. As the journalist Derek Thompson has remarked, "The whiter the collar, the more invisible the product."[37] Think of management consultants, market researchers, and mid-level managers of all kinds— there are millions of these jobs spread across the country today. And in each of them distilling individual performance into one quantifiable metric exceeds our capabilities not because we haven't discovered the right measure, but because no such measure exists.

IMPERFECT MEASURES

As the above examples demonstrate, for many jobs out there today, defining performance is an ongoing, contested process, subject to bitter disagreement and power struggles among actors seeking to imprint their favored definitions on an organization. Why don't workers just quit when they disagree with their organization's dominant performance measures? Certainly, the frictions involved in changing jobs are substantial. But there is a more fundamental reason. The stakes are high because once a definition wins out at a prominent organization, it tends to diffuse throughout a particular field, as organizations mimic the practices of industry leaders. That's what happened in journalism, as entity after entity began chasing clicks— and rewarding those who produced the most effective bait.

It is more-or-less true in my profession, as well. Despite whatever attempt a Texas A&M administrator might make to frame professor performance in revenue terms, the dominant standard among research universities is individual research productivity. Publishing early and often, and especially in highly respected outlets, is the key to success in modern academia. That doesn't mean it should be or that the metric is accepted by everyone, or that open debate about it as a key criterion doesn't continue across higher education. But once the Harvards and Princetons of the world coalesced on the measure, all the Harvard and Princeton wannabes followed suit. And that means, if you don't accept the established measure of performance, quitting isn't an option unless you plan to change careers.

But there are occupations in which at least a general standard of performance is widely agreed upon by all relevant parties. In the case of physicians, for example, deciding on a common metric for practitioners' success should be easy. The point is to improve patients' health. But past that statement, the complications arise. Which aspect of health? Overall health? Simply performing a specialized task correctly, such as a hip replacement? What if there were other, less-invasive options available, but the physician only received payment for major surgery? Is that how we want to structure our healthcare system's incentives? A recent exposé into payment systems in modern dentistry found an egregious example of a dentist who performed far more root canals than necessary, earning him in some years nearly $1 million.[38] Recommending surgeries without carefully weighing the alternatives is a predictable consequence of a system that pays for procedures. That's the dominant system in dentistry, with the result being a profession in which widespread "creative diagnosing" leads to overcharging patients for treatments they don't need.[39] It's widespread among US hospitals, too, with many doctors receiving pay based on number of services performed.

The "fee-for-service" model common in the US healthcare sector does incentivize providers to increase patient volume. And that matters, obviously—saving one patient from a life-threatening infection is all well and good, but what about the other people in need of the physician's specialty care? Under Tony Blair's government, the UK's National Health Service increased compensation to hospitals that reduced their wait times. It's true that nobody likes sitting around the doctor's office waiting to be seen, so wait time, while not a direct measure of patient health, does capture an important component of patient well-being. But an issue quickly arose: in an effort to hit waiting time targets, hospitals held patients in ambulances before transferring them to waiting rooms.[40] Why? Time spent in an ambulance didn't count as "waiting," according to this particular performance measure.

As a result of these questions and complications, performance measures for doctors differ markedly both across and within national healthcare systems, as there isn't widespread agreement on one particular "objective" indicator of improving patients' health. The Blair Government's transformation of healthcare didn't stop with its effort to reduce hospital wait times. It also introduced a range of incentive pay schemes to health providers who met performance thresholds on various indicators. The resulting Quality and Outcomes Framework (QOF) was and remains the most extensive pay-for-performance model in healthcare.[41] At the QOF's outset, it tracked "76 quality indicators in 10 clinical domains of care, 56 process indicators, 4 measures linked to patients' experiences, and a few other factors for additional services."[42] Give the British government credit for recognizing the difficulty in distilling a doctor's mission to help patients down to a simple indicator or two. The problem is that what the system lacks in simplicity it doesn't seem to make up in effectiveness. Research from the UK and particular experiments in the United States generally find that pay-for-performance in healthcare "simply doesn't work," and that "giving doctors extra cash to do what they are trained to do can backfire in ways that harm patients' health," as one article by researchers at Harvard Medical School and the University of Pennsylvania put it.[43] We'll explore why a little later in the chapter. For now, suffice it to say that even in a field where the core goal seems fairly simple—help patients get healthy—attempts to measure each individual doctor's contribution to reaching that goal are anything but.

Despite research findings suggesting it is counterproductive, fee-for-service remains commonplace in medicine. Partly this is due to inertia. Once instituted, much of an organization's designs and practices become structured around maximizing whatever measure of "performance" has won out. In modern medicine in the United States, this includes a reimbursement system that rewards procedures performed over other potential measures of patient well-being. This institutionalization makes undoing the incentive structure in an occupation—redefining what performance means—exceptionally difficult, and the resulting inertia insures that workers past, present, and future will be evaluated and compensated based on the prevailing performance measure absent a radical disruption.

Such a disruption requires a power shift, and that's exactly what happened with the change in US presidential administrations in 2009. Early in its first term, the Obama administration took aim at the prevailing incentive system for K-12 teachers. Teaching, like medicine, is a job in which nearly everyone agrees on what constitutes performance: student achievement. Similar to medicine, there is far less consensus about how to measure that performance, and how or whether to attach teachers' pay to that measurement. The US Department of Education, under the leadership of Secretary Arne Duncan, decided it knew how to measure student performance, and designed a couple of incentive programs for districts interested in adopting its definition. The administration defined performance as changes in student achievement on standardized, statewide tests, and tasked schools with measuring these changes. It also promoted the idea that teachers' pay should be explicitly linked to this "value-added" measure of student growth.

As part of the major stimulus package passed at the height of the Great Recession, the administration allocated over \$4 billion to its Race to the Top initiative, which awarded funds to school districts that implemented a suite of education reforms, including one that tied personnel decisions regarding teachers to measures of their students' growth in the classroom. At around the same time, the administration expanded the Teacher Incentive Fund, a grant program for high-need districts that aimed to reshape performance evaluation and compensation systems among principals and teachers. It, too, rewarded those districts that attached teacher pay to its preferred measure of student achievement.[44] In a sign of the effort's impact, the number of states in which student achievement was a core feature of teacher evaluations jumped from just four in 2009, prior to the Race to the Top initiative, to sixteen by 2015. Today, nearly all states include measures of student achievement as part of teacher evaluations.[45]

The carrot part of programs like Race to the Top and the Teacher Incentive Fund linked incentive pay to teachers whose students demonstrated the most growth on standardized tests. But there was a clear stick component, as well. One of the core goals was to identify and remove underperforming teachers, with underperformance defined as a lack of improvement in student's academic growth. Past teacher evaluation systems identified very few underperformers. One study found that in most districts fewer than one percent of teachers were rated unsatisfactory, despite the fact that a majority of teachers could name at least one ineffective colleague.[46] The Obama administration hoped to change that, by identifying a higher fraction of ineffective teachers and removing them from the profession if necessary.

It turned out that school administrators rarely reached for the stick. A study of two dozen states that revamped their teacher evaluation systems to align with the Education Department's reform agenda found that in most of them the fraction of teachers deemed ineffective hadn't budged; still, fewer than one percent underperformed according to the new evaluation metrics.[47] This lack of movement had a number of underlying causes, one of which was the fact that many districts designed teacher evaluation systems that assigned lower weight to student outcome measures than to other inputs, such as classroom observations. Many teachers felt changes in test scores didn't reflect their contributions to the classroom—they rejected Arne Duncan's definition of student achievement. Many principals in cash-strapped districts lacked the resources to develop underachieving teachers' skills and were constrained in their abilities to fire them. The result was that there was little incentive by the relevant parties to label a higher share of teachers as lacking proficiency.

The new system also incentivized criminal behavior. Pressure to raise students' standardized test scores had first started building after passage of the No Child Left Behind Act in 2001, a law that sanctioned schools that didn't demonstrate significant test score growth. Race to the Top and the Teacher Incentive Fund increased the stress on principals and teachers to get their students' scores up. Many did legitimately. Many others cheated, with accounts of testing irregularities surfacing in the majority of states between 2010 and 2012.[48] A sprawling cheating scandal engulfed the Atlanta public school system, eventually implicating 180 teachers and administrators in dozens of schools.[49] A handful of teachers landed in prison for their misdeeds.[50]

Why did teachers across the country end up breaking the law so brazenly? Writing decades ago, the social psychologist Donald Campbell noted that, "The more any quantitative social indicator is used for social decision-making, the more subject it will be to corruption pressures, and the more apt it will be to distort and corrupt the social processes it is intended to monitor."[51] This seems especially true in organizations geared to complex, often idealistic missions, such as schools. In these contexts, as Muller explains, "Whenever reward is tied to measured performance, metric fixation invites gaming."[52] Many of those caught up in the scandal said they rejected the definition of student performance pushed from the federal government down to local districts. One Atlanta educator, initially enthusiastic about "what appeared to be an objective metric" of teacher performance, ultimately considered the system a deterrent to student achievement.[53] He told a panel at his termination hearing how improving test scores came to become "the underlying force behind everything we did," radically reshaping how he taught, what he taught, and why he taught.[54] Another shifted the blame away from front-line teachers, many of whom never bought into the idea that student improvement on standardized tests was the metric that captured good teaching. She redirected it upward: "The education officials and policymakers that have pushed high-stakes testing—that is who has cheated these children. That is who is guilty."[55]

Simon likely wouldn't have been surprised by the widespread teacher cheating, or by the in-vogue pay-for-performance model that precipitated so much gaming of the system. Writing in the 1930s about evaluation efforts in public schools, Simon and his coauthor, Clarence Ridley, noted that "For years standardized tests have been used as the basis for gathering statistics on pupil progress and retardation." Improvement on these tests "may give some indication that a teacher is improving her performance," but it is only one indication among many, and a preliminary one at that: "the use to which the pupil puts that knowledge is the only really significant point."[56] Measures designed to capture value-added needed to be supplemented with a range of indicators on the social health of the broader community. "The final appraisal of the school system," they wrote, "must be in terms of its impact upon the community through the individuals that it trains."[57] Capturing these contextual effects raises its own set of thorny measurement questions, leaving the authors to conclude that, "from a practical standpoint, no one is so optimistic as to believe that all these results can be directly measured."[58]

Seven decades later, Jesse Rothstein likewise cautioned against the use of just one quantitative indicator in measuring a teacher's contribution to a school system. First, there is the issue of the measure's stability. Research has found significant variation in a teacher's value-added over the course of her career.[59] Second, echoing Ridley and Simon, the use of one metric, however well measured, to capture performance has a range of unintended and damaging, if entirely predictable, consequences. One, obviously, is the kind of cheating that Atlanta and other school districts across the country experienced. Rothstein concludes that the quest for "simple quantitative measures" that capture "workers engaged in complex, multifaceted tasks" like teaching is misguided.[60] Even some proponents of the measure caution that it should not be used in isolation to capture teacher performance, but combined with other metrics, such as classroom observations by peers and principals.[61] And examples of employees cheating to boost their performance evaluations, and therefore their pay, go well beyond our schools. Green Giant, the frozen vegetable producer, once instituted an individual bonus structure at one of its plants that rewarded workers who kept a sharp eye out for insect parts in the product. Before long, there were workers inserting bugs brought from home, "discovering" them, and reaping the financial rewards.[62]

To sum up, even in those fields where there is widespread agreement about organizations' core missions, such as education, definitional disputes about how to measure mission success are common. But there is another reason to avoid a single indicator of performance, having to do with the "architecture of evaluation."[63] The design of so-called "objective" indicators of performance involves numerous decisions that influence how the indicator works in the real world. Even seemingly innocuous choices, like how many levels to include in a performance scale, have important ramifications for those being measured. A recent study compared teaching evaluations for men and women professors, capitalizing on a change in a university's evaluation metric. Under the old system, students evaluated their professors on a ten-point scale, with a rating of ten being reserved for the best, or most exceptional, teachers. The authors found that in male-dominated fields women professors received lower evaluations than men even after adjusting for a range of other relevant factors that influence evaluations. What accounted for the gender discrepancy? Stereotypes about exceptional performers or "geniuses" benefit men, who were more likely to receive a "perfect" rating of ten. When the university moved to a (seemingly less precise) six-point scale, the gender ratings gap vanished. Fewer categories to choose from eliminated the opportunity to make fine-grained distinctions, distinctions that had benefited men. A follow-up experiment where the investigators presented subjects with the same lecture transcript but varied the gender of the instructor produced a similar result: the more condensed the scale, the smaller the gender bias.[64] Another recent study found that an arbitrary change in the ratings system for equity analysts influenced which ones received the coveted "All-Star" designations from *Institutional Investor* magazine.[65] For analysts, such a designation isn't purely symbolic—it has an impact on their salary.[66]

The number of categories isn't the only crucial decision managers face when deciding how to capture their workers' productivity. There is also the question of how to ensure enough variation in the outcome for the metric to be meaningful. In the performance management literature, "leniency errors" occur when managers rank the vast majority of their employees as similarly productive.[67] This problem plagued teacher evaluation metrics, as we've seen. What managers—or school administrators—may gain in employee goodwill, they lose in information useful for making individual distinctions when setting pay. No one would accuse Microsoft of being too lenient. Borrowing a practice from 1980s-era General Electric, the technology giant ensured variation in employee evaluations by instituting a "stack" rating system, one also known as "rank and yank." Typical of many performance appraisal systems, Microsoft graded employees on a five-point scale. Less typical: managers had to construct a normal distribution (bell) curve that placed the highest number of employees in the average-performing middle and smaller percentages at both ends of the curve. Typically, if a manager wanted to give out a "five" to a standout performer, she had to balance that with a "one" for the team member contributing least. And where people landed on the curve really mattered: management handed out the biggest bonuses to those ranked highest, and "yanked" those ranked lowest right out of their jobs. This system solved the "leniency error" issue but caused its own set of problems. Most critically, workers hated it. "If you were on a team of 10 people, you walked in the first day knowing that, no matter how good everyone was, two people were going to get a great review, seven were going to get mediocre reviews, and one was going to get a terrible review," one employee told *Vanity Fair*. "It leads to employees focusing on competing with each other rather than competing with other companies."[68] Microsoft scrapped the system in 2013, replacing it with more frequent evaluations based on qualitative indicators, while granting managers greater flexibility in deciding on performance bonuses.[69]

Researchers of employee evaluation metrics tend to speak of subjective versus objective measures.[70] In the educational realm, again, the subjective ones include classroom observations by more experienced educators, and a good example of an objective measure is a class's average score on a standardized test. But no measure is a perfect, error-free indicator of a worker's contribution to her organization. The subjective input often has rigor, and the objective input often involves as much "art" as science. Better to speak of quantitative and qualitative measures, each one attempting to capture one dimension of a worker's output, and each one "relationally constructed, subject to categorical biases, and routinely contested," as Donald Tomaskovic-Devey and Dustin Avent-Holt have argued.[71] Even in data-intensive fields where everyone more or less agrees on the general goal, such as healthcare and education, assessing performance is never straightforward.

THE PITFALLS OF PAYING FOR PERFORMANCE

There are a few jobs in which the relevant parties are in general agreement about what constitutes good individual performance and the agreed-upon definition lends itself to easy quantification. Take sales, an occupation where a direct line can be traced from an individual worker's actions to the company's bottom line. Unsurprisingly, among private sector workers, the percentage of sales workers who report receiving individual performance pay is higher than in other occupations.[72]

In retail sales, new technologies provide store managers with real-time data on each floor salesperson's productivity, allowing them to match the highest performers with the shifts where they could have most impact. Ann Taylor, the women's clothier, was early to try out the new technologies. One of its stores outfitted sales employees with headsets over which managers would inform everyone of how well the store was doing that particular shift, and give a shout-out to those making big sales. The company ranked workers by their sales per hour and those with the highest rankings were rewarded with more hours and more desirable shifts. Often the least desirable shifts were the least remunerative ones—the times and days with little foot traffic. One low-ranking clerk in a Beavercreek, Ohio, store told the *Wall Street Journal* this made it hard to make her way back up, since she was stuck working shifts with fewer potential sales to make. "Computers aren't very forgiving when it comes to an individual's life," she said.[73] Another complained that the system undervalues sellers who focus on cultivating long-term customer relationships. Spending time with a customer who might not buy anything on a particular visit "no longer pays."[74]

Predictably, the spread of this software throughout retail sparked tension and resentment among many employees. So much, in fact, that one of the producers of the software, Dayforce, added a "fairness" setting for managers to adjust and scramble the algorithm a bit, adding some randomness to soften its hyperoptimization of shift assignments. Dialing up the fairness factor might not maximize sales, but could yield schedules that employees find more humane.[75] It turns out that the "softer route" might make business sense. As Dayforce CEO John Orr notes in the *Washington Post*, "If you're ruthless, you'll have a lot of turnover, they'll go work for someone else."[76] Having the ability to measure something doesn't mean those measurements should guide everything.

That's the lesson learned at Mayer Brown, the giant Chicago-based law firm. But it took a while. Some corporate law firms compensate partners in a "lockstep" fashion, where pay is mostly determined by your seniority at the firm. Others have adopted an "eat-what-you-kill" model, tying a year's pay directly to the amount of business a partner generated for the firm. Mayer Brown decided to move from one model to the other, shifting away from a seniority-based system toward one where the firm paid partners based on the business they brought in. Calculating how many hours a partner has billed her clients and the value of the business she has generated doesn't take an advanced math degree.

Yet few firms allocate pay solely on this simple equation, given the infighting, sabotage, and general feelings of inequity such a system spawns among workers.[77] Industrial psychologist Herbert Meyer argued over four decades ago that, "Since almost everyone thinks his own performance is above average, almost everyone expects the above-average increase."[78] Not receiving such a raise feels unfair.

Mayer Brown found this out the hard way when it added to its new performance pay system transparency into how well each attorney did relative to the others. The firm published the "points" allocated to partners, translating to the shares of that year's profits that would be allocated to them, with the top fifty performers appearing on the first page. In theory, this kind of leader board motivates others in an organization to raise their game. In practice, "the amount of resentment this engenders is hard to overstate," writes Noam Scheiber, who documented Mayer Brown's experience for the *New Republic*. The firm's performance pay system affected more than people's feelings, it drove behavioral changes as well. But not in the direction management intended. Partners stopped cooperating with one another, which, given what the compensation system rewarded, was perfectly rational. Since "credit was a zero-sum game," asking a colleague for help trying to land a client meant that you'd be splitting the proceeds. The behavioral changes didn't stop there. After the implementation of the new system, partners "competed aggressively not just against lawyers at other firms, but against one another," trying to poach clients from their colleagues.[79] Mayer Brown eventually backed away from the system, instituting broad pay bands that combined groups of partners into similar compensation levels.

In sales and legal services, determining exactly what each worker contributes to an organization's bottom line is comparatively easy. Compensating workers based on their contribution is anything but, as the examples above demonstrate. We should also bear in mind an important truth often buried in our quest to assign different values to workers' varying performance: most of us don't work in isolation. Our productivity is jointly produced by our contributions along with those around us. One recent study examined an occupation in which productivity could be measured rather simply: checkout clerks at supermarkets. What the authors found was that inserting a highly productive clerk into a shift raised everyone's productivity. It wasn't because this superstar jumped aisles to help her colleagues speed up their scanning and bagging. It was because having such a high performer in their midst motivated the others to work harder. As the authors put it, "mutual monitoring" and "social pressure" increase the productivity of individual cashiers.[80] This finding aligns with Pfeffer's observation that workers "do not make decisions about how much effort to expend in a social vacuum; they are influenced by peer pressure and the social relations they have with their workmates."[81] Even the most skilled workers' motivation may flag when they are surrounded by disaffected coworkers complaining constantly about their jobs. Conversely, a well-functioning team with an inspirational manager can boost the performance of its least-skilled member.[82]

LOTS OF TALK, LITTLE ACTION

As we've seen, basing compensation on a measurement of individual contributions to a business's mission is rife with definitional, measurement, and ethical dilemmas. The majority of US employers don't use it, and the overall prevalence of performance-related pay has declined. Yet in many circles today, "Questioning pay for performance is rather like questioning gravity."[83] Researchers continue to churn out studies investigating whether paying for individual performance is beneficial or detrimental to overall organizational performance.

A few have found positive benefits, albeit from samples of rather atypical occupations, such as professional hockey players.[84] One study, based on an investigation of auto-glass installers during the mid-1990s, found sizable positive effects on output per worker.[85] The general thrust of the academic literature, however, has been toward caution when implementing an individual pay-for-performance plan.[86] A recent study found elevated rates of work-related injuries in firms with individual incentive pay, which led to lower financial performance and product quality.[87] Another linked performance pay with working excessive hours, with those workers taking on punishing shifts ending up with higher rates of absenteeism.[88] A third linked performance pay to more drug and alcohol abuse among workers.[89] It turns out that attempts to disentangle each worker's distinct contribution, and to peg pay to it, often end up backfiring. As a result, despite what we tend to think, and many experts like to imply, most of us aren't actually paid for our individual performance.

What about broader performance measures? If your pay isn't tied to measures of your individual productivity, surely you're compensated according to how well your organization is performing? You might be. But for many workers, changing power dynamics occurring within and beyond their organizations' walls have severed that connection, upending the once-dominant conviction among employers that workers should share in the success of the enterprise. The next chapter tells the tale.

5 THE BOSSES' BOSS

LOW PAY IS IMPRINTED in Walmart's DNA. Prior to founding it in 1962, Sam Walton operated other stores in Arkansas. He took full advantage of a carve-out in the nation's minimum wage law that excluded retail workers from coverage, allowing him to hold wages down and keep prices low. That avenue closed in 1961 when Congress overwhelmingly passed and a newly elected President Kennedy signed legislation that both raised the nation's minimum wage and extended it to the fast-growing retail sector. Or so it seemed. Walton had a convenient workaround. The new act, HR 3935, pushed the minimum hourly wage up from $1.00 to $1.25 while covering an additional 3.5 million workers, most of them in retail, but exempted small businesses from its purview. Any company with annual sales below $1 million—lowered in 1967 to $500,000 and in 1969 to $250,000—didn't have to abide by the minimum. By 1967, Sam Walton already operated two dozen Walmart stores and their combined sales that year hit $12.7 million. But because each store had been set up as a separate entity with its own ownership structure, annual revenue for most of them fell conveniently below the large company threshold. A district attorney in Arkansas took issue with the decentralized ownership structure, and eventually a court order required that employees at three stores be compensated for double their lost wages. The company reluctantly issued checks for back pay, angering its founder. One store manager later recalled that Walton was so furious he told a group of employees, "I'll fire anyone who cashes the check."[1]

Sam Walton may have lost that particular battle, but for decades his firm would win the war on labor costs. Over the years, Walmart became the symbol for rock-bottom wages. Its pay practices are extraordinarily powerful, given its gargantuan size. Today, Walmart directly employs around a million and a half Americans. There were about 157 million workers in the country in 2019. That means that Walmart accounts for nearly one out of every hundred US jobs. Aside from the federal government, no other employer comes close.

Walmart's reach extends well beyond its direct employment figures. As the leader in a now global retail industry, every move Walmart makes influences the business practices of its direct competitors. Research has found that the opening of a Walmart in a community leads to lower pay and more meager healthcare for other retail workers, as local stores scramble to compete with the behemoth by mimicking its business practices.[2] Meanwhile all of Walmart's manufacturers have to respond to its demands, and its demands are legendary. If you're head of sales at a manufacturing company surviving largely on goods sold on Walmart shelves, you have little leverage to negotiate when Walmart tells you to cut your prices by 20 percent. Or when the company tells you to price your goods so low you can't make a profit on them, as the pickle producer Vlasic found out in the late 1990s. After agreeing to supply Walmart with gallon jars of pickles it could price at less than $3, basically a break-even price, Vlasic came to realize that sales of all its other, more profitable varieties and jar sizes were tanking as a result. It asked for a higher price, but Walmart's first response was to threaten to find another supplier for the gallon jars—and for all their other pickle products, as well.[3]

Eventually Walmart relented, to a degree, but that initial strong-arming was typical of how it dealt with suppliers again and again. The resulting price cuts came out of manufacturing workers' paychecks, and at the expense of their jobs. In the mid-1990s, less than a tenth of Walmart's merchandise came from overseas. Fast-forward a decade, and well over half did.[4] Plant after plant was shuttered in the United States as companies competing for Walmart's business off-shored their operations to take advantage of dirt-cheap labor in foreign countries. Lakewood Engineering & Manufacturing Co., a Walmart supplier, once produced fans in the Chicago area. In the early 1990s, the company's twenty-inch box fan sold on Walmart's shelves for $20. By the early 2000s, after relentless pressure from Walmart, the same fan was selling for $10. The firm increased productivity at its Chicago production site as much as possible, automating various tasks and cutting the number of workers needed to produce a fan by two-thirds. When those cost savings weren't enough, the company opened up a factory in China. Owner Carl Krauss explained that he had no choice: "I have the same respect for American workers, but I'm going to do what I have to do to survive."[5] As Walmart's product mix has shifted in recent years toward groceries, it is now the packaged goods producers feeling the heat—and not just those in the pickle business. In February 2017 meetings with major vendors, including Procter & Gamble, Unilever, and Kraft Heinz, Walmart asked for 15 percent cost reductions to help it win a price war with global rival Aldi.[6] Those discounts benefit you when you're buying a bottle of ketchup. But they don't emerge from the ether—somewhere, workers are getting their paychecks squeezed.

It was a shock to many, then, when the company decided early in 2015 to raise its base pay rate for its "associates" (Walmart-speak for its workers) to a minimum of $9 per hour, 24 percent higher than the federal requirement. One of its top rivals, Target, countered soon after, worried that it would lose out in recruiting and retaining workers if it didn't match Walmart's pay.[7] The White House cheered Walmart's move.[8] Many worker advocates hoped it would spur wage growth more broadly for retail workers. The fast-growing economy surely contributed to Walmart's break with its usual orthodoxy; retailers in general were having trouble finding and retaining workers. In fall 2015, the nation's unemployment rate improved to 5 percent—half of its level in October 2009, the worst month of the Great Recession.

This backdrop of a humming economy encouraged other corporate leaders to take a worker-friendly stance. Doug Parker, CEO of American Airlines, decided to act on the pay gulf that had opened up between his pilots and flight attendants and those at competing airlines. Whether or not he felt it was unfair that his employees were getting paid less for doing the same work, his company now faced a greater risk that its best people would leave for employment elsewhere. So, two years before the company's existing contract with these unionized employees was due to run out, he announced pay increases to reduce the gap. For his efforts, as Matthew Yglesias of *Vox* put it, "Wall Street freaked out"—and not from joy.[9] The market responded to the $350 million this added to annual operating expenses with a 5.2 percent hit to the company's share price. Not content with punishing just one firm for its transgression, investors sold more than they bought of all airline stocks that week, sending a clear message about the sector's rising costs and who should bear the brunt of lower profits. As a JPMorgan Chase analyst remarked, Parker's decision "establishes a worrying precedent in our view, both for American and the industry." An equity analyst at Citi echoed the lament, complaining that "Labor is being paid first again. . . . Shareholders get leftovers."[10]

What's so curious about that complaint is how utterly disconnected it was from the reality of the past few decades. Shareholders, in fact, had feasted on ample "leftovers" since the late-1970s when a new norm of equity defined "fairness" as shareholders getting first dibs on the available pie. As a result, many CEOs placed workers on a starvation diet. Some did this by design, as in Walmart's case, where low pay was long part of the company's formula for beating competitors on price. But many others felt compelled to do it. Just as the *Washington Post*'s Steven Pearlstein noted that most executives "would be thrilled if they could focus on customers rather than shareholders" and privately "chafe under the quarterly earnings regime forced on them by asset managers and the financial press," so, too, many would rather reward workers if their own livelihoods didn't depend on putting shareholders first.[11]

If you're a worker in a publicly traded firm, you're not likely to find a major shareholder skulking through the halls of your workplace, peeking into your desk, and monitoring your efficiency to ensure everything is running smoothly. But they are watching operations nonetheless, and they are staking claims on more and more of the organizational revenue. Shareholders now comprise an incredibly powerful set of actors in the claims-making process, and their hugely consequential influence on non-executive workers' pay is often overlooked in ongoing debates about wage stagnation and rising inequality.[12] These effects are direct, as firms redistribute organizational revenue upward to please shareholders. They are also indirect, as pressure to cut operating expenses to the bone leads to layoffs, automation, and offshoring. Either way, the growing trend toward prioritizing one set of stakeholders over all others has hurt workers' livelihoods.

The rare firms that decided to buck the trend faced withering resistance from financial analysts. The giant retailer Costco, for example, has long been known for paying decently and offering a robust benefits package. In a sector dominated by its rival, Walmart, whose gravitational force has most competitors scrambling to hold labor costs down, Costco's anomalous approach make it all the more unique. It's an approach that has not escaped the attention of financial analysts. "Public companies need to care for shareholders first," one commented. "Costco runs its business like it is a private company."[13] Another gave this blunt assessment of how the company's long-standing CEO, James Sinegal, treats his employees: "He has been too benevolent."[14]

THE ORIGINS OF THE MYTH

Do public companies need to care for shareholders first? In a word, no, and for the middle decades of the twentieth century, most didn't. This also happened to be the period in which wages grew the fastest for the widest swath of American workers. During this postwar, pre-globalization era of American economic growth, different corporate practices reigned. Instead of seeing the value produced for the shareholder as paramount, managers of profitable corporations were more likely to favor internal stakeholders. This "managerial business model" gave hired executives wide latitude to make decisions and, with ownership well separated from management, the focus was more on product quality and job creation.[15] Within the overall goal to grow the business profitably over the long term, the expectation was that shareholders would see sufficient returns—but managers were more directly concerned with the needs and demands of workers and customers, and the local communities whose respect they wanted to earn. Indeed, some corporate leaders explicitly ranked the interests of investors least deserving of management's protection. In 1950, Robert E. Wood, the brigadier general who had led Sears, Roebuck at that point for over twenty years, told a gathering of business leaders that the "four parties to any business" were "by order of their importance" as follows: "customers, employees, community, and stockholders."[16]

So what changed? How did shareholders leapfrog from the back of the line to the front, and increasingly come to subsume so much of the attention and strategic planning of corporate leaders? Two factors reshaped power relations among key actors, upending existing business practices and ushering in a new set of norms governing the distribution of organizational revenue. First was the increasing stress many leading American firms felt in the mid- to late 1970s as a combination of forces began eating into profits and the companies' primacy atop the global hierarchy of businesses. These included the opening up of global trade as nations such as Japan and Germany emerged from the wreckage of World War II into manufacturing powerhouses. Not helping were the dual oil shocks that would strangle the US economy. Rising energy prices simultaneously decreased the demand for goods and increased the costs of producing them. Households had to spend a larger portion of their budgets on gas and heating expenses, leaving less room for other purchases, while soaring energy prices left many factories struggling to keep the lights on.

Second was a new business philosophy that radically shifted what was seen as equitable in corporate operations. It would gain some early eager adherents among America's class of corporate leaders scrambling to survive an economy that no longer seemed to play by the established rules. The philosophy emerged from, at first, a rather small yet influential section of the academy. In 1970, Milton Friedman was six years away from receiving his Nobel, but already had a level of influence in policy and business circles the vast majority of academics can only dream of. Writing in the *New York Times Magazine,* Friedman derided corporate managers of his day who wanted to direct more of their firms' profits toward "social responsibility" projects. It was enough contribution to society to provide quality goods and jobs. Whatever money a manager spent on such projects took away from other possible recipients: "Insofar as his actions raise the price to customers, he is spending the customers' money," Friedman wrote. "Insofar as his actions lower the wages of some employees, he is spending their money." Of course, stockholders were the other group whose ability to spend that money on whatever they deemed worthy was being curtailed by this "pure and unadulterated socialism." A corporate executive could direct his own money to favored social goals, Friedman insisted, but in his role as "an employee of the owners of the business," he could not claim the right to tax them for those purposes: "He has direct responsibility to his employers."[17]

Friedman's polemic on the obligations of the hired executive connected directly to work other economists were doing at the time to develop what came to be known as "agency theory." From these scholars' perspective, the issue was that managers did not behave like owners. But steps could be taken to better align their interests as "agents" of the owners with the interests of the "principals"—the shareholders—who had entrusted them with running their businesses. The priorities of these parties didn't necessarily converge, especially to the extent that corporate managers took seriously the interests of other stakeholders in and outside the firm. As high inflation and low growth drained corporate coffers during the 1970s, shareholders felt the pinch. The disco era might have been a high point for bell-bottoms and big collars, but it was a "lost decade for investors."[18] That made solving the principal-agent problem all the more urgent.

For Friedman and like-minded economists—including Michael Jensen, William Meckling, and Eugene Fama—the obvious way to align the interests of top executives with their firms' investors was to change the structure of their pay. Compensating corporate managers in company stock would instantly sharpen their focus on one particular aspect of the firm's performance: its stock price. Soon, any recalcitrant CEOs, the ones clinging to the old managerial business model, had activist shareholders to shake them out of their slumber.

The word *activist*, when it comes to investment firms, should not conjure up images of lefty types pressuring companies to stop polluting or to close down sweatshops in faraway lands. These activists are deep-pocketed investors who take an unusually active interest in how the companies they invest in are managed. Rather than take a pass on the shares of a company that is not maximizing its shareholder returns, they buy up its shares and then, based on their substantial ownership stakes, "pressure executives to make changes to 'unlock value' and drive share prices higher."[19] That pressure got ugly for the most unruly pupils in the 1980s with the rise of hostile takeovers. These maneuverings, in which one firm takes control of another over the objections of the targeted firm's management, represent what one former Shell CEO called "the dark side of capitalism."[20] Nothing spelled the end of the managerial business model more than managers being ousted by restless shareholders who felt they weren't getting the best return on their investments.

From this potent combination of a frustrated investor class and an emerging economics theory came a decisive power shift among owners, executives, and workers that now gave the owners—the firm's shareholders—the upper hand. The replacement for the managerial business model was a new approach, shareholder capitalism, and it radically transformed American business during the late decades of the twentieth century. As its starting point, shareholder capitalism took it as an article of faith that a company should be run to maximize returns for its shareholders. What that meant in practice was that managers focused on boosting return on equity, and often over short time periods. Quickly the habit of punishing firms that missed quarterly targets became the norm on Wall Street. Just ask JetBlue's former CEO, David Barger, who had the nerve to try to retain the airline's reputation for premium service, and ignored analysts' calls for it to copy other airlines' customer-unfriendly practices like charging for checked bags and Wi-Fi. With analysts complaining loudly about JetBlue's lower profitability, the company's board opted not to renew Barger's contract. A few months later, the newly installed CEO capitulated, reining in a plan to add more legroom and adding fees for internet use and every checked bag.[21]

And whereas diversification and empire building were all the rage in the decades after the Second World War, turning "lean and mean" was the new name of the game.[22] Underperforming portions of a company were to be jettisoned as soon as possible, to allow it to focus on its "core competencies"—those activities that produced the best return on equity. This fissuring once signaled a company in distress.[23] But increasingly, Wall Street rewarded the firm that laid off workers, narrowed operations, and focused like a laser on strategies to pump up its share price.[24] Firms were finding it was harder and harder to escape the gaze of activist investors. As those investors grew increasingly powerful, they widened their target list.

The Timken Company, a producer of bearings and specialty steel, anchored Canton, Ohio, for much of the twentieth century.[25] After setting up shop there in 1901, it grew through five generations of members of the Timken family, providing good pay and benefits packages to thousands of the city's residents. Its community impact went well beyond the wallets of its workers. The company's charitable arm, the Timken Foundation, paid for the construction of Timken High School in the 1930s, and would pour millions more into the school in the 1990s to shore up flagging graduation rates. It also provided funds to regional arts initiatives, healthcare facilities, and other cultural endeavors. The company was, to quote the superintendent of the city's school district, "the cornerstone of the community."[26]

Leadership at the firm believed in investing in its community, and focused on the long term in its business operations. The goal was steady, smooth profits regardless of the economic season. Steel is a cyclical product, prone to boom and busts. The bearing business is more reliable. Thus the beauty of producing both: the company could bank high earnings during steel's boom periods to protect them when prices collapsed, all the while counting on reliable returns from the bearings operation.

Alas, this increasingly anachronistic way of operating would bump up against the exigencies of shareholder capitalism. The activist investment firm Relational Investors set its sights on Timken in 2012, buying more and more of the company's stock. Relational Investors and its allies wanted the company broken into two distinct firms, one focused on steel, the other on bearings. The idea was to unlock value by letting each side serve its different purposes for investors. Those seeking a higher risk / return profile could put their money into the steel business, those seeking less volatility could invest in the bearings business. As Relational cofounder Ralph Whitworth put it in 2013, Timken's stock had "more potential as two independent companies."[27] Eventually, the activists got their wish, splitting the venerable firm into two. And Whitworth would win his bet. Wall Street cheered the move, and Relational walked away with nearly $200 million after selling its shares of the Timken Company (now the bearings operation) and TimkenSteel (the steel firm) at a steep profit. Relational timed its exit well. Since the spinoff in the summer of 2014, as of this writing, the Timken Company's stock is up 10 percent—a decent return. But TimkenSteel's is down over 200 percent. And for the first time in Timken history, the chief executive of the bearings company is not a Timken family member.

The story of Timken reveals another characteristic of the financialization of our economy, one that shifts risk and uncertainty from firms to average workers. One of Relational's key allies in its battle to break up the manufacturer was the California State Teachers' Retirement System, or CalSTRS. This giant investment fund manages the pensions of a quarter million California state-employed educators, and owned millions of dollars' worth of Timken stock. It, too, wanted a higher return on its investment. In microcosm, observed Suzanne Berger, these were the workings of "a financial system in the U.S. where California teachers have to protect their pension funds by hurting manufacturing in Ohio."[28]

Milton Friedman's 1970 rebuke to corporate America has reached its half-century mark. It was meant to challenge a self-serving class of CEOs too ready to support social causes with other people's money. But its explanation of the more fundamental "principal-agent problem" would gain adherents among many in the economics profession, and from there, quickly jump over ivory tower walls to the practical-minded investors, financial analysts, traders, and journalists happy for a new rationale to give shareholders a greater claim on company profits. It was a turnabout that took hold so spectacularly that CEOs seemed powerless in the face of their financial overlords' demands. Describing his 1997 decision to shed his company's production facilities and boost return on assets, Sara Lee's CEO put it bluntly: "This is what they want. . . . Wall Street can wipe you out. They are the rule-setters."[29] Shareholders gained power in staking claims to organizations' revenue. And their power spread quickly as firm after firm mimicked the early converts to the conception of the publicly traded company as primarily a financial investment vehicle.

Shareholder capitalism is, at heart, an *idea*—not a fact of nature, not a law enshrined in the Constitution—and the resulting set of business practices that it sparked are not immutable characteristics of capitalism. Indeed, they would appear foreign and downright bizarre to many American business leaders of the mid-twentieth century. And yet the core premise behind shareholder capitalism—not only that a business should yield attractive shareholder returns, but that it must be managed to maximize them—has in recent decades reached the point where it is practically taken for granted by executives, business journalists, and management scholars.

Nelson Schwartz is a thorough, dogged economics reporter for the *New York Times,* and his 2014 story of the Timken breakup was a source for material in the recap above. But he made one telling mistake in the tale. "As in all publicly traded companies," he wrote, "TimkenSteel's board and top executives have a fiduciary duty to shareholders to maximize both profits and investor returns." He was wrong: their fiduciary duty is simply to apply sound business judgment. But his inclusion of that line spoke to the reach of an idea whose rise was abetted, protected, and then institutionalized by a set of powerful actors in business and the academy. Steven Pearlstein, his counterpart at the *Washington Post*, accurately described shareholder capitalism as "an ideology . . . that has no basis in history, in law, or in logic. . . . Legally, no statutes require that companies be run to maximize profits or share prices."[30] Cornell Law School's Lynn Stout agreed: "Chasing shareholder value is a managerial choice, not a legal requirement."[31] Rick Wartzman is a former White House reporter for the *Wall Street Journal* and business editor for the *Los Angeles Times,* where he helped shape a series on Walmart that would win the paper a Pulitzer Prize for National Reporting in 2004. He's also the author of *The End of Loyalty,* an exploration of the change in corporate philosophy at major US firms during the second half of the twentieth century. When I asked for his perspective on this notion that corporations "have a fiduciary duty to shareholders to maximize both profits and investor returns," he didn't hesitate: "It's bullshit." Wartzman noted that courts give executives and boards of directors broad freedom to choose their objectives under a doctrine known as the "business judgment rule." He also pointed out that the

Business Roundtable, an organization composed of the CEOs of America's leading companies, explicitly rejected the theory of shareholder primacy in 2019. Instead, the Roundtable's members endorsed the idea that they should "lead their companies for the benefit of all stakeholders."[32] Asked Wartzman: "Do you really think they'd have gone on the record saying that if they had a fiduciary duty to maximize shareholder value?"[33]

ALL ABOARD THE GRAVY TRAIN

"I wrestle over how to build shareholder value from the time I get up in the morning to the time I go to bed," Coca-Cola's former CEO, Roberto C. Goizueta, said in 1990.[34] "I even think about it when I am shaving. But I use an electric razor, so I think I'm safe."

Chasing shareholder value was an obsession more and more managers would choose. Some didn't like the new way of doing things, including Bill George, the former CEO of the medical device maker Medtronic. Critiquing the "short-termism" rampant among activist investors, George pointed to the inevitable drop in research and development that comes along with this outlook: "Activists think long term is twelve months and the first thing that goes is the stuff that pays off in five to ten years."[35] Others embraced the new philosophy wholeheartedly, including Goizueta. In the mid-1990s, he had a computer installed in a meeting room adjacent to the executive suite that tracked Coca-Cola's stock prices throughout the trading day. Reportedly the CEO could often be found there: "Unaware of the employees passing down the hall behind him . . . he was oblivious to everything but the green light coming from the screen."[36] For disciples like Goizueta, part of the allure of focusing solely on stock price likely lay in its simplicity. No longer would you have to account for a range of factors, some crudely measured, others not measured at all, to gauge your performance. How could you even tell whether you did right by your community, or your workers, more this year than last—or more or less than other companies? What were the correct measuring devices? Wall Street provided one convenient, universally applied metric and tracked it constantly to measure your success: the firm's stock price.

In *The Protestant Ethic and the Spirit of Capitalism,* Max Weber theorized that predestination—the Calvinist belief that God had already chosen who would be saved and damned—created a psychological crisis among its adherents, who cast about desperately for signs that they were among the "elect." Over time, many believers coalesced around one particular sign of eventual heavenly ascent: economic success. Doing well financially, it was thought, meant God was smiling down at you, providing a route to achieving some peace of mind despite the essential uncertainty of Calvinist doctrine. Like the number flashing across Goizueta's screen, economic success provided a clear sign of favor or disfavor from above, offering some semblance of control over one's fate. A similarly deep uncertainty was making American corporate leaders anxious in the era when agency theory was being hatched. As one article puts it, "the stagflation of the 1970s, a decade of lackluster stock market performance, and the specter of Japanese domination of auto and high technology manufacturing had sent America's Fortune 500 companies on a spiritual quest."[37] This new theory offered a diagnosis of what was wrong with the management model, and its prescribed remedy of better principal-agent alignment turned the firm's stock price into that same kind of transparent marker of salvation.

Bringing matters solidly down to earth, the more specific prescription to tie executives' pay to their firms' stock valuations definitely focused CEO attention on Wall Street's concerns. The spread of stock options as a component of executive compensation packages tended to win over any CEOs still skeptical about the shareholder value revolution. Options allowed executives to buy company stock at a future date at the price of the stock when the option was issued. For example, an executive whose company was trading at $30 per share in 2018 could be granted options allowing a certain number of shares to be purchased at that price in, say, 2021. Of course, those shares could then be sold at their new market price for a tidy profit, assuming the share value had risen. (If the share price fell between 2018 and 2021, the executive would simply not exercise the option, and at least would lose nothing.) The point was to give the executive extra incentive to make decisions that would cause the stock price to rise. Across the next two decades, the effect was that stock options would prove incredibly lucrative; during the bull runs of the 1980s and 1990s, many CEOs found themselves fantastically rich.

Top executives have not always had such inordinate pay advantages. Yes, they have always earned more than their subordinates.[38] But there have been periods, notably in the post–World War II decades, when average worker pay grew at a faster rate than the pay of executives.[39] In the mid-1960s, the typical American top executive earned about twenty times as much as the typical American worker. That sounds high. Yet by the turn of the twenty-first century, the typical head of a multinational company was making four hundred times that of an average worker, according to one measure that factored in the value of stock options at the time they were granted. The ratio has since fallen from its peak in 2000, but it remains, historically and cross-nationally speaking, astronomical. Depending on how one accounts for the value of stock options, today a CEO of a large firm earns anywhere between 224 and 271 times that of the average worker.[40] Measurements vary, but no matter the estimate, the United States stands out in the gap between what our corporate titans take home compared to typical, non-executive workers.

GEORGE ROMNEY WAS A SUCCESSFUL GOVERNOR of Michigan during the 1960s and unsuccessful challenger to Richard Nixon for his party's nomination for the presidency in 1968. Later appointed by Nixon as Secretary of the Department of Housing and Urban Development, he would leave politics for good in 1973 after the two repeatedly clashed over the direction of urban policy, and Romney became "a pariah" in the administration.[41] But preceding all that public service was a career in business that in a key way typified corporate behavior at major US firms during the World War II era. Romney was president of American Motors Corporation, a car manufacturer, between 1954 and 1962. He was paid well by the company, making this son of a carpenter a millionaire during his time at the helm. But Romney consciously and consistently held his pay down. During the lean year of 1957, he cut his pay in half. When fortunes for the firm rebounded a few years later, Romney refused a raise over the objections of the company's board. During one five-year period, with the company flush with cash, Romney repeatedly rejected bonuses granted by his firm. In all, Romney would leave over $2 million in today's dollars on the table.[42] Why? Well, the CEO felt his current compensation was enough, believing no executive should earn more than $2 million a year.[43] When Romney first realized he was a millionaire, he told his biographer that he lost his equilibrium for a moment, saying that the achievement of such worldly success is often when "most people lose out."[44] He didn't like the feeling and the temptations it engendered, so he remained a rich man, but not an extravagantly rich one, very much of his time.

His son, Mitt, would become extravagantly rich, exhibiting no moral qualms about accepting all the cash on offer. In key aspects, Mitt's career trajectory matched his father's: a successful stint in business followed by much success in the political realm, including the governorship of Massachusetts, his party's nomination for the presidency in 2012, and election to the Senate. But unlike the firm headed by his father, Mitt's company didn't actually make things. Bain Capital, the company Mitt Romney would lead off and on during the 1980s and 1990s, is an investment company known for its use of the private equity model. Private equity firms use their investors' money to buy and sell companies. The goal is to acquire companies, unlock their value, and then sell them at a steep profit. Common strategies for private equity firms include heavy borrowing, the transferring of debt to acquired companies, and the restructuring of acquired firms to reduce labor costs, resulting in layoffs. As Rosemary Batt and Eileen Appelbaum write, this approach "represents an extreme version of the shareholder value model of the firm," one in which "companies are viewed as assets to be bought and sold for the purpose of maximizing profit—rather than as organizations to produce goods and services."[45]

Bain Capital has made a lot of profit by buying and selling a lot of companies. Some of these bets worked out for nearly everyone involved: an early investment in the office-supply retailer Staples resulted in the rapid expansion of that business and a healthy $11 million return on Bain Capital's investment.[46] Many others led to crippling layoffs at firms now saddled with unpayable debts, as in the case of American Pad & Paper, or Ampad, which Bain acquired in the early 1990s. Loading the firm with debt and management fees would eventually bring the company down, and hundreds of manufacturing workers would lose their jobs. Bain and its investors, meanwhile, pocketed nearly $100 million on the deal. For Mitt Romney and other private equity managers and investors, it was hard to lose. The investor and business school lecturer Howard Anderson once offered this colorful description: "The private equity business is like sex. When it's good, it's really good. And when it's bad, it's still pretty good."[47] All this good and bad business would make Mitt Romney very rich, with an estimated net worth between $190 and $250 million.[48]

As a society, our collective imagination hasn't fully caught up to the reality of our corporate leaders. When asked, Americans guess that CEOs make about thirty times that of average workers. And that ratio is much higher than what Americans think CEOs *should* earn. A 2014 study found that Americans believed the ideal pay ratio between a CEO and an unskilled worker should top off at about seven to one. As those researchers conclude, "respondents underestimate actual pay gaps, and their ideal pay gaps are even further from reality than those underestimates."[49] I'd say so. Even at the height of worker power in the United States—in the decades following World War II—executives made a larger premium than people think they should today. Survey research finds the vast majority of Americans are upset about dramatic disparities in compensation between corporate bosses and average workers, even at the level they vastly underestimate that gulf to be.[50] Campaigning for his party's nomination for the presidency in the fall of 2015, Donald Trump capitalized on this sentiment, echoing outrage over outsized pay packages for CEOs: "You see these guys making these enormous amounts of money, and it's a total and complete joke." He added that, these days, CEOs "get whatever they want."[51] That might be a slight overstatement, but today's CEOs certainly get an enormous amount. This is somewhat paradoxical given that much of the original impetus behind the rise of shareholder capitalism was to rein in the power of CEOs. But by shifting corporate leaders' compensation away from salaries to stocks, the move to align the interests of CEOs and shareholders had the side effect of enabling "top-level managers to enjoy unprecedented degrees of wealth."[52] In terms of compensation, shareholder capitalism has been good for our corporate titans. Executives of the past like George Romney earned a lot. But compared to today's CEOs, what Romney brought home was embarrassingly little. His son wouldn't risk such embarrassment.

WHEN SHAREHOLDERS COME FOR YOUR PAYCHECK

Randy Johnson was a worker and union steward at a small plant in Indiana during the years in which Bain Capital was busy restructuring Ampad. Founded in 1888 in Massachusetts, the company a hundred years later was struggling. Its restructuring was based on a strategy to capitalize on its strong brand and grow by buying up other office-supply businesses, consolidating their operations to achieve scale economies, and shutting down facilities deemed to be redundant. After Ampad acquired the assets of a hanging file folder manufacturer in Indiana from Smith Corona, the new management promptly alerted 258 union workers there that their employment was terminated but they could reapply for jobs doing the same work in the same location. There was a catch, or rather, a series of them: wages would be lower, work rules would differ from what the union had formerly negotiated, and now employees would have to cover half of their healthcare costs.[53] After unsuccessful efforts to negotiate acceptable terms, the workers went on strike in September 1994. But that high-risk move backfired: within six months, the new management closed the plant and had all its equipment shipped to a new facility out of state. All the employees were out of work. As Johnson recalled:

"What I remember the most were the guys in their 50s, breaking down and crying."[54]

The rise of stock option compensation and other practices that accompanied the shareholder capitalism revolution presented America's corporate leaders with win–win pay scenarios. Even getting fired could prove lucrative, with "golden parachute" severance packages diffusing through executive contracts starting in the 1980s.[55] Michael Ovitz, for example, lasted all of fourteen months as president of Disney in the mid-1990s. His termination came with a major upside: a $140 million severance package, or $10 million for every month he was on the job.[56] For workers like Johnson, however, the new rules of the game presented them with lose–lose scenarios: accept steep pay cuts or lose your job. The experience of Johnson and his coworkers was not atypical among companies bought out by private equity. Analyzing thousands of manufacturing companies acquired by equity firms between 1980 and 2005, a group of economists found that two years following the buyout, earnings per worker averaged 2.4 percent lower than at otherwise similar companies. Job losses in those first two years post-buyout tended to be higher, too, although most of these were counteracted by the simultaneous addition of new jobs. As the authors observe, the combined effect of job loss and job creation is to "catalyze the creative destruction process."[57] Other research shows that companies unworried about the threat of takeover tend to pay their workers comparatively well.[58]

Of course, creative destruction is the force at the heart of capitalism, and private equity's defenders argue that increased creation along with a dash of destruction was exactly the recipe needed to invigorate US businesses in the late twentieth century. Private equity promises to take over "underperforming firms . . . reforming their operations" to put them on a path to profitability while "acquiring healthy businesses and then injecting capital and management exper-tise to enable them to expand further," according to the authors of a typical industry-sponsored report from 2008.[59] But what seems inar-guable is that average workers bear the brunt of this economic churn, in the form of greater job reallocation and lower wages.

Private equity is now a huge force in the contemporary economy. In a single decade, from 2003 to 2013, private equity firms invested over $3.6 *trillion* in US companies that employed approximately 7.5 million workers.[60] These millions of employees have been directly affected by a shift in business governance to prioritize financial per-formance turnarounds often at the expense of worker paychecks. To be sure, most of us do not work for organizations backed by private equity. Still, the influence of the private equity model extends far beyond the companies acquired by firms like Bain. Private equity takeovers send a powerful message to corporate leaders trying to manage according to their own judgment of what is best for the com-pany: get in line, or you could be next. Many executive teams don't want to risk their own careers, and, as a result, mimic their peers and behave according to the imperatives of the present system of finan-cial capitalism that "favors the finance sector over the non-finance sector, financial investments over investments in production, and shareholders and top executives over workers and other citizens."[61]

The rise of the shareholder capitalism model is part of the tri-umph of finance over other domains of business in America. When people speak of the financialization of the US economy, they are not only referring to the massive share of GDP represented by financial sector firms but also the fact that firms outside that sector—firms ranging from American Airlines to Sara Lee to Walmart—are in-creasingly "responsive to and disciplined by financial rather than product markets."[62] The discipline that financial markets dole out to companies removes much managerial discretion over which set of stakeholders to prioritize when it comes to distributing profits. In this way, it simplifies matters for many corporate leaders, who, like Coca-Cola's Goizueta, can focus on strategies to pump up their firms' stock prices. It also leaves another group of stakeholders out in the cold: companies' workers. Wall Street doesn't appreciate distributing profits downward, or otherwise departing from what is increasingly seen as the sole mission of a company: to return every available penny to shareholders.

Shareholder capitalism is a system, at heart, of income redistribution away from today's workers and toward executives and investors.[63] As such, it is deeply implicated in decades of wage stagnation for millions of American workers. Its rise affects average worker paychecks in a variety of ways. One is the most dramatic and disruptive: the removal of the paycheck itself. As shareholder capitalism spread far and wide, executives whose pay was tied to share performance resorted to tactics that would immediately boost profits. Rather than go the longer and less sure route of growing the top line, many companies took the shortcut to improving the bottom line. To reduce costs, and appeal to investors looking for a higher rate of return on assets, they opted for layoffs.[64] The payoff came quickly. Of course, for the workers involved, so did the pain. Increased mergers and acquisitions activity also spurred layoffs, as redundant workers of the newly created entity were shown the door. Research finds, too, that layoffs often anticipate a potential merger, as firms struggle to shore up their financials rather than leave themselves vulnerable to being swallowed by a competitor.[65]

Surely all this disruption to workers' livelihoods at least produced more profitable companies with more money overall to distribute—right? After all, higher profits were the goal behind all the shareholder value tactics. Alas, the record is mixed. Neil Fligstein and Taekjin Shin find that at least one tactic, seeking scale economies through mergers and acquisitions, actually diminished profits on average. What then explains such widespread use of that tactic? Fligstein and Shin conclude that, similar to how pay practices often spread, "mergers and layoffs may be ritualistic and imitative."[66] Firms adopt these strategies because they seem like the thing to do, because other firms are doing it, and they can be presented plausibly to Wall Street analysts as value-producing moves.

Layoffs most directly affect the pay of those suddenly out of work. They also exert downward pressure on the pay of all employees in the industries where the layoffs occur, by increasing the ranks of job searchers, thereby reducing the bargaining leverage of the employed. No industry better illustrates these dynamics at work than airlines, which underwent a dramatic restructuring following deregulation in 1978. Deregulation was meant to open the industry to greater competition by reducing barriers to entry. Increased competition would benefit consumers through lower ticket prices and more flying choices. Fast-forward to the present, and four carriers control 80 percent of all flight routes in the United States.[67] Whether deregulation caused the airfare price decline remains disputed—some analysts maintain that prices were falling prior to the policy, and point to decreased fuel costs as the source of the drop.[68] What nobody disputes are the deteriorating conditions for those who work in the airline industry.

What happened? First, a series of bankruptcies in the industry led to concentration. They also led to mass layoffs—20 percent of all full-time jobs in the industry vanished in the first five years of the twenty-first century. And the remaining workers—pilots, flight attendants, baggage handlers, maintenance workers, and others—suffered severe pay and benefit cuts.[69] Maintenance workers took it on the chin, with nearly one-third of them losing their jobs since 2000 because airlines began flying their planes abroad for cheaper, out-of-country repair work. Pay cuts as deep as 40 percent in a range of occupations within the industry were not uncommon. Sara Nelson, president of the Association of Flight Attendants, recently told journalist David Dayen that the pay was "not for a middle-class income anymore."[70] (The US Bureau of Labor Statistics pegged the average pay in 2019 at $56,640 per year, and the bottom 10 percent of attendants brought home less than $30,000.) As for pilots, while the average one at United, American, or Delta makes well over a hundred thousand in annual salary, starting pay for pilots at regional carriers can be as low as twenty thousand.[71]

Certainly your average flyer isn't crying out for airline consolidation. The primary cheerleader backing that development has been Wall Street. Concentration in the airline industry shifts power away from consumers—you can't bargain-shop for a Nashville–to–Boston ticket if United is the only carrier offering one. A 2014 research note from Goldman Sachs highlighted the lucrative potential of growing market concentration in the airline industry. In its "Dreams of Oligopoly" section, the analysts extolled the virtues of betting on an industry with few players: "a smaller set of relevant peers faces lower competitive intensity, greater stickiness and pricing power with customers due to reduced choice."[72] Points for honesty, I suppose. And with workers in the industry firmly in retreat, these analysts rightly saw that the "pricing power" accruing to a consolidated set of airlines meant that much of the resulting profits would go to one set of stakeholders above all: the airlines' shareholders.

Today, many critics of increasing industry concentration point to the effects that oligopolies—such as the one that currently dominates our skies—have on depressing workers' wages.[73] Especially when combined with employer collusion around the kinds of no-poaching agreements we explored in Chapter 3, industry concentration can remove leverage for workers seeking higher pay. But highly concentrated industries can also treat their workers well. We know this because many once did. The US auto industry in the post–World War II years was dominated by a handful of firms, including George Romney's AMC. Workers on the line enjoyed steadily rising pay and generous benefits negotiated by the powerful United Auto Workers (UAW) union. For the first time, millions of manual laborers could live comfortably, swelling the ranks of the nation's middle class. The phenomenon wasn't limited to autos, either—in other highly unionized industries, workers actually benefited from oligopolistic market structures.[74] It was when concentration combined with the pressures of shareholder capitalism and the removal of unions that it became detrimental to workers' paychecks, because together these reshaped the power dynamics in claims-making. And increasingly this combination, alongside diminished employee power, is the reality for American workers.

THE LEGISLATIVE PATH PROVED tough sledding for President Donald Trump and his allies in Congress during the first year of his presidency. But the Republican leaders could trumpet one unequivocal achievement: the passage of a massive corporate tax cut that the president signed just before the 2017 holiday break. Among other changes to the tax code, the Tax Cuts and Jobs Act lowered the official corporate tax rate from 35 percent to 21 percent, while also reducing taxes on individual earners, especially for those at the top of the income distribution. Touting the legislation, President Trump made a prediction: "All of this, everything in here, is really tremendous things for businesses, for people, for the middle class, for workers."[75]

Businesses would soon line up to offer their thanks—and to provide some early evidence to substantiate the president's claim that the legislation was tremendous for workers and not just shareholders, as many of the bill's critics claimed. Throughout early 2018, company after company announced one-time bonuses, and, on rarer occasions, worker pay raises due to their reduced tax liabilities. During the month of February alone, nearly a hundred US firms broadcast plans to pass along some of the windfall to workers.[76] CVS Health increased its minimum hourly wage to $11; AT&T, Discover, and American Airlines dished out $1,000 bonuses to their workforces.[77] In a letter to employees announcing the bonuses, American Airlines CEO Robert Parker and president Robert Isom noted that the decision wasn't an obvious one: "This is not an action we take lightly when balanced against the returns our shareholders / owners demand and deserve. But we believe it is the right thing to do for our team, which ultimately benefits our shareholders too."[78]

Lost amid the initial blitz of headlines was the reality that the portion of the tax savings being passed along to workers paled in comparison to what firms were handing out to their demanding "shareholders / owners." Researchers at the Academic-Industry Research Network looked at over forty firms in the S&P 500 stock index that announced, to much fanfare, that their workers would see higher pay thanks to the tax cut.[79] They discovered that the amount handed over to shareholders exceeded that given to workers by a factor of thirty. These companies promised their workers over $5 billion in pay increases, whether through bonuses (which accounted for the lion's share of the total) or annual raises. That's a hefty sum, to be sure—but a pittance compared to what shareholders saw. Since the bill passed through the Senate, these same companies announced nearly $160 billion in stock buybacks, one particularly popular means of redistributing revenue to shareholders.

When a company buys back a portion of its outstanding shares, the prices for the remaining ones go up as the total number of available shares goes down. Investors holding the leftover shares reap the benefit. Companies used to shy away from such a practice—it carried the taint of bearing a close resemblance to illegal share price manipulation. But a 1982 ruling by the Securities and Exchange Commission, headed by Reagan appointee and former Wall Street banker John Shadd, dispelled these concerns.[80] Rule 10b-18 granted corporations "safe harbor" against manipulation charges—and ever since, major US firms have used more and more of their profits to purchase their own shares. In just one five-year period—1985 to 1990—the number of stock repurchase programs announced by US firms more than tripled.[81] And for good reason, at least from the CEOs' perspective: Wall Street once reacted negatively to stock repurchases, reading them as an indicator that the firm had no good investment options. But by the 1980s, with the ethos of shareholder capitalism now dominant, that attitude flipped and companies that announced stock buybacks could expect Wall Street to applaud.[82] In 1980, companies spent 5 percent of their profits on buybacks; by the mid-1990s, that fraction had quadrupled.[83]

American Airlines won't announce what fraction of the savings from the tax bill it is returning to shareholders—in fact, it is currently being sued for the lack of disclosure.[84] But in 2017, the firm handed over (or "returned," in revealing financial industry parlance) $1.7 billion to its shareholders through dividends and stock buybacks.[85] Dividends represent the portion of profits a company issues directly to its shareholders, and together with stock repurchases they account for an ever-growing portion of total profits. In 2005, after the Bush administration announced a corporate tax holiday for firms earning income abroad, an estimated $300 billion poured into the United States from overseas. Of that, over 90 percent went into shareholders' pockets.[86] Morgan Stanley analysts estimated that over 40 percent of the savings from 2017's Tax Cut and Jobs Act would go to dividends

and share repurchases. Another 20 percent of the corporate savings
would be spent on mergers and acquisitions, while slightly less than
that would go to investment. And for the workers? Only 13 percent
would go to bonuses and wage increases—in spite of all the prominent press announcements.[87]

Sears Roebuck, the venerable American icon that revolutionized
retailing through its ubiquitous catalog and mail-order service, is now
Sears Holdings. The company is headed by former Goldman Sachs
trader Edward Lampert. Lampert's vision couldn't be more different
than that of his mid-twentieth century predecessor, Robert Wood,
who ranked shareholders dead last among the company's stakeholders.
Under Lampert's watch, stock repurchases approached $6 billion
between 2005 and 2010—more than the company earned over the
period.[88] Debt ballooned. The once iconic brand shuttered hundreds
of stores, declared bankruptcy in 2018, and reemerged as a mere shell
of what it had been. Workers who remain have endured pay cuts.
Lampert will come out okay, however. His hedge fund is one of
Sear's largest creditors, charging millions in fees and interest payments.
Should the retailer go belly up, it could seize valuable collateral. As
a former vice president of Sears Holdings told *Business Insider,* "He's
moving money from one pocket to the other pocket, and he's protected himself on both sides."[89] Nice work, if you can get it. Lampert's
subordinates at Sears couldn't.

How did Wall Street react to Walmart's uncharacteristic move
to raise its workers' pay back in 2015? Shareholders dumped the company's stock, leading to the company's largest one-day share drop in
a quarter-century.[90] This punishment was announced in the nation's
business press for other employers to see, sending a clear message to
firms who might have wanted to buck the prevailing trend and not
mimic peers who prioritized shareholders to the detriment of other
company stakeholders. Nine in ten Americans live within ten miles

of one of the nearly five thousand Walmart locations in the United States.[91] In 2018, the company's revenue exceeded $500 billion—more than the gross domestic product of Norway, Ireland, or Austria that year.[92] And yet, even Walmart can't escape shareholder pressure or the punishments that follow when a firm strays from the now-dominant ethos that shareholders come first when it comes to divvying up the company's resources. The result is that workers' wages get squeezed, regardless of the workers' individual performance.

Despite shareholder's increasing power, certain jobs—take, for example, orthopedic surgeons—still offer hefty rewards. If our pay isn't a reflection of our individual performance, maybe it stems from fixed characteristics of our jobs? Or perhaps this is true at least for workers in occupations that have the power to restrict entry, limit competition, and thereby extract more rent? Like the human capital model, this explanation—which links pay to inherent characteristics of the types of jobs we do—overlooks how important organizations are to determining who gets what and why. As we will explore next, in Part III, there is enormous variation across place and time in average pay levels in our jobs. Good jobs are often bad, and bad jobs are sometimes pretty good.

PART III

PAYING FOR THE JOB?

6 WHEN GOOD JOBS GO BAD

LITTLE BRINGS DEMOCRATS and Republicans together in our hyperpartisan age. For the last few Congresses, there has been no ideological overlap between the parties: the most conservative Democrat is more liberal than the most liberal Republican, and vice versa.[1] But in recent years there is one issue that unites office-holders on the right and left, one that has become a trope for aspiring politicians on the campaign trail. It's the well-worn call to bring back "good jobs"—specifically, manufacturing and other types of manual labor, like construction and mining. Accepting his party's nomination in 2004, then-Senator John Kerry promised new incentives to rejuvenate the manufacturing industry.[2] Rallying his supporters in the lead-up to the 2008 presidential race, GOP nominee John McCain offered his perspective on what most workers want: "a good job in their hometown . . . a plant gate to walk through and a paycheck to count on."[3] In his 2013 State of the Union address, President Barack Obama bragged about some of the economic achievements under his watch: "Caterpillar is bringing jobs back from Japan. Ford is bringing jobs back from Mexico. . . . And this year, Apple will start making Macs in America again."[4]

Nobody has hammered away at this theme of bringing back manufacturing and other manual labor jobs more than President Donald Trump. Speaking at a rally in North Carolina two days before the presidential election, he declared: "We're going to bring back the miners and the factory workers and the steelworkers." Sometimes the President added his own distinctive spin on the issue, emphasizing the humiliation of manufacturing decline in the United States. Introducing his nominee for vice president, Trump veered off script: "We also need to bring back in this country—because we see what happened—our industry, our manufacturing, our jobs. They've been taken away, like we're babies."[5] Trump recognized how powerful an exhortation this was. Speaking to a panel of manufacturing CEOs early in his tenure, he proclaimed, "Bringing manufacturing back to America, creating high-wage jobs, was one of our campaign promises and themes, and it resonated with everybody." He went on to declare that nothing would distract his administration from fulfilling this frequent campaign promise: "Everything is going to be based on 'bring our jobs back'—the good jobs, the real jobs. They've left, and they're coming back."[6]

The conflation of "manufacturing" with "high-wage"—of "good jobs" with factory work—extends beyond the ranks of our elected officials. A 2012 survey asked a thousand Americans whether they believed that manufacturing was very important to the nation's economic prosperity and standard of living. Nine in ten responded "yes" to both questions. The survey also asked what type of facility respondents would support to create a thousand new jobs in their hometown. Of the seven types listed—among them, facilities for energy production facility, healthcare, and retail—support for a manufacturing facility ranked number one.[7]

Where does this idea come from? Why the attachment to factory work—with its jobs that are often exhausting, repetitive, and downright dangerous? Why is it that we intuitively know that when our politicians promise to bring back "good jobs" they mean manufacturing jobs and other types of manual labor? It's because these were the jobs that once offered a decent, reliable wage and with it a path to the middle class for Americans lacking a college education. People have watched many of these well-paying jobs disappear—and they want them back.

GONE BUT NOT FORGOTTEN

In mid-twentieth-century America, manufacturing accounted for about one out of every three non-agricultural jobs. Today that number is approximately one in ten.[8] Auto production once led the way: in 1950, one out of every six jobs in the country was connected to the industry.[9] Now there are fewer than a million people employed by auto and auto parts makers, far less than the number of Walmart workers. Other blue-collar occupations took a similar hit. On the campaign trail in 2016, candidate Donald Trump promised to "put the miners back to work."[10] He found receptive audiences for this message in locales across Appalachia and the Midwest, where mining once served as the economic bedrock supporting entire communities. That bedrock had long since crumbled. Since 1990, the number of miners overall has fallen by nearly 40 percent. The decline of coal mining has been particularly steep, with employment in the occupation collapsing by two-thirds between the mid-1980s and today.[11] The number of steelworkers—another oft-invoked occupation during the 2016 campaign—decreased by 44 percent between 1990 and 2018.[12]

Remembrances of the halcyon days of our blue-collar past are usually incomplete. They grow hazy with time, and often ignore the racial and gender bias pervasive in many of these occupations. They also tend to forget how degrading, physically demanding, and outright alienating these jobs often were. A *New York Times* article published on Labor Day in 1970, titled "Blue Collar Blues," describes discontent among workers who, despite attaining middle-class status through substantial real wage growth, felt they had become "forgotten Americans."[13] Absenteeism and turnover rates in the auto industry spiked during the 1960s and early 1970s, with many workers complaining of the monotony and alienation so often felt working on the assembly line. As one autoworker lamented to a reporter: "There's only three ways out of here. You either conform and become deader each day, or you rebel, or you quit."[14]

Today's recollections do get one thing right: these were occupations that tended to pay well, and tended to offer some security and reliability for a wide swath of the workforce that had not gone to college. This was true for African-Americans as well as whites. Despite the racism African-American workers faced in many plants, a factory job remained the golden ticket for the hundreds of thousands of African-Americans making the journey north into the manufacturing hubs dotting the Midwest and Northeast. Detroit was once home to dozens of auto manufacturing plants as well as defense industry factories. The city's African-American population grew by over half a million between 1930 and 1970.[15] Many of these new arrivals came in search of manufacturing work that paid comparatively well and offered generous benefits. Nationwide, autoworkers' pay far outpaced that of the average private sector worker up through the 1970s.[16] Manufacturing workers as a whole outearned nonmanufacturing workers in the private sector by 15 percent as late as the 1980s.[17] Part of the worker alienation that popped up during the 1960s and 1970s may have been the disconnect between the rising standard of living many blue-collar workers enjoyed and the realities of the workplace. While wages rose dramatically in the post–World War II decades, life on the factory line or in the mines remained relatively unchanged.

Change was coming, rapidly, that would upend both the experience of blue-collar work and the remuneration for it. Massive developments in the global economy during the 1980s and 1990s

radically transformed life for millions of working-class Americans—
and not for the better. First, the opening up of global trade markets
ratcheted up competition in select US industries, such as auto. No
longer the only players around, suddenly US automakers had to
compete with a glut of imports from Europe and Japan. In the 1960s,
nearly every car on America's streets had been produced by a US
automaker.[18] By the end of the 1970s, domestic firms' share had
eroded, accounting for three out of every four new cars sold in the
United States, a decline that continued in the decades to come.[19]
Add to that the dual energy shocks of the 1970s, with rising gas costs
eating into demand for new cars, and one result was that US producers' profits dropped precipitously. Smaller profits reduced the
ability of automakers to expand their workforces, and sharpened
competition among labor, management, and owners for their slices
of a shrinking pie. A similar story occurred in the steel industry, as
European and Japanese mills embraced innovative technology in
their postwar rebuilding. More recently, cheap Chinese imports
further undercut domestic producers' market share, causing more
drastic declines in US steelworker jobs. During the first decade of
the twenty-first century, US steelmakers eliminated over fifty thousand positions, or nearly 40 percent of the industry's total number of
jobs in 2000.[20]

Even more important than globalization, rapid technological
change automated factories across the country, allowing employers
to shed scores of now-redundant workers at an alarming clip. What
often gets lost in the ongoing debates about manufacturing decline
is that manufacturing *production* continues to increase; it's the jobs that
have been lost. Since the mid-1980s, US manufacturing output has
expanded by 80 percent.[21] Employment in goods-producing jobs,
meanwhile, has fallen substantially, especially as a fraction of total
employment. In the mid-1960s, about 20.5 million Americans worked

in the goods-producing sector—comprising factory workers, construction laborers, and miners. In 2018, the same number did—despite a total labor force that had more than doubled in size.[22] At the end of the 1970s, nearly five million more Americans worked in manufacturing, construction, and mining than today. Where did those five million jobs go? Some were shipped overseas. Others—especially in the Midwest and Southeast—vanished due to the glut of Chinese imports.[23] But as Harvard's Lawrence Katz says, "clearly automation's been much more important—it's not even close."[24] One study estimates that increased productivity—largely due to automation—accounts for nearly 90 percent of the jobs lost in manufacturing in recent years.[25]

Again, consider steelmaking. Popular coverage of the industry's recent crisis emphasizes China's role in undercutting US firms. Less prominently featured—but actually more impactful if you're a steelworker in the United States and have recently lost or are worried about losing your job—is the role of technological change. In this case, it takes the form of the "minimill."[26] Minimills turn scrap metal into steel, bypassing the traditional step of making steel from scratch. The arrival of minimills jump-started productivity, and today it takes just one-and-a-half worker hours to produce a ton of steel, down from ten worker hours in the 1980s.[27] As a result, despite cutting most of its workforce since the 1960s, the industry has held its shipment volume steady. The force of this technological revolution was enough to overcome the inertia in the industry's pay-setting by shifting power toward those employers who could—and would—shed scores of workers from the payroll. As the technology spread, firms mimicked one another in cutting headcount and holding down wages for remaining workers, who had lost much of their claims-making ability in this fast-changing industry.

A similar dynamic occurred across a broad range of goods-producing industries. Robert Stillwell, from Evansville, Indiana, didn't graduate from high school but still found a steady, well-paid job at an auto parts maker, until his work was automated: "I used to have a really good job . . . until it got overtaken by a machine, and then I was let go."[28] Stillwell wasn't alone. Auto manufacturing plants used to have thousands of employees toiling under one roof. In Dearborn, Michigan, in the early 1940s, sixty thousand workers walked through the gates of Ford's sprawling River Rouge facility on a daily basis.[29] Post-automation, Ford's workforce total at that site has dwindled to about 5,500.[30] Indeed, the entire state of Michigan today employs less than forty thousand autoworkers.[31]

As it turns out, it was pretty easy to bemoan the boring days inside the factory gate when you had a steady job. The "blue-collar blues" sung by manufacturing workers in decades past might sound positively cheery to the millions of working-class Americans searching for jobs today that pay as well as those manufacturing, steelmaking, and mining jobs once did.

THEY'RE BACK!

Between spring 2010 and spring 2012, as recovery kicked in after the Great Recession, US factory employment grew faster than overall employment, marking the first time that manufacturing job growth had outpaced overall growth for a two-year period since the 1970s. The development led *Bloomberg*'s Justin Fox to declare, "The factory job is back—or has at least stopped disappearing."[32] Given the prior decades in which millions of manufacturing workers had seen their jobs outsourced, automated, or simply vanish as firms struggled to compete in a rapidly changing environment, the news was welcome—and trumpeted by politicians eager to claim credit for the development. During his final State of the Union Address, in 2016, President Obama boasted of a "manufacturing surge that's created nearly 900,000 new jobs in the past six years," and spotlighted the auto industry for its "best year ever."[33] A few years later, it was Trump's turn to cheer manufacturing's return. Never shy to claim credit for positive developments real or imagined, he wasted no time when General Motors decided to close an overseas plant. "GM Korea company announced today that it will cease production and close its Gunsan plant in May of 2018, and they're going to move back to Detroit," he announced in a meeting on trade issues with members of his cabinet and other elected officials. "You don't hear these things except for the fact that Trump became President."[34]

Alas, the President got a bit ahead of this particular story, as GM had no actual plans to shift the production capacity of the shuttered plant to American shores.[35] But plenty of other firms did, including General Electric, which recently "reshored" a water heater production plant from China to Louisville, Kentucky, and Ford, which shifted production of its F-650 and F-750 truck lines from Mexico to Avon Lake, Ohio.[36]

Much of the actual credit for the reversal goes not to the heroic actions of our elected officials, but to developments thousands of miles away. Following China's entry into the World Trade Organization in 2001, Chinese imports flooded the US market, squeezing US-based manufacturers in the Midwest and Southeast.[37] Labor cost differentials between the two countries spelled the end of many domestic plants, and motivated the surviving ones to extract concessions from workers. In 2006, manufacturing workers earned $17 more per hour in total compensation in the United States than in China.[38] But from 2005 to 2016, factory wages in China tripled, substantially narrowing the compensation gap between Chinese and US workers.[39] This trend and other changes in the Chinese labor market, such as strike activity by workers—once unheard of—changed the calculus for many US employers. As industry consultant Hal Sirkin told the *Washington Post,* "Companies are realizing it's not as easy to do things in China as they thought."[40] So some decided to bring production back home. A 2015 survey of large US manufacturers' executives found that nearly a third were considering increasing production in the United States over the next five years. The same survey found that the share of executives reporting that they were "reshoring," or bringing jobs back from overseas, had more than doubled in just a three-year period.[41]

WHEN REUTERS REPORTER TIMOTHY AEPPEL visited a small industrial city in the Midwest in 2017, he was struck by the fact that its people weren't calling for more factory jobs: "The problem, for many workers here, is one of quality, not quantity."[42] The workers of Elkhart, Indiana, had suffered grievously during the Great Recession. While unemployment hit double-digit rates unseen since the early 1980s all across America, in their town, population fifty-one thousand, it soared to 20 percent.[43] Given its cluster of recreational vehicle manufacturers—Elkhart's moniker of "RV Capital of the World" is well-earned—the fortunes of Elkhart rest on the demand for recreational vehicles, and during the Great Recession, demand plummeted.

Today the RV business is booming, and the unemployment rate of Elkhart stands at 2 percent, lower than the national average. Manufacturing jobs are readily available to residents eager to work production lines. The only issues? The work itself is physically taxing, pay is low, and hours are highly unpredictable. Kirsten Southern, a thirty-four-year-old mother of three employed at two different plants, says the work "tears your body down after a while."[44] Cassidy Davies, a veteran of numerous RV plants, agrees: "I really don't know how long I can do it, because you're beating the crap out of yourself every day."[45] Davis is twenty-nine.

Even in the twenty-first century, "beating the crap out of yourself" is unavoidable in many manufacturing jobs. Some offer a (usually low) hourly base rate of pay supplemented by bonus pay if production targets are met—a strong echo of the "piece work" pay system, in which pay was purely based on what you produced, common in an earlier era of manufacturing. Many of the Elkhart RV plants operate this way, with employees anxiously working as quickly as possible to maximize their take-home pay. The frantic pace of the job takes its toll. Annual staff turnover exceeds one hundred percent in many plants. Up until World War I, many auto production plants paid primarily for piece work.[46] With hundreds of small businesses making up the nascent industry (most of them very short-lived), and plenty of other growing industries seeking workers, labor turnover in auto was also rampant; as late as 1928, it exceeded that of any other industry.[47] At International Harvester's tractor assembly plant in Chicago, long-standing worker frustration with the group-based piece-work system helped launch early unionization efforts in the 1930s.[48]

The story of Elkhart and its manufacturing renaissance illuminates a key reason for the return of manufacturing jobs, one no politician wants to trumpet. Eroding labor standards on our shores has made the United States an attractive destination for firms looking to cut costs. While the average Chinese factory worker has seen her earnings rise in recent years, her American peers have on average seen their earnings fall. Average pay in the auto industry was once

30 percent higher than average private sector pay. Today, these rates are essentially the same.[49] Auto parts suppliers are leading the way downward. Today, the majority of autoworkers in the United States work not for name-brand firms such as Ford, GM, Honda, or Volkswagen, but for the firms that supply these companies' parts. Increasingly, the pay and working conditions of a supplier's employees bear little resemblance to those of autoworkers in the days of the Treaty of Detroit—the early 1950s period of rising wages and extensive benefit packages. They more closely mirror the bad old days of auto production in the early twentieth century.

THE NEW DETROIT

The parts jobs are also increasingly far from Detroit. In Alabama, for example, auto parts makers now employ twenty-six thousand workers, helping to fill the jobs gap opened by the erosion of the state's once-vibrant textile industry. The proliferation of auto parts suppliers across the state helps boost Alabama's employment numbers. But it doesn't do much else for the workers in the plants, where "Pay is low, turnover is high, training is scant, and safety is an afterthought," according to a recent investigation by *Bloomberg Businessweek*.[50] Reco Allen found out the hard way what the combination of scant training and poor safety standards can generate on the factory floor. He took a job as a custodian at Matsu Alabama that paid $9 per hour. Matsu is an auto parts facility in Huntsville owned by the Matcor-Matsu Group, a Canadian car parts manufacturer. But Allen didn't work for Matsu, at least not technically. Technically he was an employee of Surge Staffing, a temporary help agency that provided labor to Matsu. As a custodian, Allen had no business on the production line, but Matsu had fallen behind on its quota for Honda and needed extra manpower. Here we see how demands from one organization, Honda, to another, Matsu, alter the work environment of a third, Surge Staffing. All of a sudden Allen's job tasks changed dramatically without any commensurate change to his pay. That's how Allen found himself—with no formal training—loading bolts into a press. Soon he found himself trapped inside the press, his arm pinned by a die cutting machine, for an hour. Eventually freed, Allen lost his right forearm after surgeons, worried about the risk of gangrene, eventually amputated it.

After Allen's 2013 accident, Surge Staffing learned that Matsu routinely "provided no hands-on training . . . ordered untrained temps to operate machines, [and] sped up presses beyond manufacturers' specifications."[51] The Occupational Safety and Health Administration (OSHA) fined Matsu $103,000 for its flagrant health and safety violations. The company argued that Allen was trained to operate the plant machinery, but failed to follow procedure. Allen sued and won a seven-figure settlement. It didn't compensate for what he went through, as he told Peter Waldman of *Bloomberg Businessweek:* "I'd rather have my arm back any day."[52] As a privately held company, Matcor Matsu does not make its revenue figures public. But the recent opening of a new facility in Mexico suggests the company weathered the financial penalties for Allen's injuries just fine.

It's not just Alabama where auto parts suppliers are popping up: the entire US South is now dotted with them. They share the same characteristics as Alabama's. Nakanishi Manufacturing Corporation supplies bearings to Toyota. In 2015, a worker at its Winterville, Georgia, facility suffered third-degree burns across his upper body when a fire at the facility overwhelmed him. It was the fifth fire in the plant's dust collection system.[53] The penalty? A $105,000 fine levied by OSHA—a drop in the bucket for a company that announced a $4.5 million expansion of its Georgia facilities the following year.[54]

By 2013, median manufacturing wages were 8 percent less than the overall median, despite productivity rates in manufacturing that far exceeded the economy-wide average.[55] Fully a third of families with at least one production worker receives means-tested government assistance, substantially higher than the overall rate. The authors of a recent study of manufacturing workers' reliance on government safety-net programs reach a sober conclusion: "Historically, blue collar jobs in manufacturing provided opportunities for workers without a college education to earn a decent living. For many manufacturing jobs, this is no longer true."[56]

What happened? As Elkhart's experience makes clear, this is not a textbook case in which jobs are in short supply and desperate workers are competing with one another, bidding down starting wages. It's also not the case that wage declines map neatly to productivity trends. If anything, the opposite has occurred: productivity in the industry keeps rising while wages head south. Two interrelated developments, each augmenting employers' power vis-à-vis their workers, helped turn good manufacturing jobs bad. One was the waning of the key institution that ensured workers got their fair share of a company's surplus. Labor unions were once a ubiquitous feature of manufacturing, construction, mining, and other "good" jobs of the past. They have largely been eradicated from these occupations. Their decline owes much to, and also reinforces, the second major development augmenting employers' power: reclassification, or, as many have argued, misclassification. Reclassification involves casting your workers as something other than employees—often as independent contractors. In the eyes of the law, these designations matter. Many workplace rights and protections we have in place, from minimum wage requirements and eligibility for overtime pay to the ability to bargain collectively with one's employer, are limited to workers classified as employees.[57] As we'll see, over the past few decades, a massive reconfiguration of the employer-employee relationship through reclassification has put workers on the defensive in industry after industry. Both union decline and reclassification shifted the terrain of the claims-making process, making it more difficult for workers to have their claims validated—or for workers to press a claim for decent pay in the first place.

What about the roles of automation and globalization in turning good jobs bad? They, too, altered claims-making within firms, especially in industries where the prospect of operations shifting overseas was no idle threat. A union demanding double-digit pay increases for its members is playing with fire in a rapidly changing industry where employers feel no reluctance to search the globe for cheaper labor. "Made in America" used to be the mantra, but once that norm eroded, employer after employer mimicked those firms that had first figured out how to manage offshore production. Automation, meanwhile, slowed the growth of blue-collar jobs. The slack demand for manufacturing labor helped employers drive hard bargains over pay and benefits and left workers increasingly unprotected. Along with outsourcing, then, automation reconfigured claims-making dynamics within many organizations. And both combined with union decline and aggressive reclassification efforts to set blue-collar workers back on their heels in contract negotiations.

But outsourcing and automation shouldn't be seen as determinative forces. Both are just tools which employers can use—or choose not to use—to gain power over workers in negotiations over the distribution of revenues. Different claims-making environments can alter the ways in which these dual forces affect workers' paychecks. For example, research finds that unions can protect workers in jobs most at risk of automation, lowering the likelihood of being laid off.[58] Technological change and workplace relocation aren't confined to this country—these are forces affecting all mature economies. Yet,

manufacturing workers elsewhere—for example, in Germany—
haven't been nearly as negatively affected by globalization and outsourcing as their US counterparts. Comparatively strong unions and
less worker reclassification go a long way in explaining the divergent
trajectories. As we'll see, not all the good jobs of yesteryear can be
outsourced—nor have many, as of yet, been automated—but all of
them have experienced significant deunionization and reclassification,
and steep declines in worker pay.

BIG LABOR GOES SMALL

Stockton, California, in the aftermath of the Great Recession, made
headlines when it became the largest US city in history to declare
bankruptcy. (Detroit would take over the top spot when it declared
bankruptcy in 2013.) Stockton's 320,000 residents had grown used to
bad news: gang problems, homelessness, and empty storefronts were
just some of the issues confronting a city that, in the words of Peter
Goodman of the *New York Times*, "has long functioned as a display
case for the wrenching troubles afflicting American life."[59] Among
the businesses that had closed its gates was a DaimlerChrysler distribution facility located just south of the city's airport, one of many
casualties brought on by the economic downturn. So state and local
officials cheered when the electric car manufacturer Tesla Motors
chose a site just outside Stockton for a modest parts manufacturing
facility in the spring of 2014. Brook Taylor, Deputy Director of
California's Office of Business and Economic Development, announced that the state was "excited that Tesla is expanding their
footprint in California."[60] The manager of the town where the
431,000-foot facility was located agreed: "We're ecstatic over the
fact that Tesla's going to be in town and expanding part of their
operation here."[61]

Fremont, California, sits about sixty miles southeast of Stockton. It, too, contains a Tesla factory. That's about all the two cities share. Fremont is booming, with an unemployment rate of 2.5 percent, below the national average. Nevertheless, Fremont couldn't escape all the ravages of the Great Recession, and the city saw its unemployment rate spike to 9 percent in June 2010. Part of the increase could be pinned on the closure of one giant auto facility, the New United Motor Manufacturing plant, which had occupied 5.5 million square feet in the city's southwest corner for just over twenty-five years. Nummi, as it was called, had been a unique joint venture between Toyota and GM employing close to five thousand workers. Before Nummi, the same location had housed a General Motors assembly site from 1962 to 1982. Now the facility sprang back to life for the third time as Tesla founder Elon Musk chose it as the perfect place to locate his firm's core production facility. As in Stockton, elected officials celebrated Tesla's decision. Fremont Mayor Bob Wasserman championed the rebirth: "When Nummi said it would close, the land was dead," but with Tesla's announcement, "the land became alive" again.[62] Today, Tesla has brought the number of workers there up to ten thousand, double the size of the Nummi workforce, contributing to Fremont's impressively low unemployment numbers.[63]

The residents and officials of Stockton and Fremont were understandably excited about landing a Tesla facility. These were to be good jobs—archetypical auto manufacturing jobs—the types of jobs that once anchored so many communities in the nation's heartland. And Tesla was cutting-edge, the future of manufacturing, helmed by an "economic visionary . . . hailed for solving the world's great challenges with panache."[64] Elon Musk, who cofounded the company in 2003, made his first million in the mid-1990s after ditching his pursuit of a PhD in physics to start an internet company with his brother. He later sold the firm, Zip2, to Compaq and pocketed $22 million in the transaction. But a bigger payday came a few years later after Musk merged his online financial transactions company, X.com, with Confinity to create PayPal. When eBay bought PayPal in 2002, Musk walked away with $180 million.[65]

While these early ventures didn't tackle humanity's most pressing crises, later ones did. According to the US Environmental Protection Agency, over a quarter of the United States' greenhouse gas emissions come from transportation activities, specifically through the burning of fossil fuels to power our cars, trucks, ships, airplanes, and trains.[66] The sales success of Tesla's all-electric vehicles—the company turned its first quarterly profit in 2013—proved that it's possible to run an economically profitable car company while reducing this key source of pollution. With a bit of luck, future sales growth would nudge the company's gas-guzzling competitors to move in a greener direction, too. Meanwhile, as if to hedge his bet on saving Earth from environmental catastrophe, Musk also founded SpaceX, a company whose day-to-day business is building rockets and launching payloads into space, but whose long-term vision is to go to Mars—and in so doing, make the human race a "multiplanetary species."[67] At this writing, SpaceX is valued at over $20 billion. Recently, Musk helped establish Neuralink, a corporation developing ways to implant devices to help people function better after serious brain injuries such as strokes.[68]

So Tesla wasn't just any source of factory jobs trumpeted by the local officials in Stockton, Fremont, and the surrounding locales. It was the company of the future, an automaker that could simultaneously invigorate the region's manufacturing base and make the world a better place. What these communities and their leader likely failed to detect is that, for all Musk's efforts to improve this world and to prepare for life on another, he's no fan of the living wage.

By 2017, Tesla's market value surpassed that of Ford, and the company couldn't roll enough cars off its assembly lines to keep up with soaring demand. Yet, setting aside the equity awarded upon hire to production workers and bonuses in the form of stock options and restricted stock units, average hourly pay at the Fremont facility was significantly below the national average for the industry. Journalist David Dayen reported that the first-level production workers at the plant earned between $17 and $21 per hour, while the national average for such workers was $29. These low hourly wages in an extremely high-cost area result from Tesla workers' lack of bargaining power. Unlike their counterparts at Ford, Tesla workers are nonunion, and aggressively so. Dezzimond Vaughn was a well-regarded worker at the production facility south of Stockton. Then he became active in a unionization effort and suddenly his performance ratings dropped, leading to his termination in October 2017. The rumors of union-busting didn't end there. Michael Sanchez, another Tesla worker, claims he was fired not long after Vaughn for distributing pro-union leaflets outside the plant, a practice protected by law. His case in currently under investigation by the National Labor Relations Board (NLRB).[69]

Musk has inserted himself directly into Tesla's opposition to unionization, stating his view that it pits managers and workers against each other. The NLRB alleges that, in a 2017 meeting at the plant, he "solicited employee complaints about safety issues and impliedly promised to remedy their safety complaints if they refrained from their union organizational activity." To the NLRB, that sounded like illegal interference with employees' right to self-organization.[70]

Musk appears to really believe that Tesla is a "fair and just company," and the work experience, as well as the total compensation package, of Tesla production associates beats that of other automakers. In a lengthy email to workers he countered the claims of "a recent blog post promoting the UAW"—the United Auto Workers, the union attempting to organize his facilities—offering evidence of Tesla's commitment to excellence in four categories: safety, compensation, work hours, and fun. On the last point, he promised "a really amazing party once Model 3 reaches volume production later this year," and more to look forward to:

> There will also be little things that come along like free frozen yogurt stands scattered around the factory and my personal favorite: a Tesla electric pod car roller coaster (with an optional loop the loop route, of course!) that will allow fast and fun travel throughout our Fremont campus, dipping in and out of the factory and connecting all the parking lots. It's going to get crazy good.[71]

Good jobs in decades past offered steadily rising wages, comprehensive healthcare, and a raft of other benefits. Today, most of those perks are gone. But if you're a lucky Tesla worker, there's always frozen yogurt and high-speed roller coaster travel around the factory. Crazy good, indeed.

The nation's unionization rate peaked in the 1950s when, for a brief period, about one out of every three wage and salary workers belonged to a labor union. This was also the time in which economic inequality reached historic lows, and relative wage gains for average workers outpaced those at the top of the income distribution. Today about one-tenth of American workers are organized, and in the private sector, where Elon Musk plies his various trades, it's roughly one in twenty. You could fill a small apartment with the articles and books written on organized labor's demise. A porch addition might be necessary, as scholars continue to churn out analyses investigating just what caused the drop in representation rates and what unions' losses mean for broader trends in economic inequality.[72] Prominent explanations for the decades-long drop in union memberships include deindustrialization and the related forces of globalization. Unions in the United States were anchored in core manufacturing industries like steel and auto. Technological change allowed employers to automate many processes, leading to layoffs and slower employment growth in highly organized sectors. Pressure from foreign competition spurred US employers to search for cheaper labor overseas or in nonunion areas of the United States, further decreasing many unions' leverage vis-à-vis management.

But unionization rates fell not just in jobs subject to offshoring and automating. As Figure 6.1 makes clear, union decline was much more widespread. The figure displays unionization rates for full-time, private-sector workers for four major occupations between 1973 and 2016. (Prior to the early 1970s, unionization was not tracked at an occupation-specific level). Few occupations automated as rapidly and as extensively as mining, and production workers bore the brunt of rising manufacturing powerhouses abroad. Unionization rates for both occupations fell off a cliff. Over a third of all production workers belonged to a labor union in the early 1970s; just 13 percent do today. Miners are fast disappearing from the US economic landscape, and the few that remain are much less likely to be organized than in decades past. Fewer than one in ten mining jobs are unionized today.

The remaining two occupations either cannot be outsourced or haven't felt the full impact of technological changes. In construction, people can't send their houses to China to have their roofs replaced, but unionization rates in the industry fell by over 60 percent between 1973 and 2016. In transportation, as of yet, robots don't rule the road—and still, union representation rates followed a similar trajectory as construction's during the period.

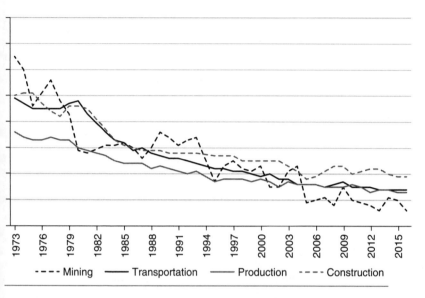

Figure 6.1 Unionization rates for full-time private sector workers, 1973–2016

These broad-based losses point to an explanation of union decline that extends beyond globalization and automation.[73] Here we need to look at a profound power shift between employers and unions that altered the bargaining landscape across the United States. Beginning in the 1960s, and increasingly throughout the 1970s and 1980s, employers mounted a frontal assault on organized labor, aiming to rid existing workplaces of unions and prevent the formation of new ones. They were aided in their efforts by a growing political coalition of anti-union lawmakers who stymied efforts by unions and their allies to update an increasingly toothless labor legal regime. Globalization and technological change proved effective tools in those industries' undergoing transformation. Many employers used the threats of outsourcing and automating the jobs of unionized workers to stifle organizing drives. What the legal scholar Mark Barenberg terms "the disintegration of employers" aided anti-union efforts, as well. Instead of vertical integration, combining many factors of production in a single organizational entity, companies chose atomized structures in which many activities were outsourced to other firms specializing in those tasks.[74] The complicated supply chains that resulted hindered unionization attempts. At any given link in the chain, the central company could sever its ties to a firm whose workers had mounted a successful union drive, and swap in a new nonunion one. Large, vertically integrated firms also had much larger workforces, presenting richer targets for labor organizing campaigns, given their many potential members. Going through the long process of organizing for the much smaller firms, each one making up a single link in a long chain, often wasn't worth the cost.

Employers had plenty of other resources to draw upon, too, including a fast-growing collection of consultants and law firms whose practices focused on fighting unionization attempts, and a legal landscape in which the paltry penalties for labor law violations were often worth the cost if a firm was intent on being union-free.

The cost to US workers was steep. Decades of research finds that the "union wage premium"—the pay boost a union member receives that a similar, nonunion worker does not—averages about 15 percent.[75] Union membership pays off well for members even after factoring in union dues, which average between one and two percent of wages.[76] Union-negotiated contracts, for a time, institutionalized inertia: multiyear contracts, in some cases extending to half a decade, insured that no matter the occupant, jobs paid a particular wage for a sizable period of time. And pattern bargaining in certain major industries, in which a union-negotiated contract at one firm extended to others in the industry, institutionalized mimicry.

Former members were not the only workers hurt by union decline. A growing body of research finds that nonunion workers' pay was higher in times when and places where unions were strong.[77] These "spillover" effects occur because a densely organized labor market also poses challenges to nonunion employers. Workers at an unorganized plant surrounded by unionized competitors can use the threat of unionization as a bargaining chip in negotiations over revenue. And union-negotiated contracts often served as key templates for mimicking in highly organized locales. Also, unions' cultural role as a set of organizations arguing for pay equity between top-level management and average workers was at its strongest when organized labor was a "ubiquitous presence" in the United States.[78] Debates continue about the causes of union decline and the precise impact organized labor's demise has had on rising inequality. But regardless of how much weight one assigns to a particular explanation for union decline, or how widely one believe unions' spillover effects spanned, researchers working in this area agree on one thing: unions helped make a certain set of jobs good. And their disappearance throughout wide stretches of the country and major industries in the economy go a long way toward understanding how good jobs got to be so bad.

TEMP NATION

In 2000, Phillip Hicks made the decision to accept a job 140 miles from his family at the giant Toyota plant in Georgetown, Kentucky.[79] Dealing with that distance would be hard, but "I could stand on my head for a year or two for a $20-an-hour job with benefits," he told the *Washington Post*. Unfortunately, he didn't end up making that much, because he didn't work for Toyota—at least not technically. Instead, the temporary help agency Manpower hired him and paid his wages. Through an arrangement with Toyota, Manpower provided much of the workforce for the company's Georgetown plant—the largest facility the Japanese company operates in the world. Hicks's pay averaged about half that of the workers lucky enough to be hired directly by Toyota. On his Manpower salary, he couldn't afford his family's health insurance premium. He received three paid days off a year, total. But Manpower told him not to worry. A year or two of strong performance, and Toyota would bring him onto their payroll, doubling his hourly wage, and offering health, retirement, and dental insurance. Four years later he was still a Manpower worker.

In the years after World War II, the temporary help industry branded itself as "women's work," meant for middle-class, predominantly white women to gain a little spending money without relinquishing their core domestic duties.[80] As a typical advertisement that ran in the mid-1960s stated, "She leads a double life . . . And loves it! She's a temporary office worker when she chooses . . . and a homemaker all the time!"[81] Kelly Girl Service, White Collar Girl Service, Western Girl Service, and a host of other firms emphasized this explicitly feminine image, in part to avoid providing much of what was expected of the mid-twentieth-century employment relationship: decent pay and generous benefits.[82] The strong norm in America was that men were the breadwinners of households. The temp service business model assumed its employees didn't need the kinds of perquisites that came with their husbands' or fathers' jobs.

Coupled with the industry's focus on women was its focus on white-collar jobs, especially secretarial. By the early 1960s, however, some temp firms sought to branch out into stereotypical "men's work." Early in its existence, Manpower—the firm that would hire Hicks decades later—mostly hired women. Its popular "Girl in the White Gloves" advertising campaign cemented the idea of temp work as women's work in the public's consciousness. The campaign proved so successful that a problem emerged when the firm wanted to attract clients to its manual labor division. To combat the discrepancy between its prevailing brand and the new type of worker it was targeting, the firm launched a reprisal of the "Girl in the White Gloves" advertisement. The famous woman clad with gloves remained, now pictured next to a pile of wood and saying: "Me unload lumber? Heavens, no. I'm Manpower's 'Girl in the White Gloves.' And my job is helping you temporarily with office work." The ad then pivoted: "But Manpower does have hundreds of experienced men . . ." A smaller picture showed a man performing the task the 'Girl in the White Gloves' was so unwilling to do.[83]

But the real entry of temp firms into blue-collar work would occur later. In 1990, blue-collar workers made up just over a quarter of the temporary help workforce, but less than one percent of all production workers were paid by these staffing agencies. Over the next decade, temp work exploded nationwide, doubling in size to just under four million.[84] The composition of the temp workforce changed just as rapidly. In manufacturing, the number of temp workers grew by a million between 1989 and 2000, from approximately 400,000 to 1.4 million.[85] The expansion of temp production workers more than made up for the loss of traditional manufacturing jobs during this period. During the 1990s, employment in manufacturing fell by four percent, despite an economy that was rapidly expanding by decade's end. If we count manufacturing workers provided by temp agencies, employment in production actually *rose* by 1.3 percent. It turns out that not all of our manufacturing jobs were offshored or automated. Many were just reclassified.

Today, temp staffing agencies remain a vital component of our manufacturing workforce. They are also a major reason good jobs turned bad. What they share with their mid-twentieth-century temp predecessors are the low wages and meager benefits offered to workers. Where they depart is in their "temporary" nature. Many temps today, like Phillip Hicks, toil for years, all the while awaiting reclassification so that they can receive their paychecks from the company for which they actually produce goods. While they wait, they are at the mercy of a group of agencies that try to outbid their competitors with promises of lower labor costs. There are now an estimated seventeen thousand temporary help staffing firms in the United States, all competing to win contracts from companies like Toyota.[86] Offering a lower rate is a key way to best your rival, and lower rates mean lower paychecks for the workers provided by the staffing firms.

Some of these employers excuse their low pay by pointing to "natural" economic forces over which they purportedly have no control. By the early 1990s, Manpower had grown into one of the largest private employers in the country, with more than half a million Americans on its payroll. When asked about the low pay endemic to the temp industry, Manpower's CEO at the time, Mitchell Fromstein (creator of the "Girl in the White Gloves" advertising campaign back in the 1960s), gave this response: "We are not exploiting people. We are not setting the fees. The market is. We are matching people with demands. What would our workers be doing without us? Unemployment lines? Welfare? Suicide?"[87] Invoking the seemingly unchallengeable logic of the "market" is a tried-and-true tactic in claims-making. But as Erin Hatton has documented, staffing agencies help shape this market, taking every opportunity to convince companies that shedding permanent staff is the only way to survive in the new economy. Indeed, it is an entire industry built upon the exploitation of labor, allowing companies to skirt their traditional employer-employee obligations through the reclassification of workers as temporary.[88]

As the case of Phillip Hicks demonstrates, "temporary" is a mis-
nomer for these jobs. The poor pay, lack of benefits, and lack of basic
fairness endure. Most galling to many "temp" workers on the line is
that they perform the exact same duties, working in the exact same
occupation, as the nearby worker who wears the official company
shirt. The only difference is the classification.

Matt Roberts was one of the lucky ones: after starting as a temp,
Toyota hired him directly, enabling him to enjoy the comparatively
higher pay and generous benefits the carmaker provided its permanent workforce. He watched as his temp partners on the line did the
same job as he did, but for far less: "These people are making extreme sacrifices, working second shift, no benefits, low pay. It's a
disgrace to the American dream. That's what it is."[89]

The presence of temps alongside permanent workers raises equity issues—unequal pay for equal work usually does. But the fissuring of organizational borders dilutes the impact of these feelings
of unfairness by erecting artificial boundaries between workers. Matt
Roberts experienced both sides of the divide. Unlike Matt, many
other permanent workers were never temps, and as a result their pay
referents were likely restricted to fellow permanent employees. This
type of workplace fissuring acts as another exercise of power by
manufacturing firms. Seeing lower-paid workers laboring under
the same roof reminds those lucky enough to wear the company
uniform what could happen to them should they raise a ruckus about
their own situation. Toyota, meanwhile, enjoys the savings from
contracting out much of its workforce, since temp agencies compete on the basis of lower labor costs. David Weil, former head of
the Wage and Hour Division in President Obama's Department of
Labor, literally wrote the book on the proliferation of fissuring
among US firms. In it, he's clear about who benefits when firms like

Toyota contract out so much of its workforce to staffing agencies: "Shifting work outward allows redistribution of gains upward."[90]

KEEP ON TRUCKING?

Perhaps employers in auto, steel, and other manufacturing firms needed to grab the levers of power and restrain workers' demands. After all, the entire manufacturing sector underwent cataclysmic changes during the latter decades of the twentieth century, some of which undercut American firms' market position, others of which exposed US workers to competition from workers in emerging economies. Rising imports in auto eroded domestic firms' share of the market, leading US manufacturers to search for ways to reduce costs. As seen in prior chapters, Walmart's emergence as a retail behemoth had ramifications well beyond the retail sector. A key to Walmart's famous low wages was its ability to squeeze suppliers. Soon it didn't matter how strongly you believed in the "Made in America" slogan. If you were a consumer goods maker eager for a contract with America's largest retailer, you'd be hard-pressed to keep production in the United States. Overseas labor was just too cheap.

Even those employers who maintained domestic production could use the mere threat of moving elsewhere to great advantage. Passage of the North American Free Trade Agreement (NAFTA) in 1994 provided employers with another cudgel in their battles to keep labor costs low. It's a weapon they would wield often, especially during unionization efforts. During a 1995 organizing drive at ITT Automotive in Michigan, management parked over a dozen trailers loaded with shrink-wrapped equipment outside the facility. Large signs on the side of the trailers reading "Mexico transfer job" sent a clear message to workers considering whether to organize. Not content to stop there, management flew in workers from one of its Mexican facilities to shadow its Wisconsin-based employees on one production line as they performed their duties, with the supervisor explaining that the company was "considering moving to Mexico."[91] All told, in the years surrounding NAFTA's passage, management threatened to move operations elsewhere in nearly two-thirds of unionization drives involving labor whose work could be offshored. Even when the union drive prevailed, workers sometimes lost. More than one in ten union victories was followed by the company closing the union plant and relocating. Sometimes production was sent to Mexico or other countries with low labor costs; sometimes it was shifted to American sites whose workers had been less demanding. In the mid-1990s, a Steelworkers campaign to organize workers at St. Louis Refrigerator Car Company initially looked like an organizing success when the company voluntarily recognized the union. Soon thereafter, it shuttered the plant and shifted operations to a nonunion facility in Ohio.[92] Other firms with sizable domestic workforces adjusted to the new playing field by reclassifying their workers and thereby lowering their wage bill. And that wasn't all: along with offshoring (or the threat thereof) and reclassification came rapid technological change throughout the sector, and the automation of many workers' jobs. The typical worker faced a sometimes explicit, often implicit, dual threat: speak out to demand higher pay and your job may be sent elsewhere or replaced by a robot.

These developments dramatically altered the claims-making environment in US manufacturing. Rapid automation and the opening of overseas labor markets empowered employers to depress wages among their remaining US workers. Pressures from the newly empowered shareholder class gave employers more reasons to cut costs. Some saw it as necessary to staying in business; changes in product markets, such as Walmart's relentless cost-cutting, have repercussions for labor markets. Thus, the growing power of retail giants over their manufacturing suppliers in turn increased the power of supplier firms over the labor pool. So, too, did increased competition in once-protected industries like auto. As auto executives felt the squeeze from overseas, they squeezed their employees. Interorganizational power shifts triggered intraorganizational power shifts. Wages for non-executive workers fell as a result.

But that can't be the whole story of how good jobs went bad. It is not simply the case that diminishing workers' power was a necessary corrective to survive in a rapidly changing sector. Worker power—the ability to wrest a fair share of organizational surplus—also diminished in industries that haven't undergone much change at all.

RON CARRABIS, reflecting in 2017 on his career driving long-haul trucks, advised others to steer clear of the occupation he had given three decades to. He thought of family members in particular: "Any one of my grandkids do it, I'll kill 'em."[93] A reporter interviewing a veteran trucker in 1977 would probably have encountered a different attitude. Trucking is rarely invoked as an example of the kind of good job that workers lacking a college education used to get. But, at least in terms of pay, it should be. As late as 1980, many truckers easily cleared $100,000 a year in today's dollars.[94] During the 1960s and 1970s, average annual earnings for truckers far exceeded those for manufacturing workers.[95]

Unlike manufacturing work, you never hear calls on the campaign trail to "bring trucking back." For one thing, trucking never left. Trucking jobs can't be shipped overseas. And while the advent of self-driving vehicles poses an existential threat to the nearly two million drivers of heavy and tractor-trailer trucks on our roads, it's a worry for the future. Add in short-route delivery services, and nearly four million Americans make their living today behind the wheels of trucks. Automation has yet to transform commercial transport in ways that it has other blue-collar occupations. Technological change has occurred, to be sure. Most notably, onboard sensors continuously monitor equipment performance, and GPS-enabled electronic logging devices track location, speed, and hours spent idle. The latter constitute one example of a sophisticated class of tools also spreading across many industries beyond transportation.[96] According to one study, these new technologies "have dramatically expanded capacities for worker surveillance both on and off the job."[97] Still, they don't replace drivers—they just watch over them—and today's trucks look and act much as they did fifty years ago.

While the act of driving a truck hasn't changed much over time, the pay and working conditions attached to performing that act has—all to the drivers' detriment. In the two decades between the early 1970s and 1990s, wages for truckers fell by over 20 percent.[98] In some markets, the losses were steeper. Between 1980 and 2017, median trucker pay declined by nearly a third in Chicago and Atlanta, and by over a third in Toledo.[99] Steve Viscelli sought to understand the dynamics of this transformation. He interviewed dozens of truckers, analyzed the wages and benefits drivers earn, and learned what he could from the rather limited academic literature on this large and changing occupation. Soon, however, he decided this wasn't enough. To truly comprehend what it was like to work as a driver today, "having firsthand experience was essential."[100] So he signed up to be a long-haul trucker.

Much about the job came as a surprise. The first myth dispelled for Viscelli was the notion that trucking was an "unskilled" job. Sure, a college education isn't a condition for entry into the occupation, but getting good at managing such a massive machine, interpreting signs of malfunction, and dealing with other vehicles on the road takes serious training and practice. When I spoke to him in the spring of 2018 about his research and experience as a trucker, he impressed upon me that it takes "months to be decently proficient at operating the truck itself."[101]

I asked Viscelli if there were any aspects of the job he had not anticipated. With no hesitation, he named "the physicality of it. The sitting for twelve to fourteen hours a day, breathing diesel fumes 24 per hours a day. You're living out of that machine."[102] Anyone who believes that sitting that long, day after day, makes for relaxing work would be disabused of that notion by Viscelli's account: "I remember pain. Muscles in my back just killing me."[103]

Viscelli made clear that truckers don't forego higher pay because they prize the job's comfort and amenities. The work is long, grueling, and uncomfortable—much as it has always been. What's changed is the compensation: average driver pay has declined dramatically. Is this a matter of productivity being lower than in decades past? In trucking, unlike so many other occupations (see Chapter 4), this is a fairly easy question to answer. Individual performance can be objectively measured, and there is a general consensus on what output per hour rates as high productivity. The job involves getting a large vehicle full of goods from point A to point B without damaging the cargo (or truck, if it is company-owned) or endangering other drivers on the road. Today's technology automatically calculates the time spent between pickoff and drop-offs and flags any rule violations. As a result, employers now have precise measurements for gauging driver productivity—and it turns out, drivers today are no less productive today than in decades past. In fact, by some measures, they are *twice* as productive as drivers were in the late 1970s. So much for paying for productivity.

If productivity didn't decline, what does explain the drop in pay? As Ruth Milkman writes, the trucking industry experienced "a broader change in the power balance between labor and capital," with capital coming out ahead.[104] Two interrelated factors shifted the balance: deregulation and de-unionization. During the 1970s, a bipartisan consensus formed around the idea of deregulating the trucking industry. Barriers to entry had been high ever since passage of the Motor Carrier Act of 1935, and academic economists and right-leaning think tanks argued that the stifled competition allowed existing carriers to overcharge for their services. Much of that excess rent went into the pockets of drivers thanks to generous contracts negotiated by the powerful Teamsters union.

Rising inflation combined with the twin oil shocks of the 1970s to shift the terrain further in deregulators' favor. Ralph Nader and Ted Kennedy united with the National Association of Manufacturers and other corporate interests to advocate for opening up the industry.[105] By 1979, the Carter administration, angered over what it considered overreach by the Teamsters in contract demands, broke its silence and publicly championed the cause of deregulation. On July 1, 1980, after easy passage in the House and Senate, President Carter signed the Motor Carrier Act into law. "This is historic legislation," he said. "It will remove forty-five years of excessive and inflationary government restrictions and red tape."[106]

That law also began to remove much of what was good about being a trucker—most notably, high pay. The Motor Carrier Act reversed many of the trucking regulations put in place during the Depression. Its implementation coincided with the brutal recession of the early 1980s, fundamentally reshaping the claims-making environment within trucking companies. As a result of deregulation, thousands of new firms flooded the market, ratcheting up competition.

They did so at the same time that demand for trucked goods plummeted, with the nation's unemployment rate moving into double digits for the first time since the Depression. These massive changes to trucking's labor and service markets provided trucking firms—old and new alike—with powerful tools to drive down drivers' wage claims, and to drive out the unions that had been so successful at legitimating them. New nonunion firms in the deregulated industry could often underbid organized companies. Organized carriers responded by extracting concessions from unions during negotiations or, increasingly, subcontracting out much of their work to small nonunion companies. Many carriers did both. Owner-operators proliferated, further pressuring the remaining union firms to keep costs—and therefore drivers' pay—down.[107] In the 1970s, well over half of truck drivers belonged to a union. By 1990, only a quarter did.[108]

Trucking today offers generally low and highly unpredictable pay, takes a serious toll on the body, and keeps drivers away from family and friends for weeks and sometimes months on end. Why would anyone sign on? One tactic that many trucking firms use to lure applicants is to inflate the take-home pay a driver can expect from life on the road. Obfuscation is easy since the industry draws workers from a wide range of other low-paying jobs who enter the occupation unaware of the current realities of trucking. Viscelli explained to me how trucking firms take advantage of information asymmetries in this "labor market where people get sucked in from construction, retail—all over the place and they know next to nothing about long-haul trucking."[109] A big part of the ruse is that the memory of trucking as a "good job" lingers. As Viscelli writes, "virtually all new truckers share one belief about the job that ultimately drew them to the industry: that they will earn more money trucking than in any other available job."[110] As in so many other jobs today, the information asymmetry works in employers' favor.

Erroneous information also persuades many truckers to take the independent contractor route. Some have no choice: certain firms have simply eliminated all employee positions, "leaving workers with the choice of becoming a contractor or finding a job elsewhere."[111] Many others arrive at the idea of independent contracting themselves, attracted to the idea of being their own boss. Two-thirds of the country's seventy-five thousand port truck drivers are now independent contractors. Most soon discover that the "freedom" of being an independent contractor comes with punishing costs. Independent contractors earn thousands less per year than employee drivers.[112] It's not just lower pay that independent contractors have to endure. As an executive in the Teamsters organization puts it, "The conditions that these guys work under is like sharecropping. The trucking company tells them what crops they can plant, what fertilizer they can use, makes them pay for all their equipment, and then tells them, you're independent."[113] One independent contractor, often idled for hours in traffic—hours for which he won't be paid, since most truckers are paid by the mile—summed up his situation succinctly: "This is hell on earth."[114]

HARDHATS IN HARD TIMES

Viscelli found that many drivers were drawn to trucking after spending time working construction. This is no surprise: full-time construction worker pay has dropped about $10,000 per year, adjusted for inflation, between the early 1970s and today.[115] Like trucking, construction is a "place-bound" industry, by its nature filled with work that can't be sourced to overseas employees. And while technological advancements have certainly altered many construction-related tasks, when you need a new roof on your home, a robot doesn't come by to do the job. There are over five million construction trades workers in the United States today. According to the federal government, these jobs aren't going away anytime soon. The Bureau of Labor Statistics (BLS) projects that in the coming decade employment will grow by 11 percent among the trades.[116]

Demand for construction workers remains steady, while the pay has declined. What happened? As with trucking, a massive power shift within the industry tilted bargaining toward employers. And the shift was enabled by the same successful removal of the key claims-making resource for non-managerial workers: labor unions. According to Milkman, beginning in the 1970s, "the nation's major construction firms, along with their largest industrial customers, launched a full-scale anti-union offensive."[117] It succeeded spectacularly. A 1973 government decision paved the way for firms to establish nonunion subsidiaries alongside their organized ones, in what were termed "double-breasted" arrangements. The fraction of large contractors that had union and nonunion subsidiaries more than doubled between 1975 and 1982, eroding labor's standing by creating competition between organized and unorganized subsidiaries within the same company. As parent firms expanded their nonunion subsidiaries, unionization in the industry fell—and with it, average wage levels. By one account, the spread of double-breasted firms was the most important cause of union decline in construction during the 1980s.[118]

In the early 1970s, 40 percent of private sector construction workers belonged to a union. Today, just 13 percent do.[119] Pay for construction workers fell sharply as the number of nonunion shops rose. In the words of one Californian contractor, "Once the union was actually broken out of the business, these guys were taking a screwing, it was as simple as that."[120]

Some companies, like Walmart, have long justified their low pay by pointing to their low prices. In construction, the savings from low wages weren't passed onto home buyers or renters. In 2018, the average cost of a house in the United States was just under $400,000—close to the historical high set the prior year. Adjusting for inflation, in the three decades between 1970 and 2000, median housing values nearly doubled; median rents increased by 45 percent.[121] There are various reasons for the rise in home values, including the expansion of the average size of houses.[122] But increased pay for the people who make them isn't among those reasons.

Just as reduced labor costs in housing haven't translated to lower housing prices, undercutting construction workers' pay hasn't reduced the cost of repairing our highways. Prevailing wage laws in construction establish a pay floor for public construction projects, including for road and bridge repairs. Depending on the jurisdiction, these floors are determined by wage surveys of relevant occupations in the surrounding counties where the project is based, or by local collective-bargaining agreements. In general, they have assured that construction workers on publicly funded projects will be paid decently. In recent years, a range of states have overturned their prevailing wage laws, including Arkansas, Indiana, Kentucky, and Wisconsin. Yet a review of the relevant research indicates that overturning these laws has no appreciable effect on subsequent construction costs.[123] The savings from lower labor costs aren't going to taxpayers.

MILLIONS OF AMERICANS HAVE seen their pay stagnate or decline, and are stuck in good jobs gone bad. What's critical to remember is that there is nothing inherent about a job that makes it good or bad. Wages and working conditions are what matters. Good jobs will not return in large numbers absent a fundamental shift in the claims-making terrain—a change that puts more power in workers' hands as they fight their uphill battle against employers for a fair share of company surplus. A full reckoning of how to achieve this goal awaits the final chapter, but what is clear for now is that any solution requires resuscitating employee organizations and reversing the reclassification trend so that the organizations under whose roofs people work, and whose rules they follow, are the ones providing their paychecks.

7 BAD JOBS CAN BE GOOD

IF GOOD JOBS CAN BE BAD, then the upside is that bad jobs can be made good. And that's a good thing, too, because contrary to the political promises of many elected officials, there is little reason to believe that manufacturing, mining, and other occupations of decades past are ever again going to employ the millions of Americans they once did. Five quintessentially poorly paid and grueling occupations are cases in point, as this chapter demonstrates: retail, fast food, sanitation, meatpacking, and home healthcare. Most workers in these occupations have few resources to improve their bargaining position. Claims for a fairer share of organizational revenue go largely unmet due to a set of political, organizational, and demographic factors tilted in employers' favor. Yet for each occupation, countervailing examples exist to suggest strategies for workers and their allies to make these bad jobs good. Or at least better than what currently prevails.

Today, the combined number of retail sales workers and food and beverage servers is about ten million. And contrary to popular lore, influenced by generations of television shows and Hollywood movies, these aren't ten million teenagers, working short shifts and weekends to save for their first car. The median age of a retail clerk is thirty-six; the median age of those fast food workers handing over your lunch is twenty-six.[1] Over the next decade, the government projects we'll need nearly 600,000 more food preparation workers to keep our bellies full. And despite the rise of online shopping, we'll also need nearly 150,000 more retail workers and first-line supervisors to steer us to the right aisles in the nearly 7,500 Walmarts, Targets, Sam's Clubs, and Costcos that dot our nation's landscape.[2]

The task of cleaning up all the burger wrappers, plastic containers, and other detritus we leave behind on a daily basis is unappealing, usually low-paying, and in some settings downright dangerous. For many of the country's tens of thousands of garbage and recycling workers, for example, just finishing a shift with all ten fingers intact counts as success. Earning enough to save for a much-needed vacation or an early retirement? Nearly unheard of, at least among private-sector sanitation workers. And all of those burgers, burritos, and nuggets require people to slaughter the cows and chickens and process the carcasses. Today, approximately a quarter of a million Americans toil away in meatpacking plants, a number that is also expected to grow in the years ahead.[3] This work is dangerous as well as low-paying. Meanwhile, given an aging population, the government predicts a need for millions more nurses, healthcare aides, and other healthcare providers. Some of these jobs, like home healthcare aides, currently offer rock-bottom pay, few if any benefits, and meager protections.

There is nothing inherent about these occupations that make them bad. The poor pay, unpredictable schedules, lack of benefits, and occupational risks that characterize so many of them are not necessary features of a home healthcare aide's or Walmart worker's job. There are ways to make these jobs of today and tomorrow pay like those quintessential middle-class jobs that once sustained a large and growing middle-class. We know that this is possible, because a look around the world, between competing firms, and in our nation's own history reveals something important: so-called bad jobs are sometimes pretty good.

SAVE MONEY. LIVE BETTER?

Françoise Carré and Chris Tilly are labor researchers whose work focuses on the causes of poverty, joblessness, and low wages. In a recent book, they issue a broad indictment: "The United States has a bad jobs problem, and retail jobs are at the heart of it."[4]

In the autumn of 2014, a nineteen-year-old employee at an Oklahoma City Walmart was worried about certain colleagues of hers, whose households she knew were struggling. She asked store management for permission to place a bin in an employee break room where others could donate food items for her to pass along. On its face, there was nothing extraordinary about a canned goods collection in the weeks before Thanksgiving. But this particular drive was not for the usual community foodbank but for some of the store's own workers. The sign she posted on the bin read: "Let's Succeed By Donating to Associates in Need!!!"[5] This wasn't the first time that Walmart employees had passed the hat for coworkers. A Cleveland store had done the same in 2013. Asked for comment, a company spokesperson in Bentonville explained that this had been a store-level decision, but noted it was "part of the company's culture to rally around associates and take care of them when they face extreme hardships."[6] Unmentioned was another defining feature of the company's culture that contributed to those extreme hardships: low pay.

Walmart's reach extends beyond US borders, and not just through its global supply chain. Walmart also has stores in over two dozen countries, including over two thousand locations in Mexico. Walmart associates there earn as much as and often more than workers at competing retailers. As a study of Walmart's Mexican expansion concludes, "Wal-Mart Mexico is not a low-wage employer."[7] The pay isn't extravagant, by any means—retail wages rarely are. But

Walmart Mexico offers wages that compare favorably with its competitors and are far above the country's minimum wage. This is also true beyond Mexico. In China, Walmart labor contracts are above the industry average.[8] When Carré and Tilly undertook a comparative study of retail pay across the globe, they discovered this about the company: "Wal-Mart as a low-wage employer among retailers appears to be a less than universal phenomenon."[9]

But you don't have to travel across the Southern border or fly all the way to China to find retailers who pay decently by local standards. Costco has over five hundred stores in the United States employing 163,000 workers. There are over three times as many Costco workers as there are coal miners left in the United States today. As we discovered in Chapter 5, to some investors' chagrin, Costco treats its employees well. A report from 2007 found that Costco's wages were about 70 percent higher than at Sam's Club, the Walmart-owned wholesale competitor.[10] More recently, Costco announced a pay hike, bringing up its starting hourly wage to $14.[11] That's 27 percent higher than the starting pay of a Walmart employee. And starting pay rates drastically understate the differences in compensation between the typical Costco and Walmart worker. Why? Huge differences in turnover. As efficiency wage theorists have long held, treating workers better by paying them more engenders goodwill and greater loyalty. That certainly seems true at Costco, where annual turnover rates average 10 percent, and fall to nearly half that for workers who have been with the company for at least a year.[12] This is in an industry where turnover rates regularly exceed 100 percent. As a result of such low turnover, a typical Costco employee has been with the company for a while, and earns, on average, $22.50 per hour.[13] That's nearly $47,000 for a full-time worker—and unlike many of its peer firms, Costco does employ a sizable fraction of its workers full-time.

Does higher worker pay in low-margin businesses like discount retail lead to higher prices at the checkout line? That has been the excuse some businesses offer when confronted about their low wages. Back in 2005, facing a barrage of criticism from a range of unions and other worker advocacy groups, Walmart took out a two-page advertisement in the *New York Review of Books*. Presented as a letter over the signature of then-CEO H. Lee Scott, Jr., the ad explained what would happen should Walmart cave to pressure and raise wages:

> If we kept our low prices and raised our average wages and benefits above today's market levels by a few dollars an hour or so, we would sacrifice a hefty chunk of our profits, hurting shareholders. . . . If, on the other hand, we raised prices substantially to fund above-market wages, we'd betray our commitment to tens of millions of customers, many of whom struggle to make ends meet.[14]

For Walmart, the equation was simple: higher pay means either hurting shareholders (an increasingly treacherous route to take, as we've learned) or hurting consumers through higher prices. But in fact, the empirical literature on the relationship of pay and prices in the retail and restaurant industries presents a mixed set of findings. One study, by Daniel Aaronson, focused on the pricing patterns in the restaurant industry in the United States and Canada. After legislation raised the minimum wage in various states and provinces, the cost of restaurant food did increase. But the increase was quite modest, and limited to the period surrounding the legislative change.[15] Sara Lemos's review of existing research on minimum wages and prices makes no greater case that pay hikes lead to price hikes: many studies find a small effect and some studies find no effect at all.[16] Lemos concludes that raising the minimum wage in industries like retail and fast food "increases the wages of the poor, does not destroy too many jobs and does not raise prices by too much."[17] The red-hot economy of the late 1990s helped to produce record-low unemployment and robust wage gains throughout industries, including retail. Prices for retail goods, however, remained essentially flat.[18]

How come? As Costco has demonstrated, well-paid workers often make happier and more loyal workers, and happier and more loyal workers work more productively. As anyone who has slogged through a lousy job under a lousy boss knows, the combination of low pay and poor management is enervating. Wage increases, meanwhile, don't just motivate employees. Higher labor costs can also shake employers out of complacency, leading them to innovate more in their search for other ways to beat competitors. As Carré and Tilly conclude, "nothing gets employers thinking harder about ways to increase productivity than blocking the low-wage solution."[19]

So far, other retailers have largely eschewed innovative thinking and resorted instead to the copycat approach. As one executive in the late 1990s lamented, "When a competitor comes in, you have to mimic their operations, and you get reduced to the lowest common denominator."[20] Walmart has proven especially tempting to mimic, a fact that the company's critics have long recognized. In the spring of 2005, five members of Congress and a former Miss America joined with unions and other worker advocates to shame Walmart for the company's gender pay disparities and general low pay. As part of the "Love Mom, Not Wal-Mart" campaign, the participants signed an eight-by-eight-foot Mother's Day card addressed to CEO Lee Scott, urging him to remedy sex-based discrimination and raise rock-bottom wages. Congresswomen Rosa DeLauro of Connecticut, one of the giant card's signees, said Walmart's massive scale meant it was especially obliged to serve as a positive model for others: "certainly, as the nation's wealthiest and largest employer and largest company, Wal-Mart has a unique role and responsibility to do the right thing and set the best standard for America."[21] Having industry behemoths set higher standards is important because mimicry often leads to inertia. The pay rate they use settles in to become part of the operating model for others—an assumed factor when making business decisions. Likewise, when an industry leader changes its ways, that can motivate firms to overhaul their established practices, too.

Since that Mother's Day, Walmart has raised its base pay in the United States. Still, it remains far from setting the "best standard for America." But as the case of Costco shows, there are other models out there to mimic—ones that don't necessarily lead you to "the lowest common denominator" when it comes to pay. Nearly sixteen million Americans work in the retail industry in some capacity—fully 10 percent of all workers.[22] Given the sector's size, breaking from Walmart's domestic model would have enormous consequences not only for retail but for the overall workforce.

UNHAPPY MEALS

There's another reason why breaking from Walmart's domestic model is so important if we're serious about making bad jobs good. Major retailers such as Walmart, Target, Costco, and others compete for workers with firms in another industry known for its low pay and high turnover. Since 2000, the number of fast food establishments in the United States has grown by 40 percent.[23] Over a third of the US adult population dines daily on food from one of the quarter million fast food outlets in the country.[24] As most people who have traveled outside the United States know, manufacturing isn't the only industry to have slipped America's shores. America's fast food favorites are ubiquitous across the globe—and sometimes beyond. In 2001,

Pizza Hut spent $1 million to deliver a pie to a cosmonaut aboard the international space station.[25] Not to be outdone in the race for galaxy supremacy, Domino's countered a decade later with a plan to build the first fast food outlet on the moon.[26] No word yet on an opening date.

Flipping burgers or delivering pizza won't make you rich regardless of where you're plying your trade. This is especially true in the contemporary United States. Average pay for fast food workers in this country is less than $10 per hour, or just over $20,000 per year. If you're a single mother with two kids, that'll put you right at the federal poverty threshold. Pay is low in fast food compared to most other occupations for three key reasons. First, the claims-making space for an average worker is narrow. No advanced educational degrees or specialized certificates are required, leading to a large pool of potential replacements should your boss grow tired of your demands for a sizable raise. Second, labor costs comprise a significant portion of operating expenses, leaving less room for employers to offset higher payroll costs by lowering expenses elsewhere. In fast food, the combined cost of payroll and benefits eats up nearly half of operating expenses.[27] In auto manufacturing, by contrast, workers' wages and benefits comprise only about a tenth of the total cost of making a car.[28]

But while a Wendy's worker isn't going to get rich, there is room for her to get richer. It's not as if the CEOs of the major fast food conglomerates have to stick to their own firms' offerings to balance the family budget. In 2017, McDonald's CEO Steve Easterbrook took home nearly $22 million.[29] If he wanted to stay completely on-brand, he could have bought over four million Big Macs that year, or over eleven thousand of the sandwiches per day.[30] Fast food leads the way when it comes to CEO-to-worker pay ratios.[31] Average workers make very little; CEOs of iconic brands like McDonald's earn quite a lot. And while labor costs are a sizable fraction of operating expenses, the global brands that dominate the fast food landscape are enormously profitable. From the average worker's perspective, that's a good thing, too. High relative payroll costs combined with low profit margins put workers in the worst claims-making position: not only do employers have little room to offset a rise in labor expenses with savings from other operating costs, narrow margins mean less remaining revenue to divide up among the various claimants.

Narrow margins help us understand the third reason why workers' claims for higher pay in an industry like fast food may not be met: organizational size. Politicians' paeans to small businesses cross partisan divides. During the 2016 campaign, Donald Trump and Hillary Clinton didn't see eye to eye on much. But when it came to extolling the virtues of small businesses, their views were virtually indistinguishable. At a campaign roundtable event with small business owners held at Smuttynose Brewing Company in New Hampshire, Clinton put it bluntly: "I want to be the small business president."[32] In his 2018 State of the Union Address, Donald Trump heralded how his signature tax cut plan helped the nation's small business owners in particular: "Small business confidence is at all-time high. . . . Our massive tax cuts provide tremendous relief to the middle class and small businesses."[33]

Small businesses loom large in our collective imagination of what a strong economy looks like. And not without reason: small businesses employ nearly half of all private sector workers.[34] But, comparatively, they don't pay those workers all that well. If you're looking for workplaces where pay is high, big is generally better. This pattern holds not only in the United States, but around the world.[35] Researchers continue to debate why the number of workers in a company should prove so determinative of what they are paid. This finding is especially challenging to the traditional economics consensus in which pay is largely based on your individual skills and the resulting value you add to your company. Yet even after comparing workers with similar skills, backgrounds, and education, the "bigger is better" pattern remains.[36]

A few organizational factors stand out in the empirical literature. First, large firms remain more likely to have internal labor markets in place (despite their recent declines).[37] The development of firm-specific skills takes time, and, as a result, high turnover at companies with these structures is especially costly. To employers who don't want to lose someone in whom they've invested so much training over a long period, a tried-and-true tactic to win workers' loyalty is to pay them comparatively well. That's one reason why large firms with internal labor markets pay more than smaller firms lacking this organizational feature. Second, there are equity concerns. Large firms, on average, have more complex division of labor, with employees filling a range of jobs from the bottom to the top of the organizational hierarchy. At many small fast food establishments, a more limited number of workers can open and close the shops, maintain inventory, serve the customers, and clean up after the stores close. In major corporations, many of these discrete tasks are assigned to different workers, and, of course, larger firms have many more tasks to perform. As research has shown, when everyone from the cleaning staff on up works for the same employer, it is much more difficult to pay certain workers poorly and others extravagantly— equity concerns are too prominent.[38] Maintaining workers' sense that their company pays fairly, in practice, often requires pay compression between similarly situated workers and compression up and down the corporate chain.[39] As David Weil concludes: "As long as workers are under one roof, the problems presented by horizontal and vertical equity remain."[40]

The authors of a recent book on the matter, *Big is Beautiful,* implore politicians to redirect their attention—and rhetoric—away from small companies toward the firms that, on average, tend to treat their workers better: "if policy makers want to improve wages, they should focus their efforts on helping both existing large firms and the minority of small firms that are capable of significant growth."[41] At smaller firms, a flat organizational hierarchy combines with low profits to constrain workers' claims-making ability. And if the available pie, after all fixed costs are accounted for, is down to mere crumbs, there simply isn't money to redistribute to even the most treasured workers.

That's not a problem with our giant fast food firms, right? Steve Easterbrook's company sold a lot of Happy Meals and french fries in 2018, contributing to a net profit margin of over 21 percent. The industry average was a healthy 13 percent.[42] Given annual revenues for the company that exceed $20 billion, there was money to go around. Workers in the United States got comparatively little of it. Partly that's because, when it comes to fast food, many large companies do their best to act small. Franchising is a form of workplace fissuring where a lead firm—say Burger King—offers a franchisee the right to operate an establishment, sell its products, and use its branding. In return, the franchisee must pay the lead firm royalties based on the establishment's revenue. Leftover revenue minus other operating costs provide the franchisee with profit. The advantage for franchisees is that the business has a proven model, established product line, and corporate branding investment. The advantage for the franchisor is much higher return on assets than it could achieve owning stores and their equipment in many locations. It also doesn't have to worry about pay equity issues arising in a store crew—those are the franchisee's problem.[43] The franchise model is the third reason that fast food workers in the United States earn so little. Fissuring through the franchise model—in effect, making mighty corporations act small—is the third reason why many US fast food workers earn so little.

Fast food workers elsewhere, it turns out, get much more. Hampus Elofsson, for example, works full-time at a Burger King restaurant in Copenhagan, Denmark. There is nothing dramatically different about working at a Burger King in Denmark versus an outlet in, say, downtown Denver. The official website of Burger King Denmark features an array of products recognizable to any customer of the company's US locations, with the exception of the "Halloumi" burger, a menu item tailored to Danish tastes which substitutes fried Halloumi cheese for the beef patty. No advanced training is required to produce one, as far as I can tell.

In a 2014 *New York Times*' profile, Hampus reported receiving roughly $20 per hour for his work at Burger King. "You can make a decent living here working in fast food," he said.[44]

Assuming full-time hours, that translates to annual earnings of $41,600. The current debate in the United States is whether to raise the minimum wage to $15 per hour, 25 percent lower than Hampus earned as a fast food worker a few years ago. And yet Burger King establishments in Denmark aren't closing due to a lack of profitability. In fact, their sheer presence in that country—where union-negotiated agreements guarantee workers like Hampus at least $20 per hour—gives the lie to any claim that fast food jobs must pay poorly.

How do Danish fast food outlets survive with such high wage bills? For one thing, turnover is lower. In the Copenhagen airport's fast food restaurants, for example, over two-thirds of employees stay on for more than a year. Compare that to typical turnover rates for fast food in the United States, which reached 133 percent in 2018.[45] In the United States, chances are the maker of your favorite breakfast sandwich or specialty coffee will leave the job before a year is out. Saving on training and search costs helps Danish companies absorb some of the higher pay they dole out to employees. Prices are somewhat higher, too. In 2014, a McDonald's Big Mac cost $.80 more, on average, in Denmark than in the United States.[46] Partly those higher prices reflect higher wages. Partly they reflect the cost of benefits a fast food worker in the United States can only dream of, including five weeks of paid vacation and parental leave.

Profits are lower, too. That's another consequence of paying workers well in a competitive industry where labor costs are a large fraction of total expenses. As the general manager of the Copenhagen airport restaurants told the *New York Times,* "We have to acknowledge it's more expensive to operate." But, he noted, "we can still make money out of it—and McDonald's does, too. Otherwise, it wouldn't be in Denmark."[47] He noted with pride that "a full-time Burger King employee made enough to live on," speaking to a different sense of equity when it comes to fast food work than we usually see in the United States. What he was getting at is the notion that paying workers too little to live on is morally wrong, and if that means some profit margin has to be sacrificed to raise workers' living standards, so be it.

Currently, Burger King employees in the United States tend to earn much less than $15 per hour, let alone $20. Denver is one of the cities that has passed a $15 per hour minimum wage, which will be phased in by 2021. Nationally, median hourly pay for American fast food workers is less than half that of their Danish counterparts.[48] There are severe consequences to such disparities. Hampus sees a career at Burger King, one that can support a decent living as he climbs the corporate ladder. Anthony Moore, a Burger King worker in Tampa, Florida, has already stepped up a rung. Yet despite supervising a team of ten, he earns just $9 per hour. He's behind on his bills, and relies on food stamps to feed his two young children. Burger King's healthcare plan is beyond his reach, so he goes without insurance. He compares his situation to Hampus's: "If I made $20 an hour, I could actually live, instead of dreaming about living."[49]

Can the Danish model for fast food work be exported to the United States? In fact, an approximation of it is already here. Emeryville, California, sits sandwiched between its two higher-profile neighbors, Oakland and Berkeley. With just eleven thousand residents and no major university within the city limits, it was known mostly as the home of Pixar Studios and Peet's Coffee and Tea. In 2015, it became recognized for something other than its corporate headquarters. That spring the city council unanimously approved a bill to raise the town's minimum wage to $16 per hour by 2019.[50] As of this writing, tiny Emeryville has the highest minimum wage in the country at $15.69 per hour, set to increase to $16 per hour later in the year. The highest minimum wage in the country translates to about $32,600 a year, if you're lucky enough to work full-time. It will not make you rich, especially in high-cost coastal California. But it can make all the difference for workers toiling away at the wage floor. It certainly did for Emeryville resident Julio Payes, who had been working eighty hours a week, shuttling between jobs at McDonald's and a temp agency. Prior to the increase, "to afford basic necessities, he had to work up to 16 hours a day, seven days a week," reports Matthew Desmond. The grueling schedule had predictable consequences: "I felt like a zombie. No energy. Always sad."[51] Today, Payes still works two jobs (although he swapped out the McDonald's position for one at Burger King), but much else in his life has changed. He has cut back on his hours, gets decent sleep, exercises regularly, and actually has time to spend with his family.

Minimum wage debates often revolve around the policy's effects on employment, with the theory being that mandatory increases must depress job growth. In the real world, however, disemployment effects are awfully hard to detect.[52] In many cases it is clear from the data that minimum wage increases benefit workers and do not reduce jobs. Emeryville, with its current claim to the highest minimum wage in the country, can also claim something else: an extraordinarily low unemployment rate of 2.4 percent, substantially below the national rate. It's also a lower rate than found in many of its neighbors. The balance of Alemeda County, in which Emeryville sits, has an unemployment rate 17 percent higher than Emeryville's.[53] This is not to suggest that raising the minimum wage decreases unemployment. There are plenty of factors contributing to the fact that so few Emeryville residents are looking for work. But it does show it is possible to pay workers well—even fast food workers—without reducing jobs.

It's not the case that no consequences would result from dramatically raising US fast food workers' wages to match what those elsewhere receive. Probably prices would rise a bit and profits would decline. The lower profit margins might keep employers from opening new outlets, reducing fast food's footprint in the country a bit. What would be gained? Governments might see reduced take-up rates in programs for the poor and near-poor. Workers like Anthony could think bigger about his own and his children's future. Indeed, millions of Americans toiling away at bad jobs would gain a sense of being treated fairly, and the dignity such treatment instills. Eduardo Porter writes in the *New York Times*, "There is nothing inevitable about dead-end jobs."[54] He's right. As Hampus shows, they can offer a way forward, and a way up.

PAYING FOR DANGER?

Liberty Ashes, a private waste collection and removal company, was founded in 1977, and continues to this day to serve the greater New York City area. Between 2010 and 2016, three different sanitation workers lost fingers working on one of its trucks. More precisely, the lack of a safety latch on Truck #11 led to two severed pinkies and one severed ring finger.[55] In New York City's hypercompetitive private garbage collection industry, Liberty Ashes isn't unique in the gruesome injuries that afflict workers at regular intervals. While working for a competitor, Viking Sanitation, Alex Caban was smashed in the head by a winch falling off a container. It left a deep indent to go along with various scars and other physical reminders that he holds one of the most dangerous jobs in America.

At least Alex didn't die. In 2018, the last year for which we have complete data, "refuse and recyclable material collectors" had the fifth-highest fatality rate of any occupation.[56] Fifty-seven garbage collectors died on the job across America that year.[57] In the first three weeks of 2019, thirteen more died.[58] The occupation regularly outranks policing and fire fighting in its percentage of workers who die on the job. In the academic literature, the theory of compensating differentials maintains that dangerous jobs must offer workers higher pay than safer jobs that require similar skill sets.[59] After all, why would anyone choose to risk life and limb if safer alternatives offering the same pay were available? By this logic, the nation's 115,000 garbage collectors must be well compensated, given the daily hazards they face during the hundreds of pickups they make each shift.

In reality, the work for many is generally "dangerous, brutal and poorly paid."[60] The medium hourly wage for garbage collectors is $17.40 per hour. In the broader context of bad jobs, that's pretty good. A worker lucky enough to be employed full-time at that rate will clear $36,000 a year. But the median obscures significant variation in the industry. Some private collection companies offer an hourly rate barely above minimum wage. Others pay a flat fee, with no benefits, regardless of the time it takes to complete the shift. According to the

Bureau of Labor Statistics, a quarter of all collectors earn less than $13.12 per hour; one out of every ten earns $10.30 per hour or less—effectively a fast food wage.[61]

Garbage collection and fast food share another defining characteristic: wage theft. In the New York City commercial waste industry, the practice where an employer deliberately withholds wages that the worker is legally entitled to "is rampant."[62] It's also rampant in fast food, with one recent study finding that 14 percent of workers in the food and drink service industry report receiving less than minimum wage, a clear indication of wage theft.[63] In 2017, the national chain Carl's Jr., to take just one example, had to pay back nearly $1.5 million to its workers in Los Angeles after the city found the company had paid workers less than Los Angeles's minimum wage.[64] Yet workers don't die operating the fry machine at Carl's Jr. People do die collecting our trash. Can something be done, or are these risks inherent to the job?

We can think of the law as institutionalized power. But it is not simply a reflection of existing power differentials. It is also, and often more significantly, a "major means through which power is exercised," as a study of the role of laws in structuring the economy concludes.[65] The law carries an independent force that can upend existing power dynamics, which explains why many battles to change the law are so hotly contested. Labor law is no exception. Power as expressed through the law is a crucial means by which employers are able to get their way in conflicts over their employees' wages and working conditions.

OSHA—the Occupational Safety and Health Administration—is our government's workplace watchdog, setting health and safety standards, investigating abuses, and levying fines on offending firms. It was created in 1970, after a years-long effort, and the effect was to institutionalize power for workers, who now had a federal agency to look out for them when employers violated the nation's workplace health and safety requirements. This particular form of institutionalized power has its limits, however. Consider the story of SeaWorld, the marine-themed amusement park chain, which has faced negative scrutiny in recent years over its treatment of captive orcas (commonly known as killer whales). A popular documentary released in 2013 led to calls to boycott the parks, which ultimately pressured the company to end its orca breeding program and phase out theatrical shows in which the animals performed. It also led to a major fine after executives understated to investors the negative impact of the film on the firm's finances. Misleading or lying to investors is illegal, and SeaWorld paid the price: on September 18, 2018, the Securities and Exchange Commission (SEC) fined the company $5 million for "untrue and misleading statements or omissions in SEC filings, earnings releases and calls, and other statements to the press."[66]

That wasn't the only whale-related controversy engulfing SeaWorld. In 2010, one of its orcas drowned a trainer, leading to an OSHA investigation. OSHA found fault with the company for exposing workers to preventable dangers on the job, including drowning (the same animal had previously killed a trainer at a different park). An administrative law judge and the agency's review commission upheld OSHA's decision. SeaWorld appealed, and eventually the case ended up before a panel of the DC circuit court. The company lost again (future Supreme Court Justice Brett Kavanaugh was the lone dissenter), with the court deciding that "SeaWorld had violated its duties as an employer by exposing trainers to 'recognized hazards' when working with killer whales."[67]

All that was left was for SeaWorld to pay OSHA's penalty. All $12,000 of it—a fraction of a percentage point of its earlier SEC fine. And actually $12,000 is a *high* penalty for OSHA. Absent evidence that a company acted willfully to put an employee in danger or is a repeat violator, the maximum fine OSHA can levy is just over $13,000 per violation. Not long ago, the maximum was $7,000. That's the amount OSHA fined Flag Container Services, a Staten Island trash collection firm, after a dumpster missing a safety latch crushed a worker to death in 2014.[68] In both of these cases, OSHA decided the actions of the firms weren't willful, just negligent. But even willful wrongdoing isn't that costly, as codified in the law. The maximum fine for this severe category is $132,598 per violation—about three percent of the SEC penalty SeaWorld paid.[69]

SeaWorld's CEO, Jim Atchison, was forced out in 2014 after all the backlash. He didn't leave empty-handed. His severance package of $2.6 million was over two hundred times the amount his firm had to pay for its worker's drowning death.[70] The law both reflects and structures power relations in our economy. It's also an expression of our economic values. The huge gulf between the SEC penalty and the OSHA fine "pretty much sums up the contrast between how we view investors versus workers in this country," in the words of labor lawyer Andrew Strom.[71] So sure, the establishment of OSHA shifted power to employees in US workplaces. A bit.

But back to garbage collection. Safety violations are endemic to the industry not because they're inevitable but because, as in the case of discouraging unionization efforts, the costs to employers of violating our labor laws are so low. The chances of being caught in the first place are low, too. OSHA's budget has remained relatively unchanged in real terms since the late 1970s, despite a dramatic increase in the number of firms operating under its watch.[72] As a result, many employers take advantage of an existing legal regime to save on costs by not upgrading equipment or offering adequate training.

The law is not the only thing enabling employers to exert power over workers in the dangerous world of private garbage collection. A characteristic common to many workers in private collection companies is a criminal record. Alex Caban's past includes several felony convictions. He'd much rather work a job that isn't so dangerous and offers better pay, but many employers screen out convicted felons. He's not alone, as Kiera Feldman reports: "for many men with a criminal record, private sanitation is one of the few jobs they can get."[73] This characteristic reduces the likelihood an employee will speak out against an employer who cuts corners on safety or doesn't pay the worker what he is owed. And it reduces the likelihood a worker will quit in the face of mistreatment, or over a denied raise. There simply aren't enough other employment choices.

Like retail and fast food, garbage collection need not be a bad job. How do we know? For a lucky segment of the industry, it isn't. In New York City, private collectors serve business customers, and work at night. But the city has a fleet of its own, and its trucks and workers collect the trash and recyclables at residences during the day. The job still involves garbage, but that's about the only thing it shares with the nighttime operations. Across the nation, public sector collectors have a much lower job-related death rate.[74] Public sector garbage collectors also enjoy much higher pay. In New York City, a job with the Department of Sanitation offers solid middle-class wages. In 2014, starting pay was about $34,000 a year, increasing to nearly $70,000 after five-and-a-half years on the job.[75] Experienced drivers can make $90,000 a year. Training is extensive, and managers and employees adhere to safety regulations.[76] The difference between collecting trash at night and collecting it during the day really is like night and day. Demand for a job with the Department of Sanitation is extraordinarily high. After an eight-year hiatus, the city offered its sanitation civil service exam in 2015. Nearly seventy thousand people signed up to take it. The city hired about five hundred of them.[77]

If anything, working for a private collection company with a business client base may be a more difficult job calling for a higher skill level, given the frenetic pace drivers and their helpers must maintain. And it's certainly more dangerous to work the commercial side. What then accounts for such a huge gulf in wages and working conditions? City employees can't point to a lack of possible replacements when bargaining for higher pay, given that the sanitation department turns away tens of thousands of people each hiring cycle. Two organizational characteristics shift power relations within the city's sanitation service. First, of course, it's a public sector organization. There remains debate about whether public sector workers outearn their private sector counterparts, with recent studies suggesting that certain segments of the government workforce—especially workers at the highest skill levels—are underpaid compared to their private sector peers.[78] In the case of trash collectors in New York City, this finding doesn't hold. That's because another organizational characteristic, unionization, also boosts city trash collectors' pay. City sanitation workers are part of a powerful union, Teamsters Local 831, which negotiates the terms of the collectors' wages and working conditions.

In a situation where one union negotiates with just one employer—in this case, the city—the union is able to exert more leverage than in industries in which a number of small unions are spread across numerous small sanitation companies. The city doesn't need to worry about being undercut by low-wage nonunion rivals, since there aren't any competitors for residential trash pickup. This allows for more generous labor contracts compared to highly competitive markets where rivals can underbid firms on labor costs. And while city agencies must be mindful of how their budgets affect residents' tax burdens, New York City remains, comparatively speaking, a union-heavy and union-friendly town. If the city were to reduce trash collectors' pay down to that of the nighttime private collectors, there would likely be a public backlash with electoral implications.

On the private collection side, garbage collection remains a dangerous job without a detectable compensating differential. Indeed, within the broader occupation we see that the highest-paid collectors tend to work in less dangerous environments, essentially opposite of what the theory predicts. And it's not just garbage collection that combines dangerous conditions and low pay. As one study into the relationship between wages and workplace fatalities concludes, the "observation that workers exposed to higher levels of work-related fatalities are usually those with low pay" has become "commonplace."[79] Despite the "commonplace" findings, the theory of compensating differentials keeps its strong hold on the public imagination. This empirically discredited idea frequently emerges as an excuse for persistent pay gaps between men and women. For example, former tech executive Steve Tobak observes, "Men are far more likely to choose careers that are more dangerous, so they naturally pay more."[80] If anything, today's dangerous jobs pay less.

What does the theory of compensating differentials get wrong? First and foremost, it ignores power. Dangerous working conditions often emerge in precisely those labor markets in which employees' claims-making abilities are severely constrained by certain characteristics, such as a criminal record or immigration status. The characteristics bear no relation to whether the workers can perform the job—but they bear a large relation to the workers' alternative employment options, and therefore their claims-making ability to pressure employers to pay them more and make their workplaces safer. Dangerous jobs and low pay often go hand in hand because employers use power differentials based on available resources at their disposal—including a lax regulatory environment and the precarious legal standing of many of their workers—to pay their workers poorly and skimp on equipment upgrades and monitoring. And once a few firms with a sizable market share act this way, competitors feel pressured to mimic their practices, institutionalizing the worst of all worlds when it comes to worker treatment.

WELCOME (BACK) TO THE JUNGLE

Surveying Chicago's meatpacking plants during the early twentieth century, muckraker Upton Sinclair came to a realization: "Things that were quite unspeakable went on there in the packing houses all the time, and were taken for granted by everybody."[81] With the publication of *The Jungle,* first in serial form in 1905 and then as a book the following year, Sinclair spoke about what was previously unspeakable, and shocked a nation into action. President Theodore Roosevelt quickly signed the Federal Meat Inspection Act (FMIA) and the Pure Food and Drug Act (also known as the Wiley Act) into law in 1906. The FMIA, among other provisions, mandated inspections of animals pre- and post-slaughter, and authorized the Department of Agriculture to carry out the monitoring.[82] The Wiley Act banned the manufacture and distribution of adulterated or mislabeled food and drugs, and would eventually lead to the creation of the Food and Drug Administration.

Neither law did much for the workers whose plight Sinclair showcased. The book's accounts of unsanitary meat aroused the most uproar; accounts of workers being maimed and dying from the job inspired no comparable response. During a 1956 speech celebrating the fiftieth anniversary of the FMIA, the former general counsel of the American Meat Institute remarked: "There is nothing in which the American public is more interested than a tender piece of wholesome meat."[83] Sinclair's famous lament about the reaction to his pathbreaking book—"I aimed at the public's heart, and by accident I hit it in the stomach"—spoke to a comparative disinterest by the public in the wholesomeness of the work involved in getting that meat from the farm to the grocery aisle.[84]

Work in a Chicago meatpacking business was "dangerous, bloody, and occasionally life-threatening, with long hours [and] low wages," according to labor analyst Daniel Calamuci.[85] It still is. No industry undermines the theory of compensating differentials like meat processing, which has hundreds of thousands of employees working on its lines in the United States today. Most of them are classified by the Bureau of Labor Statistics as "Meat, Poultry, and Fish Cutters and Trimmers." Their median hourly wage of $12.14 is about a dollar higher than retail salespeople's. Their *mean* hourly rate is actually lower than retail workers—indicating that meat processing is an occupation without much variation in pay. Retail workers at the ninetieth percentile—those who outearn 90 percent of their occupational counterparts—make nearly $20 per hour. Cutters and trimmers at the ninetieth percentile of their occupation make $2 less per hour, on average.[86] Slightly higher up the occupational chain in our nation's slaughterhouses are the nation's seventy-seven thousand "Slaughterers and Meat Packers." This category describes the workers directly involved in killing the animals, and those performing the most precise cuts. They earn about $27,500 annually, or just over $13 per hour at the median. Mean hourly earnings for these skilled slaughterhouse jobs are on par with those of retail sales workers.[87] That is where the similarities between the jobs end. Amputations in meatpacking are common, with one estimate suggesting that two occur in a typical week. Fingers are the most likely to go, but incidents of severed arms, toes, and legs aren't unheard of.[88] Apart from such gory accidents, more routine physical ailments that come from working fast and repetitively afflict a sizable portion of the workforce. A 2014 study of one poultry processing plant found that one out of every three workers suffered from carpal tunnel syndrome.[89] Another study of a Midwestern pork processor found that a similar fraction experienced traumatic injury within just six months of employment.[90]

And while a report commissioned by the Government Accountability Office in 2016 indicated that the injury rate in meat processing plants had fallen in recent years, the authors cautioned that underreporting and other data quality issues hampered their investigation.[91] Underreporting seems to be a problem among one particular group of slaughterhouse workers: immigrants, who comprise roughly a third of the occupation.[92] Largely Hispanic, and many lacking legal status, these workers are unlikely to confront their employers over unsafe working conditions or low (or stolen) pay out of fear of exposure. That was what the researchers who studied injuries in the aforementioned Midwestern pork plant concluded after their data showed significantly lower injury rates for Hispanics compared to other racial and ethnic groups: "These findings suggest that either Hispanics are very safe employees or they underreport injuries. We make the case for the latter."[93]

While the dominant nationalities differ—the slaughterhouse workers Sinclair chronicled were largely Lithuanian—the basic reality remains of powerful plant owners employing a disproportionately foreign-born workforce. Just as Sinclair did in the first decade of the twentieth century, chroniclers of these workers' plight today also bemoan the fact that Americans are more attuned to their "tender piece of wholesome meat" than to the employment conditions in our slaughterhouses.[94] Today, however, many consumers are sensitive not only to the quality of their meat, but to the conditions the pigs, cows, turkeys, and chickens lived under prior to being killed. When Oliver Gottfried of Oxfam America, an anti-poverty organization, spoke with poultry workers, one of them asked, "If they can care this much about their animals, why can't they care about their people?"[95] Despite the growing demand for cage-free eggs, humane killing methods, and larger crate sizes for pregnant pigs, NPR's Peggy Lowe notes, "there is still little outcry about conditions for workers who produce our meat."[96]

Maybe there is something inherent about meat processing that renders the occupation low-paying and highly dangerous? Our own history suggests otherwise. Sandwiched between Sinclair's time and the present day were a few decades in which slaughterhouse work was, all things considered, well compensated and not as risky. From the end of World War II up through the 1980s, the pay for meatpackers often exceeded average wages in manufacturing; indeed, according to John Brueggemann and Cliff Brown, "Meatpackers became some of the nation's best-paid industrial employees."[97] In 1970, for example, cutters and trimmers earned nearly $24 per hour in today's dollars, roughly double what they make today. Front-line slaughterers took home nearly $26 per hour.[98] For a full-time worker, that averages out to over $54,000 a year—solid, middle-class earnings.

What happened? Powerful unions altered the claims-making environment by presenting a united front against the major meatpacking firms. This was no easy feat, given a workplace deliberately managed to inhibit worker solidarity. Employers used language and other cultural divisions to retain their workplace power by inhibiting worker solidarity—it's hard to get together to share grievances when you can't communicate. They were explicit about this strategy. In 1904, John Commons toured a Chicago plant and was startled to find that all the recent hires were Swedish. A manager explained the strategy: "it is only for a week. Last week we employed Slovaks. We change among different nationalities and languages. It prevents them from getting together. We have the thing systematized."[99]

The efforts of the United Packinghouse Workers of America (UWPA) and the Amalgamated Meat Cutters (AMC) finally got the workers together. By the 1960s, these two unions represented nearly all slaughterhouse employees outside of the South. This density allowed for industry-wide wage bargaining and safety standards that all major employers adhered to. But by the 1980s, most of these hard-won gains had been lost. In 1985, the annual injury rate in the industry topped 30 percent, meaning that for every hundred slaughterhouse workers, thirty suffered an injury requiring more than just first-aid.[100] This rate is quadruple the average across the private sector. And no pay raise compensated workers for the danger. Real wages peaked in the late 1970s, and declined precipitously throughout the 1980s and 1990s.[101]

IBP, one of the major meat processing companies, led the charge away from the highly-organized, largely urban industry structure that predominated during the World War II decades. Other companies mimicked IBP, relocating to rural locations, deskilling many positions, and shifting to nonunion labor. As anthropologist Donald Tull told the *Nation,* "IBP set the trend and other companies followed." Soon, the companies "were all locked in this dance together."[102] By the turn of the twenty-first century, that dance produced an increasingly nonunion workforce once again fractured by a kaleidoscope of nationalities. At one IBP plant in Washington state, 90 percent of the workers were immigrants. Many hailed from a range of Latin American countries, while others had traveled from Laos, Vietnam, and Bosnia.[103]

There are bad jobs, and then there is the worst. Working the line at a slaughterhouse can be awful. Cleaning up what remains is even more horrible. We don't have a great idea of the overall injury rates among meatpacking sanitation workers because the industry is so fissured. Major meat processing companies including Perdue and Tyson contract out much of their cleanup work, and, conveniently for the firms, the government doesn't require the Tysons of the world to report its contractors' injury data. Indirect evidence suggests slaughterhouse sanitation is an incredibly dangerous occupation made worse through the combination of fissuring (making it harder to track safety violators), diminished worker power (much of the labor force is undocumented), and, our old friend, financialization. A remarkable 2017 *Bloomberg Businessweek* investigation into meatpacking sanitation crews unearthed the dangers involved in working for Packers Sanitation Services, the country's largest meat processing sanitation contractor. Of fourteen thousand firms tracked by OSHA, Packers had the highest levels of severe injuries. The company's amputation rate was five times that of the rate for all manufacturing workers. One Packers worker nearly lost an arm after getting caught in a conveyor belt trying to clean fat from a railing: "The radius and ulna bones could be seen sticking out of her arm, in shards."[104] Prior to the accident, she was making just over $200 per week—about $10,500 annually. Packers' average hourly wage is under $12. And how did the firm compensate her for her gruesome injuries? By firing her.

Shortly thereafter, a private equity firm took over Packers. Like so many private equity transactions, this one relied heavily on debt. To pay back its investors, the company needed revenue, and fast. As David Michaels, former director of OSHA, asked rhetorically, "Are they reducing costs to pay debt by pressuring workers to work faster? That's a common danger with highly leveraged companies."[105] It's a common danger that leads to dangerous workplaces.

In 2018, American companies produced over a hundred billion pounds of red meat and poultry—a record high.[106] Notwithstanding

Burger King's recent unveiling of its meatless "Impossible Whopper," the average American still consumes over two hundred pounds of animal meat each year.[107] Assuming no drastic change in the typical diet, getting all those chickens, pigs, and cows from farm to table will take a lot of sawing, skinning, deboning, and cleaning up. And while automation has transformed the industry before, leading to the deskilling of cutting jobs that once required experience and considerable expertise, current government estimates do not suggest the wholesale roboticization of meat processing anytime soon. In fact, the number of slaughterhouse workers is projected to grow at a modest rate over the next decade. Those sizzling steaks and juicy hamburgers still require, at some point in the chain, human labor.

NOT CARING FOR CAREGIVERS

In a 2011 speech, President Barack Obama told the story of Pauline, a home healthcare worker: "When we met, she was getting up every day at 5:00 AM to go to work taking care of an eighty-six-year-old amputee named Mr. John. And each day, she'd dress Mr. John and help him into his wheelchair. She'd make him breakfast. She'd scrub his floors. She'd clean his bathroom. She was his connection to the outside world." The president called what Pauline did "heroic work, and hard work."

While we'll continue to need hundreds of thousands of slaughterhouse workers, we're going to need millions of home care aides. These are the people who visit the homes of our nations' elderly and disabled to help them bath, dress, and ensure they are getting adequate nutrition and exercise. The home-based direct care workforce is comprised of nearly three million workers. Add in nursing assistants, who generally do not visit patients at their homes but perform many of the same duties as home-based aides, and there are nearly five million workers today washing, cleaning, and cooking for the most frail and vulnerable among us.

Demand for these workers has risen rapidly. Between 2006 and 2016, the number of home care aides doubled. That influx won't be enough to meet future needs. Paul Osterman of MIT calculates that unless we take immediate steps to lure more workers in to the field, we'll be short 350,000 home healthcare aides by 2040.[108] Current staffing problems suggest we've already reached a "national crisis," according to the policy director of PHI, a nonprofit research and advocacy group for elderly and disabled Americans.[109] Skyrocketing demand for home care workers should have at least led to rising pay for this disproportionately female and foreign-born workforce. With employers scrambling to fill open positions, workers could have bid up earnings by forcing employers to compete for their labor. At least that's what a standard economics textbook would lead one to believe. In 2005, before the recent boom in home care employment, median hourly pay for home care workers was an inflation-adjusted $10.21. A decade later, when a swelling workforce still wasn't enough to meet demand, median hourly pay was $10.11.[110] So much for that textbook.

A full-time worker earning $10.11 an hour would gross $21,000 a year. Not enough to lift a family of four with one breadwinner out of poverty, but higher than the actual annual earnings of home care workers who are not self-employed. In 2015, median annual earnings for these workers was just over $15,000.[111] What accounts for the discrepancy between median hourly and annual pay? Fewer than half of home care aides employed by an agency work full-time. The low hourly pay and lack of full-time schedules leads to exceptionally high turnover rates in an occupation where getting to know patients and mastering their needs takes time and practice.

These turnover rates exact a toll on patients. Roy Potter suffered from post-polio syndrome, and required a home care aide to help him in and out of bed when his wife no longer had the strength to handle these tasks herself. Over a span of two-and-a-half years, a dozen different aides showed up to help Mr. Potter with his daily routine. His exasperated wife pointed to the inefficiency of it all: "A new person would come, and I'd have to walk them through everything all over again."[112] Ai-jen Poo is executive director of the National Domestic Workers Alliance (NDWA), an organization that advocates for housecleaners, home healthcare and other domestic workers. She knows what happens when it's too hard to find full-time work at a decent hourly rate: "We end up losing some of our best caregivers to fast food and retail."[113] While high turnover takes a toll on patients, low pay in the industry exacts a payment on taxpayers. Patricia Walker was a certified nursing assistant in Florida employed by a home care company. Despite a rapidly improving economy—the state's unemployment rate fell from 10 percent to just under 5 percent between 2011 and 2016—she never received a raise during her time with the agency. She turned to government assistance to make ends meet, relying on nearly $200 worth of food stamps each month.[114] According to one estimate, nearly half of households with an employed home care worker rely on government assistance.[115] A quarter live in poverty.[116]

Why do we care so little for those we trust to care for our loved ones? The demographics of the home care workforce provide a partial explanation. Nearly 90 percent of home care aides and certified nursing assistants are women. Over a fifth were born outside of the United States. And half the workforce is African American or Hispanic.[117] Rejecting claims for higher pay on the basis of ascribed characteristics such as gender, race, or national background is both illegal and commonplace, lowering workers' power in the organizational claims-making process.[118]

Another contributing factor is the source of funds many families rely on to afford a home healthcare aide: Medicaid. Medicaid covers the cost for roughly half of the $300 billion we spend annually on long-term care needs, such as home health aides. Raising aides' pay means increasing the reimbursement rates that Medicaid offers home care agencies, a move many states have resisted. But paying poverty-level wages to those who care for us when we are most debilitated is as shortsighted as it is cruel. We know this because of research showing what happens when we treat this "bad job" better. Between 1996 and 2002 wages for home care workers doubled in the San Francisco area. Unionization and a living wage ordinance pushed up pay while adding benefits such as health and dental insurance to home care workers' contracts. Annual turnover rates fell by more than 50 percent.[119] Lower turnover and an expansion of the services home care workers are allowed to provide could offset the higher reimbursement rates needed to pay workers adequately. Estimates suggest that well-trained home healthcare aides could help save hundreds of billions of dollars through better management of chronic health conditions, which could lower hospital visits and readmissions.[120]

San Francisco shows how power dynamics can interact with norms of equity regarding the pay of home healthcare providers. A coalition of unions, worker-backed advocacy groups, and sympathetic lawmakers felt existing pay rates for home healthcare aides and other low-wage workers were fundamentally unfair. They pushed through a living wage initiative that altered the claims-making environment for low-wage workers. Standard pay for home healthcare aides increased from the existing minimum wage of $4.25 per hour to $10 per hour.[121] Instead of conceiving of the work as "in the same category as teenage babysitters," as President Obama lamented in 2011, lawmakers and worker organizations redefined it as an occupation worthy of dignity through a living wage. Workers stayed on the job longer as a result.

TODAY, SAN FRANCISCO remains more of an exception to the low-pay rule. As the former president remarked, "many homecare workers are forced to rely on things like food stamps just to make ends meet. That's just wrong. In this country, it's inexcusable. They deserve to be paid fairly for a service that many older Americans couldn't live without."[122] Home healthcare is work many of us rely on to get by, not only as patients but as family members and friends who cannot afford to miss work to take constant care of our loved ones. But we also rely on the work of those who serve us food, sell us our clothes and other household items, slaughter the animals we consume, and haul away the garbage we produce. Right now, in these industries, power is tilted decisively toward employers who take advantage of a claims-making environment in which workers possess few resources. These are the "bad jobs" of today, but they can be better. We know, because in certain places, and at certain periods in our history, they have been.

PART IV

TOWARD A FAIRER WAGE

8   RETHINKING INEQUALITY

ANY EXPLANATION OF RISING inequality in the United States must contend with three fundamental realities of pay in our age: fairly flat earnings for average American workers, runaway gains for the economic elite, and growing pay differences among workers with similar skills and occupations.

From 1979 to 2018, median hourly wages for American workers have grown, in real terms, by an anemic 14 percent, driven by increases among women.[1] For men working full-time, real median annual earnings actually declined by 2 percent.[2] For the bottom 90 percent of workers, real annual earnings grew by just over 20 percent—a decent-sized increase, led largely by sizable gains among the upper-middle class. Yet this improvement was positively minuscule compared to what was happening at the top. In 1979, the average earner in the top one percent took home just under $280,000 a year in today's dollars. Today, that average is nearly $719,000.[3] And even those out-sized gains look puny from the vantage point of the peak of our current economy. The tenth-of-a-percenters among us—those who earn more than 999 of every 1,000 Americans—average $2.75 million in annual earnings, a 343 percent increase relative to the late 1970s.[4]

Skyrocketing pay at the top and moderate pay gains in the broad middle of the distribution mean that the compensation gap between a typical member of the working class and a member of the economic elite has become a yawning chasm. In 1980, the average income of someone in the top one percent of the income distribution was twenty-seven times higher than the average income of someone in the bottom half. Over the next three decades, that ratio nearly tripled.[5] Now the average one-percenter makes eighty-one times the average income of the bottom fifty percent.[6]

Meanwhile, recent research zeroes in on the third distinctive feature of recent inequality trends: the importance of one's workplace. Organizations, it turns out, are a primary driver of rising pay disparities. This research reveals that workers with similar human capital, and workers in the same occupation, are paid quite unequally by different employers. A team of labor economists analyzed earnings inequality in the United States between 1977 and 2009. They found that "most of the increased variance in earnings among individuals is associated with the increased variance of average earnings among the establishments where they work."[7] They therefore advised other researchers "to pay attention to the places where people work as well as to their skills in studies of inequality."[8]

So pay disparities have grown in large part because our workplaces are paying similar workers differently. From this book's account of pay-setting, this shouldn't come as a surprise. Our paychecks bear the name of our employer, after all, and it is actors within organizations who decide on the number on our paycheck. And it is in these workplaces that we marshal our resources to make claims on a slice of the available pie. But this is a surprising finding both for adherents of a human capital model of pay determination and for those who see our pay as largely a function of our occupations. Indeed, these two core understandings of pay determination, one emphasizing the role of individual performance, the other seeing the basis of pay in characteristics of occupations, provide inadequate explanations for what President Obama famously called "the defining challenge of our time."[9]

SKILL-BIASED TECHNOLOGICAL CHANGE

Jan Tinbergen, born in 1903 in the Hague, Netherlands, completed a doctorate in theoretical physics in 1929. He soon gravitated toward economics after early politicization as a member of the youth wing of the local Socialist party. "In retrospect," he later wrote, "I wonder whether I would have been clever enough to contribute to modern physics; anyway, my interest went to helping to change society."[10] Thus began a decades-long career as one of the founders of econometrics, reaching a capstone in 1969 when he was awarded the first Nobel Memorial Prize in Economics along with Ragnar Frisch. Since his death in 1994, journalists and academics have credited the Dutch physicist for devising the "Tinbergen norm," which maintains that a firm's productivity suffers when the top executive's pay is over five times that of its lowest-paid worker.[11] Thanks to the long-delayed implementation of an SEC ruling, we can now assess how well companies adhere to a version of this standard. As part of the 2010 Dodd-Frank Act, the government ruled that a publicly traded firm has to disclose the ratio between its CEO's salary and the median pay of company workers. Eight years after passage of the Act, companies finally began to comply. The ensuing disclosures revealed a collection of companies nowhere close to reaching a five-to-one ratio. Take the department store chain Kohl's, which stood out for its eye-popping revelation: the firm's CEO earned over twelve hundred times more than the company's median employee. At Starbucks, chief executive Kevin Johnson's compensation is so high that he need work only two hours to make what his typical barista brings home in a year.[12]

By any accounting, Tinbergen's norm has been shattered. Even those firms with the lowest pay ratios exceed it—and again, bear in mind that the norm credited to Tinbergen specifies a five-to-one ratio between the chief executive and *lowest* paid worker, not the median one. In 2017, the head of J. B. Hunt Transport Services earned just fifteen times that of the median J. B. Hunt employee, one of the lowest ratios among major US firms, and still a ratio three times larger than a Tinbergen-style norm would suggest.[13]

Surprisingly, Tinbergen may never have put this standard on paper. As Broer Akkerboom observes, "Everybody uses the Tinbergen standard," and yet "The Tinbergen standard does not exist" in Tinbergen's actual writings.[14] Tinbergen's published work does recognize the self-dealing that goes into pay-setting among the corporate elite, where boards of friendly fellow executives determine compensation packages. As he wrote, "manager compensations are the result of a 'market' where the same sociological group is acting on both sides. . . . This creates a 'monopoloid' situation, containing an element of power."[15] But even in this article he fails to mention a pay ratio to which corporations should adhere to maintain high productivity.

Tinbergen did write extensively about income inequality, yet in this area of his research we find a perspective consistent with a standard skill-biased technological change explanation. He does not emphasize power dynamics or argue for drastic pay compression within firms. In fact, his research on inequality inspired the title of Claudia Goldin and Lawrence Katz's seminal book, *The Race Between Education and Technology*.[16] Lawrence Summers blurbed that book as "the definitive treatment of changes in income distribution and their causes" and, both inside and outside the academy, it remains the most influential theory of rising inequality.

The skill-biased technological change theory is also an explanation of rising inequality that is perfectly congruent with the theory of pay determination that emphasizes individual human capital. The idea here is that the individual worker has a stock of human capital that can be augmented by education or job-related training. Workers, by mastering new skills, especially those required to work with new technologies, can earn higher wages. That was the experience for large segments of the labor force in past periods of technological change, as the educational system expanded to endow more and more Americans with the requisite skills to qualify for higher-paying jobs in a fast-changing economy. As a result, inequality didn't rise, as increasing human capital raised the productivity, and therefore the earnings, of millions of working- and middle-class Americans.

According to this perspective, in recent decades, as workplace after workplace has been transformed by information and communications technology, the educational system hasn't kept up. Rising demand for advanced skills met with a decreasing supply of high-skilled workers. Computerization eliminated many middle-skilled jobs of the past, while creating a whole new set of high-skilled jobs that paid well to those fortunate few with the human capital necessary to perform them. The plight of the bank teller exemplifies the disruption computerization caused to millions of workers. Across the decade of the 1970s, the number of bank tellers grew by 85 percent, even as the newly invented automated teller machine began its spread.[17] By 2018, it had dropped by more than a third, and the Bureau of Labor Statistics in 2018 was projecting a 12 percent further reduction over the next decade. A new generation of enhanced ATMs is now combining with online banking to eliminate any need to transact business in person.[18] As this and other occupations hollow out following the introduction of new technologies, new roles—for software analysts, coders, and many other recent arrivals on the economic scene—become the good-paying jobs, and all require advanced skills.

From this view, rising inequality stems from technological changes outpacing educational attainments. Skill-biased technological change privileges those with scarce, hard-to-acquire skills. Workers with the means to master new technologies bid up the price of their labor. Others who had been in the middle core of the income distribution find themselves out of work due to automation. Some make the transition with retraining, pluck, luck, and ingenuity. Others don't, and join the expanding base of those left behind. These workers, lacking the skills to qualify for more high-paying positions, crowd into segments of the job market not currently at risk of being automated. Think here of dishwashers, home healthcare aides, and janitors—jobs that do not require a college education, and jobs that so far have been relatively untouched by advances in technology. For adherents of the skill-biased technological change explanation of inequality, these bottom-end jobs pay poorly because of the low human capital needed to perform them, and because of the overabundant labor supply that results as technological disruptions push many formerly mid-skill workers downward.

For decades, versions of this explanation dominated academic and political discourse about rising inequality. The skill-biased technological change theory is that double rarity among academic ideas: not only did it penetrate and influence elite discourse and decision-making, it united the mainstream political left and right. In 2006, as President George W. Bush announced the release of a new "state of the economy" report, he invoked the theory to explain why the income gap had grown: "The reason is clear: We have an economy that increasingly rewards education, and skills because of that education." He went on to offer a solution that supporters on both sides of the aisle could rally around: "The key to rising in this economy is skills— and the government's job is to make sure we have an education system that delivers them."[19]

Ben Bernanke was that unusual political appointee in our polarized age who spanned Republican and Democratic administrations, serving as chair of the Federal Reserve under Presidents Bush and Obama. He, too, subscribed to the belief that the chief cause of rising inequality was a growing skills gap between those who had acquired the requisite education to thrive in our high-tech economy and those who hadn't. Speaking to the Greater Omaha Chamber of Commerce in 2007, Bernanke argued that "the larger return to education and skill is likely the single greatest source of the long-term increase in inequality," and advocated for "policies that boost our national investment in education and training" to reduce rising pay differentials.[20] In his 2015 State of the Union address, Obama likewise warned of the consequences of an education system no longer keeping up with the demands of a fast-changing economy: "America thrived in the twentieth century because we made high school free, sent a generation of GIs to college, trained the best workforce in the world. We were ahead of the curve. But other countries caught on. And in a twenty-first-century economy that rewards knowledge like never before, we need to up our game. We need to do more."[21] Since 2015, inequality has only gone up. Apparently, there's still more to do.

Sizable cracks in the explanation have recently opened. Adherents frequently cite growth in the college wage premium—the earnings advantage that college-educated workers enjoy—as evidence for the theory. Yet that growth has slowed considerably in recent years as inequality continues to rise.[22] Moreover, a college degree isn't a guarantor of a high wage, automatically opening the doors to those who earn one. It's time we began seeing educational credentials not as an automatic driver of pay, but as a resource that can be used to stake a claim for higher earnings. Powerful actors within our organizations must validate that resource for it to be effective. Sometimes, making a greater investment in education is not very helpful at all to an individual. It wasn't all that long ago that economists and others worried about workers with *too much* education. That may sound ludicrous from our current vantage point, given the saturation of messages about the importance of a college degree. But we need only look back to the 1970s to find Richard Freeman publishing his influential book *The Overeducated American*.[23] It documented a falling income return on a college education that was puzzling people at the time. As Freeman showed, the post–World War II expansion of colleges had yielded a rising supply of college graduates, resulting in a glut of degreed Americans entering a job market with too few jobs that required post-secondary education. During this particular period, then, a college degree was not worth as much as a claims-making resource.

Today, study after study demonstrates just how much a college degree pays off in the form of an average wage premium, and many believe this proves the explanatory power of the skill-biased technological change model. A typical college graduate earns 80 percent more per year than a worker who ended her education following high school.[24] A college credential has emerged as a must-have resource in many claims-making environments. Yet as Freeman highlighted, its value is hardly constant. In 1950, for example, the economic return on a college degree was at its twentieth-century nadir, representing less than half of its average worth today.[25]

Not only does the value of a college degree vary over time, it also varies across types of workers and types of workplaces. For example, over 20 percent of those in the top quintile of earners never finished college. (Steve Jobs and Bill Gates are famously among those who dropped out before finishing undergraduate programs). Meanwhile, over 15 percent in the bottom quintile do have degrees.[26] Today there are millions of college-educated Americans in jobs that don't require a bachelor's, leading one contemporary journalist, echoing Freeman, to declare that "America has an overeducation problem."[27] That statement may be hyperbolic, but it speaks to a real issue. There is evidence, for example, that employers are increasingly requiring a bachelor's degree not because of the human capital supposedly gained from attaining the credential, but just because they can. More and more positions that didn't require a college education in the past, and that haven't changed appreciably in terms of task complexity, call for a bachelor's today. In office and administrative service positions, for example, currently about one in five workers has a bachelor's degree. Yet nearly half of all job postings in this category say the degree is required.[28] Employers faced with abundant applicants increasingly use the credential simply as a screening-out process, not as a precise indicator of someone's human capital.

What all this variation makes clear is that the relationship between educational credentials and pay isn't predetermined. Like all resources brought to bear in the claims-making process, it is but a potential source of higher pay. Its influence depends on how powerful actors within organizations weigh it against other resources used in pay-setting. In recent years, higher education degrees have become quite influential. Part of that rising influence may be traced to the advanced skills and training a degree confers, and the increased productivity that results when these highly trained workers apply their skills to high-tech jobs. But part of it reflects its role as a simple screening device for employers who have the power to pick and choose from a pool of qualified applicants. After all, research demonstrates that many college careers don't actually coincide with learning much of anything.[29] In many cases, some of the college wage premium should be attributed to credentialism, pure and simple.

Another part of the apparent influence of education on pay determination has nothing to do with the educational system itself or the credentials it bestows. The rise of the college wage premium coincided with the steep decline of what historically has been the most influential resource that workers lacking a college education bring to the pay determination process: union membership. Unions provided these workers with a means of negotiating higher pay; numerous studies confirm that unions' ability to redirect organizational resources toward their members was and remains substantial.[30] So substantial is this power, in fact, that the mere presence of unions within labor markets shifted the claims-making environment toward workers even in firms without collective bargaining. In times and places where unions were strong, some employers granted higher pay and generous benefits packages to ward off a unionization drive; others simply mimicked what peer firms were doing, or raised pay to compete for good employees, thereby spreading union wage rates across wide swaths of the workforce.[31] The removal of this key pay-setting resource from workplaces across the country shifted the claims-making terrain within organizations and, in the absence of union bargaining, the college degree became an increasingly important resource for workers seeking higher pay.

Absent union power, those at the bottom of the economic ladder who lack educational credentials to bid their wages up now have few resources to negotiate an increase in their paycheck. At the very least, they do have the fallback of a government-mandated pay floor, in the form of a minimum wage. One problem is that the federal minimum wage, stuck at $7.25 per hour, has seen its real value fall precipitously from its peak in the late 1960s. And while the majority of states have set minimum wages higher than this, twenty states have not. In 1968, a full-time worker earning the federal minimum wage took home the equivalent of $20,600 a year. Today, that same worker earns just over $15,000—not enough to lift a two- or three-person household above the poverty line.[32] Our failure to increase the minimum wage disproportionately affects workers without a college education. As a result, even if there were no change in the importance of a college degree in pay determination, the declining value of the federal minimum wage means that the college wage premium necessarily widens.

More recently, the skill-biased technological change theory of rising pay gaps has attracted scrutiny within and beyond academia for reasons other than the role of the college wage premium. In that 2007 address extolling its explanatory power, even Bernanke granted that skill-biased technological change isn't the sole explanation; he also highlighted union decline and the falling real value of the minimum wage as other contributors to rising inequality.[33] Other research questions whether the jobs polarization implied by the theory, in which technological changes destroyed many mid-skill and middle-paying jobs while creating more at the top and the bottom, occurred at the precise time that inequality was rising.[34] The theory can't account for dramatic pay changes in jobs that haven't undergone significant technological change and that do not require advanced degrees. Construction workers earn thousands of dollars less per year today than they did decades ago. Yet much of the work hasn't been automated, doesn't require a college education, and isn't overrun with qualified job applicants that could explain lower pay than in past periods. If anything, there is currently a labor shortage in the industry.[35]

Most importantly, the theory does a poor job accounting for the explosion of incomes at the very top of the earnings ladder. According to a growing chorus of scholars, our corporate, financial, and professional elites have been able to exploit a growing set of rent-generating opportunities. As Angus Deaton argues, "rent-seeking has turned almost entirely in favor of the elite."[36] Even supporters of skill-biased technological change concede the theory's limitations when it comes to explaining compensation trends among the upper class.[37] For example, if skill-biased technological change explained rising CEO pay, then you'd have to presume the contemporary CEO class has acquired a set of specialized skills that, in combination with technological advances, produced a stunning increase in their individual productivity. Such an account ignores, among other contributing factors, the substantial evidence linking rising CEO pay to the growing power of shareholders, as covered in Chapter 5. It also ignores how CEO pay has far outpaced stock market value, the key measure of CEO performance under shareholder capitalism.[38]

OCCUPATIONAL-BASED INEQUALITY?

What can a more occupational-based understanding of pay determination tell us about inequality trends in the contemporary United States? One advantage of focusing on rent-seeking behavior by occupational incumbents is that it gets us closer to the grubby real world of pay determination. It's less abstract and sterile than the analysis of stocks of human capital and their relationships to new technologies that is commonly found in the skill-biased technological change literature. There is no ignoring the empirical reality of rising rents resulting from, for example, the explosion of licensing requirements in many occupations over the past few decades.[39] And given that the US labor movement largely organized workers along occupational lines, the unions' decline can be seen as a form of rent destruction among the working and middle class, contributing to wage stagnation.[40]

But the licensing story has its limits. Licensing requirements for established professions like law, accounting, and medicine extend far back, well before inequality began to rise. More recent occupations that have erected licensing barriers include, in some states, barbers and massage therapists.[41] These aren't exactly segments of the labor market one would pinpoint as the epicenter of our new Gilded Age.

So while we might find it odd that in certain jurisdictions barbers and "shampoo assistants" must be licensed, that fact isn't very informative about broader trends in who is earning what and why. After all, according to Bureau of Labor Statistics data, median weekly earnings in the occupational category of "hairdressers, hairstylists, and cosmetologists" were just $545 in 2018, essentially the same, when adjusted for inflation, as two decades prior.[42]

And an occupational-based account of rising inequality has to confront the fundamental fact of large and growing pay dispersion *within* occupations. For workers with a bachelor's degree or higher, for example, most inequality is between workers in the same occupation; within-occupational inequality has grown substantially since 1980.[43] Inequality within the managerial and professional occupations is especially high in the United States.[44] Other research suggests that increasing pay rate dispersion within occupations is not just a US phenomenon, but is occurring in other advanced economies, as well.[45]

This is not to suggest that occupations have nothing to do with rising inequality. In the modern occupational landscape, some stand out for their ability to define and police boundaries, and for their comparatively low levels of inequality among members. Inequality among teachers and engineers, for example, has resisted dominant trends and remained relatively stable since the early 1980s, at least among men.[46] Moreover, research shows that inequality has grown not only within occupations, but between them.[47] What an occupational perspective blinds us to, however, are changes within the primary site of pay-setting in our economy: organizations.

ORGANIZATIONAL CHANGE AND RISING INEQUALITY

The fundamental story of rising inequality over the past generation is a massive power shift within US workplaces away from employees and toward employers and shareholders. This process has played out unevenly across the organizational landscape, accounting for some of the variation in pay among similar workers we see in the United States today.

The unevenness can be seen, for example, in the spread of fissuring. Fissuring doesn't affect all firms in an industry simultaneously. At any given time, some firms embrace fissuring while others continue to resist. Custodial work was one of the first occupations that firms fissured out, with company after company outsourcing it to contractors and subcontractors during the 1980s and 1990s. Yet by 2000 still less than half of all custodians worked for a contractor—the majority remained employed by the company whose premises they cleaned.[48] What this means is that, at any given moment, some firms have fissured out various functions; others retain them in-house. You may be working for a university as a custodian and receive your paychecks from that university while your twin sister cleans buildings for a rival university and gets paid by a janitorial staffing agency. You benefit from working for a large organization employing people in a range of occupations, from the college president on down: vertical equity concerns ensure that your pay isn't dramatically lower than workers on rungs near you. Your sister works for a lean staffing agency with low profit margins that employs only other low-paid contract custodians. Horizontal or vertical equity issues aren't salient when everyone is paid poorly. Research finds that the wages of building cleaners and other frequently fissured occupations like security guards are significantly lower for contract workers than for workers employed directly by the companies that need their work.[49] As a result, as the fissuring process plays out across the organizational landscape, wages grow apart between otherwise similar workers in those occupations susceptible to fissuring.

There is also growing evidence of changing corporate cultures, especially within our large firms. Even absent fissuring, research suggests that workers at the bottom end of the organizational pyramid aren't benefiting as much from internal equity considerations as they did in the past.[50] Why would this be? Scholars cite a shift in norms in which powerful organizational actors have redefined the firm as "something more akin to a bundle of contracts" instead of as a "social institution."[51] A social institution implies a shared endeavor with shared obligations, one in which outsized pay disparities violate a norm of equity. A bundle of contracts implies just that: a set of autonomous workers each negotiating pay in isolation from one another. As there is substantial heterogeneity in corporate cultures, there is likely substantial heterogeneity in how quickly firms adapt to these changing norms. As a result, a worker at one enterprise may still benefit from a more social understanding of the company, while an otherwise similar one may be paid less at a firm that has embraced an ethos in which every worker is out for herself and the core goal is to maximize profits for management and shareholders.

These normative shifts don't occur randomly. The change in corporate culture over the past few decades is the result of the broad embrace of shareholder capitalism documented in Chapter 5. From the academy to the policy world to powerful corporations, influential actors urged firms to adopt an understanding of the firm that prioritized the claims of shareholders above other stakeholders. Some firms readily embraced the call, while others continue to resist— although for the latter it's an increasingly lonely fight. And as we've learned, equity concerns don't simply disappear when shareholders demand a greater share of organizational revenue. Fissuring became an effective strategy for many firms to satisfy shareholder demand and deal with the morale issues that accompany sizable pay disparities between coworkers.

Fissuring and the related embrace of a shareholder-value conception of the firm help us understand stagnant pay for many non-elite workers, especially those lacking college degrees. Meanwhile, seeing the staggered spread of these processes across the corporate landscape helps us understand why not all of these workers suffered in the same way simultaneously. But what about rising inequality among highly paid workers? Here, too, we see substantial differences between organizations, with widening pay differentials among workers in similar elite occupations.

Organizational differences seem to have exacerbated earnings inequality among highly educated workers through the adoption of pay-for-performance practices. As noted in Chapter 4, individual performance pay remains relatively uncommon. But the broad category of performance pay, which includes profit-sharing, and of which pay for individual performance is a subset, did increase during the 1980s and 1990s.[52] This is especially true for salaried positions. Unsurprisingly, inequality among workers is higher in performance pay jobs, and the growth in inequality in these jobs increased faster than in positions that did not allocate pay this way.[53] The effect of performance pay on inequality was especially large among high-earners in managerial and professional positions.[54] Among those in the 90th–99th percentile of the earnings distribution, the spread of performance pay practices accounts for nearly all the rise in inequality.[55]

There is also an increasing tendency of high-skill workers to sort themselves into high-paying firms.[56] This growing segregation seems especially true in large companies. Combined with the fissuring out of less skilled tasks, certain large firms today (think here of some of the tech giants) are highly segregated in terms of the educational background and skill levels of a typical employee. To the extent these firms already paid well, and thus were able to attract top talent, workers at the firms benefit. And to the extent the concentration of skilled workers boosts the firm's productivity and the employer shares some of the resulting revenue increase with her employees, these workers benefit further. Simultaneously, the pay of other highly educated workers who may lack the specific skill set, requisite connections, or knowledge of an opening at these large high-paying companies suffer, widening inequality at the top of the distribution. Some of this sorting is deliberate, some of it occurs by happenstance. Recent research reveals what most workers already know: certain firms pay well and others don't. "There are 'good firms' that pay higher wages, holding constant worker ability," note the authors of a summary of research into firm effects on worker pay. And "obtaining employment in those firms depends to a significant degree on luck."[57]

POWER IN THE NEW GILDED AGE

Among the tech titans of our age, fissuring is ubiquitous. The majority of workers at Google do not work for Google.[58] Today, Google employs just over 100,000 workers directly and over 120,000 through temporary staffing arrangements and contracting firms. Former CEO Eric Schmidt once explained how this kind of arrangement helps Silicon Valley's richest firms avoid calls to reduce the pay gap between their highest- and lowest-paid people: "Many tech companies solved this problem by having the lowest-paid workers not actually be employees. They're contracted out. . . . We can treat them differently, because we don't really hire them." Schmidt found the system "sort of offensive," but pointed to how mimicry had institutionalized the practice: "it is the way it's done."[59]

The tasks of temps and contractors go well beyond cleaning offices and maintaining security. Many work side by side with permanent employees on such high-skill projects as developing the firm's artificial intelligence assistant.[60] Google is not alone among its Silicon Valley peers. Estimates suggest that contingent employees comprise nearly half the workforce at technology companies today. According to Pradeep Chauhan, who runs a site that helps workers find contracting positions in technology firms, fissuring is "creating a caste system inside companies," where the contingent workers earn significantly less and enjoy fewer workplace protections than the companies' core workers.[61] This practice is a key contributor to growing pay disparities between workers with similar skill sets in the same occupation.

Contrast the present reality at a firm like Google with the practices of a technology giant of yesteryear, Eastman Kodak. Gail Evans worked at the Rochester, New York, firm back in the 1980s, starting off as a custodian.[62] Unlike in many workplaces today, her paycheck came from the company in whose building she worked, and being employed by it directly helped her in multiple ways. As an Eastman Kodak employee, she was entitled to company benefits, including a month of paid vacation and reimbursement for any tuition she paid to take college-level courses. That part-time education paid off handsomely thanks in part to Eastman Kodak's internal labor market. Having earned her college degree while working as a custodian, she was promoted to a position in information technology. From that position she advanced up the corporate ladder—and in 1987 was named chief technology officer for the entire company.

Her equivalent today at companies like Google or Apple encounters a vastly different labor market. As a custodian, most likely her employer is not the powerful and profitable tech firm whose offices she cleans but a staffing agency. Paid vacation and defrayed college costs? Opportunities for advancement? Extremely unlikely, given the disadvantageous bargaining position she's in. Staffing agencies compete on labor costs, so her employer has a strong incentive to keep her compensation low. And she won't benefit from equity considerations since her firm employs only low-wage service workers.

Fissuring has several roots, but a clear one is the rising power of shareholder capitalism over corporate decision-making. When the only stakeholder deemed worthy of attention—and one with the power to punish—demands your firm focus only on "core competencies" and keep your labor costs low, you're likely to comply. As a result, firms across the United States have "reorganized production processes to focus on maximizing shareholder value,"[63] according to Eileen Appelbaum, in part by consolidating lead firms and decentralizing much of the production process out to a range of subcontractors and service providers. Drawing in firm boundaries to include a small workforce focused on core competencies and contracting other employees helps companies "circumvent internal equity constraints," freeing them to direct revenue upward toward shareholders and senior management.[64]

The short-termism endemic to shareholder capitalism works against the adoption of internal labor markets, whose benefits tend to emerge over the long run.[65] As a result, Steve Jobs may well have wanted to keep his custodians in-house and offer generous pay, benefits, and opportunities for advancement to all his workers (although available evidence suggests otherwise).[66] But when powerful investors demand a growing share, most contemporary CEOs comply. And when powerful firms fissure out large portions of their workforces, upstarts and competitors follow suit, mimicking the organizational decisions of industry leaders. Over time, inertia sets in, and the workforce bifurcates between lucky employees enjoying high pay and generous perks, and unlucky contingent workers who earn less and have little opportunity for advancement. Between 2005 and 2015, "alternative work" jobs accounted for nearly *all* of the net employment growth in the United States.[67] These are the contract work, temporary help, freelance, and other types of jobs that offer little stability and often low pay. Between the mid-1990s and today, the total employment share of such jobs grew by approximately 50 percent.[68]

Of late, researchers have linked a growth in corporate concentration to widening pay disparities.[69] A classic example is the company town of the late-nineteenth and early twentieth centuries where a single employer provided the paychecks for the town's residents—and often the lodging through company-owned barracks, and goods and services through the company-run store. When there is only one option for work, you're at a distinct bargaining disadvantage. There is no bidding up your share of organizational revenue through offers from competing firms, because there are no competing firms. Company towns in the textile, mining, railroad, and even, in the case of Hershey, Pennsylvania, confectionary industries ranged from "genially paternalistic" to "outright exploitative."[70] But in all of them employers had enormous power to determine how the firm's revenue would be distributed. Today, it's much rarer to find a literal single firm town—although it's worth noting that Facebook is currently constructing Willow Village, a planned community for Facebook employees. (No word yet on whether the company will pay their Village workers in scrip).[71] Yet research has documented a reduction in workers' job options in many labor markets, giving employers the upper hand in setting pay for their workers, often to their workers' detriment.[72] Using data from 2010 to 2013, José Azar, Ioana Marinescu, and Marshall Steinbaum find that the typical labor market is highly concentrated, and the most highly concentrated labor markets offer lower wages than markets with more options for workers.[73] Add to growing market concentration all the ways in which many employers collude with one another, create information asymmetries, and raise the costs for quitting through the proliferation of noncompetes, and you have the present situation: the close approximation of a company town, given its lack of meaningful options for workers looking for a better deal. What unites these and other organizational changes is that they are increasingly popular and effective means to shift power away from workers toward employers and shareholders. As other research has found, while the typical labor market is highly concentrated, most of us don't work in highly concentrated labor markets.[74] Yet pay stagnation prevails in both types—evidence of how power has shifted in contemporary workplaces.

RISING ECONOMIC INEQUALITY has a number of well-documented, corrosive effects, including the ways in which it distorts our democracy. Americans recognize the growing economic divides. According to a 2012 Pew poll, over 60 percent of respondents report that the "gap in living standards between middle class and poor people has become wider," up from just 39 percent in 1986.[75] Three-quarters of Americans agree with this statement: "It's really true that the rich just get richer while the poor get poorer."[76] Belief in the cherished American ideal that hard work pays off is far from universal. In 1987, approximately a third of Americans with a high school degree or less agreed that "hard work offers little guarantee of success"; by 2012, that fraction had grown to 45 percent. A quarter of college graduates expressed the same pessimistic viewpoint in 2012, a 32 percent increase since 1987.[77] Inequality has left many workers without the means to live a comfortable, dignified life, and left many others questioning the bedrock principles upon which this nation stands.

This book argues that wages and salaries are determined within organizations, and that the process is guided by the four forces of power, equity, mimicry, and inertia. Rising inequality reflects fundamental power shifts within our organizations that have disadvantaged ordinary workers and benefited the elite. If this book's account is correct, and workers' wages are a function of whether they happened to luck into "good" workplaces, then refusing to reverse that fortune is a moral outrage. The same is true if pay derives not only from skills and hard work but from broader power dynamics over which the worker has little control; if it comes down to whether an employer happens to feel bound by norms of equity in the organization, or has mimicked the organizational practices of a rival who feels no such compunction; or if it is owing to the stubborn fact that the worker was discriminated against in an earlier position, and inertia means that initial depressed wage forms the basis of the wage offer that follows. In none of these cases is it justified to refuse people who work hard the wages that would allow them to live comfortably—or, conversely, to reward with stratospheric salaries those lucky few who have access to all of the key resources that affect pay-setting. We must reject both the unfair punishments and the unfair rewards as equally outrageous. The next chapter presents a path forward.

9 TOWARD A FAIRER WAGE

A FAIR ECONOMY in which work actually pays and a privileged few don't run off with outlandish shares of organizations' revenues requires three major changes: raising the pay floor, expanding the middle, and lowering the ceiling. For far too long, a narrow range of policy options has dominated discussions of potential remedies to rising inequality. These options rested on an underlying model of pay-setting that viewed wages and salaries as approximating individuals' marginal contribution to their firms. Fearing disruption of the "free market," policymakers have largely exempted employers and other key organizational actors—most notably, shareholders—from proposals to reduce inequality. Instead, the focus has been on posttax and transfer programs. Not only is the prevailing view of pay determination wrong, it needlessly constrains actions we can take to provide much of the labor force with a raise, reverse the tide of runaway compensation at the top, and thereby actually reduce inequality.

Finally, some scholars and lawmakers have begun to challenge this antiquated vision, advocating a range of measures to address inequalities in the labor market itself. These new ideas fall under various headings. One is "predistribution."[1] Another is "marketcraft."[2] What unites many of them is that they aim to shape income distributions prior to taxes and transfers. Other ideas use the tax system itself to affect the pretax distribution of income.[3] All see markets as inextricably linked with the state, not as a separate entity. All recognize that markets are ongoing productions involving rules and regulations created, managed, and actively organized by government actors. It's a matter of who benefits from a particular market arrangement, and for the last half-century, the benefits of these arrangements have flowed disproportionately upstream. Labor market reforms of the types detailed below are, as a result, long overdue, and vital steps if we are going to move toward a fairer income distribution, one that adequately rewards all those who work hard while not privileging the few with so much.

RAISE THE FLOOR!

At the federal level, recent attempts to roll back rising inequality have been anemic, at best. Efforts to increase the value of the federal minimum wage, last updated over a decade ago, have hit the brick wall known as the Senate. There such legislators as Lamar Alexander not only oppose an increase in the current minimum of \$7.25 per hour, they oppose the very idea of a minimum wage. The good news for proponents of a pay floor that actually meets the basic requirements to live a dignified life is that Alexander is retiring in 2020. The bad news? Powerful Senate colleagues of his, while not advocating for abolishing the minimum wage, are in no hurry to increase it.

In 2019, the House of Representatives passed the Raise the Wage Act, which would gradually increase the federal minimum wage to \$15 per hour. The law would also index the minimum wage to changes in the median wage, so that if median pay went up in the future, minimum pay would automatically go up as well.[4] The vote—231 in favor and 199 opposed—was relatively tight, with opponents trotting out well-worn critiques about how minimum wage increases hurt employment. From the House it headed to the Senate, where Senate Majority Leader Mitch McConnell announced that the proposed increase would "kill jobs and depress the economy. . . . We are not going to be taking that up in the Senate."[5] And that was that.

Progress at the federal level therefore remains stalled despite overwhelming support among Americans for a sizable increase in the minimum wage, including majority support for raising it all the way to $15 per hour.[6] There is evidence that support extends into corporate boardrooms, too. Leaked documents presenting results from a 2016 poll of a thousand business executives revealed that 80 percent supported an increase in their state's minimum wage.[7] As the director of the polling firm concluded, "If you're fighting against a minimum wage increase, you're fighting an uphill battle, because most Americans, even most Republicans, are okay with raising the minimum wage."[8]

Yet, it is an uphill battle that those in the minority keep winning, at least at the federal level. This despite what is now a well-established body of research dispelling myths about the minimum wage frequently cited by opponents. Voting against the Raise the Wage Act, Representative Virginia Foxx of North Carolina, ranking member on the House Education and Labor Committee, echoed McConnell in decrying the bill as "job-killing," and, somewhat oddly, "income-reducing."[9] This notion that the minimum wage depresses employment, since it artificially raises pay above its "market level," is as old as the human capital model of pay determination. But, as is the case with so much of that model, there isn't evidence to support it. A recent analysis of over fifty minimum wage increases of $.25 or more per hour finds no adverse effects on employment, hours worked per week, or weeks worked per year.[10] Another study focusing on 138 state-level minimum wage hikes since the late 1970s reaches a similar conclusion.[11] A recent feature in the *Washington Post* summarizes this research: "It's now evident that, since at least the late 1970s, minimum-wage hikes in the U.S. haven't reduced employment."[12]

While they haven't reduced employment, growing evidence finds that minimum wage hikes have salutary effects that go far beyond the pecuniary. One study finds that a 10 percent increase in the minimum wage is associated with a 3.6 percent decline in suicide rates among Americans with a high school degree or less—the population most likely to benefit from an increase.[13] Another finds that recidivism rates among ex-prisoners fall as the minimum wage rises, with a $.50 increase associated with a 2.8 percent decline in the likelihood of reimprisonment within a year after release.[14] These benefits speak to the stress relief that comes from working a job that pays decently. You're less likely to make rash decisions that destroy your own life or someone else's when you don't have to worry daily about feeding your family or paying your bills.

Donna Molinari, a casino cashier, was tired of hearing that the demand for a living wage is asking too much. According to her, "Making a living wage isn't luxurious, it's living!"[15] The benefits of raising the pay floor extend to our physical as well as mental health. Like Molinari Jeannine Nixon worked at a casino, as a customer relations representative at Resorts World Casino in New York. She was making about $12 per hour—40 percent more than the federal minimum wage. Yet she still described her life as "awful. . . . It was horrible, especially health-wise. . . . I had some surgery, and I was supposed to get some blood tests, but I couldn't get them because I didn't have money for co-payments. You know, it was a struggle."[16] Nixon would have benefitted from the state's subsequent minimum wage increase but it turned out something even better happened: her workplace unionized. The resulting contract lifted her hourly wage to $22.80 and provided decent healthcare insurance, allowing her to visit specialists, have a long-delayed surgery, and deal with an esophageal issue that was making it difficult to eat and drink.[17] Earning a living wage has instilled in her "pride knowing that I can pay my own bills."[18]

Presently, at the federal level, a fanatic minority wedded to a vision of the labor market as archaic as it is destructive to low-wage workers holds back progress for millions of Americans. The good news for some low-wage workers is that many states are circumventing the federal impasse (and, in rarer instances, workplaces like Nixon's are organizing). In recent years, a majority of states along with two dozen cities have raised their minimum wage above the federal rate of $7.25 per hour.[19] Seven states have already passed laws to bring their wage floor up to $15 per hour.[20]

Who will these increases help? Workers in prototypical "bad jobs" such as restaurant and food service occupations, along with retail salespeople, will benefit.[21] Cooks, waiters and waitresses, and other occupations at the bottom rung of our nation's economy will get a long overdue raise that will bring their pay closer to the minimum needed to live without the constant worry that comes with barely making ends meet. Vanessa Solivan, a home healthcare aide in New Jersey, enjoys her work, especially the job's prosocial nature. As she summarizes it, "I get to help people."[22] But the pay—between $10 and $14 an hour—isn't adequate. She and her three children shuttle between cheap motels and living in her car, joining the ranks of the "working homeless": employed Americans whose wages don't cover life's basic necessities.[23]

But the present reality is that many states continue to abide by the federal minimum wage. What this translates to is that, right now, if you're a McDonald's crew member in Buffalo, New York, you're guaranteed an hourly wage of at least $11.10. Stick it out for a couple more years, and your pay will increase to at least $15 per hour when the state's phased adjustment to its new minimum wage is complete. But if you decide to move to New York's southern neighbor, and pick up a fast-food job in Erie, Pennsylvania, you could face a 35 percent pay cut. The Keystone State's minimum is currently stuck at the federal level, and should it remain there, minimum wage earners will take home less than *half* of what New Yorkers will, once New York's $15 per hour minimum goes into effect.

Why don't cities and other municipalities in states that currently offer the federal minimum just go ahead and give their low-wage workforce a raise? Many can't, for the same reason that workers in St. Louis and Kansas City discovered back in 2017: preemption. These laws have proliferated in recent years as policymakers opposed to lifting wage floors seek to counter the growing momentum of the Fight for $15 movement. Currently half of all states ban cities and counties from raising wage floors above the state's minimum.[24] These include rather unsurprising conservative states such as Texas and Louisiana but also the more liberal-leaning states of Oregon, Rhode Island, and Pennsylvania.[25]

The current patchwork of minimum wage levels contributes to growing inequality between workers in low-rung occupations across jurisdictions with different wage floors. It's past time for states like Pennsylvania to follow its neighbor to the north and set a pay minimum that at least approximates the amount needed to live on without falling below the poverty line. At the very least, the state should free its local jurisdictions to take action to meet the needs of its lowest-paid workers. And it is way past time for the federal government to listen to what the American public—left, right, and center, including sizable portions of the business community—believe about the federal minimum wage: it's embarrassingly low, and due for a raise.

Unlike the logjam holding back progress on the minimum wage, lawmakers have expanded a different federal program that lifts the pay of low-wage workers. Inspired by Milton Friedman's ideas, the Ford Administration began the Earned Income Tax Credit, or EITC, in the mid-1970s. The program expanded greatly in subsequent years, and today benefits over twenty-five million workers and their family members.[26] Qualification varies by family size and employment status, but in general if you are in the labor force, have dependent children, and make between $40,000 and $56,000 annually, you may be eligible.[27] Workers without children have to earn substantially below those amounts to receive any EITC benefits.[28] A majority of states now supplement the federal benefit, including the conservative strongholds of Kansas and Nebraska.[29] The program operates by offering those eligible a credit to defray their tax obligations. Those whose EITC credit is larger than their obligations receive a check from the government for the additional amount.

It's a program that enjoyed widespread bipartisan support, and is estimated to have lifted nearly six million Americans—a majority of them children—above the poverty line.[30] Ronald Reagan expanded the program dramatically in 1986 as part of the Tax Reform Act.[31] Even Lamar Alexander is a fan. During a 2013 Senate hearing on the minimum wage, he suggested an increase in the EITC as "a more efficient way to help people in poverty."[32] Minimum wage opponents such as Alexander support the program because it doesn't interfere directly with the labor market and "artificially" distort the pay-setting process. Plus, it encourages work among the poor and near-poor since benefits are tied to employment. The 2017 Tax Cuts and Jobs Act, signed by President Trump on December 21, didn't contain an expansion to the program.[33] But in 2019, both Maine and California passed sizable extensions to the state components of the EITC.[34]

What's not to like? Well, while the program doesn't directly interfere with wage-setting, its indirect effects are significant. In particular, it operates as a subsidy to employers who pay poverty-level wages.[35] Employers offering low pay are able to attract workers who might not otherwise accept their offers save for the EITC credit. And those workers who don't qualify for the EITC—including undocumented immigrants and childless workers with incomes above the program's threshold—effectively have their wages suppressed. As Teresa Ghilarducci and Aida Farmand argue, the EITC is one reason why the United States leads peer nations in the percentage of jobs that offer poverty-level pay.[36]

It also rests on a misunderstanding of pay. There are, of course, certain industries where profit margins are low, labor costs are a major fraction of the total budget, and skill requirements for the workforce are minimal. For those jobs, asking for a $70,000 annual wage could be ruinous to the firm. But they are rarer than we usually presume. How do we know that? We can just look overseas or to certain periods in this country's past, as we did in Chapter 7. The presumption underlying the EITC is that government's role in ensuring a fair distribution of income comes after the "free market" does its work. People get what they deserve in the labor market, but those earnings may not be enough to live on, and so programs like the EITC are needed to supplement their market income. As we've learned, it's a faulty premise.

Of course, rolling back the program removes a vital posttax buffer to millions of poor and working-class Americans. That would not be a solution to raising the country's pay floor. But given its wage-dampening effects, EITC and its expansion should be seen as a complement, not a substitute, for a significantly raised minimum wage. As Jesse Rothstein and Ben Zipperer have noted, a high minimum wage prevents employers from taking advantage of the EITC by offering workers poverty-level pay.[37] The two programs work together best in tandem.

Not everyone eligible for a minimum wage increase would benefit should Congress take action, at least not automatically. There are two million domestic care workers in the United States today. This largely female and disproportionately foreign-born workforce is entitled to the prevailing minimum wage, but enforcement is spotty, especially since only one in twenty is paid on the books.[38] A 2012 survey of nearly 2,100 nannies, caregivers, and housecleaners in fourteen metropolitan regions found that nearly a quarter received less than the minimum wage and only 15 percent were offered overtime pay.[39] Enforcement of minimum standards guaranteed by state and federals law is crucial to freeing this workforce from the informal sector and improving their livelihoods and working conditions.

Some progress is being made at the state and local level, with New York, California, and the city of Seattle all enacting laws in recent years guaranteeing basic labor protections to domestics. For example, Seattle's Domestic Workers Bill of Rights, passed in July 2018, includes a new Office of Labor Standards to ensure employers abide by the law's protections. In the summer of 2019, Senator Kamala Harris and Representative Pramila Jayapal introduced a federal version of these state and city laws. The National Domestic Workers Bill of Rights simultaneously brings domestic workers under the purview of already-existing labor protections, while adding new ones such as requiring advance notice about scheduling. Crucially, given the enforcement challenges in an industry in which workers literally operate out of their employers' homes, the bill would establish a wage and standards board. The board brings together worker representatives and employers to make recommendations about minimum pay and benefits that would guide pay-setting and monitor compliance throughout the industry.[40]

This is a model strategy for other low-paying, precarious jobs, including those grouped under the "gig economy" umbrella. Ai-jen Poo's National Domestic Workers Alliance has been at the forefront of battles to raise awareness of the plight of this oft-overlooked group of care workers, and has been remarkably successful at winning concrete victories since Poo founded the organization in 2007.

Drawing the connections between the working conditions of domestics and gig economy employees, she writes: "No one understands the future of work better than domestic workers. As the gig economy has grown over the last 30 years, more and more professions look like theirs."[41] For ride-share drivers, food deliverers, and other Americans working for platforms, wage and standards boards can overcome many of the hurdles they face in traditional organizing campaigns.

It's worth noting that despite all the media attention, research finds that Uber-type jobs still account for an incredibly small share of total employment—a small share that actually hasn't increased appreciably in recent years.[42] Summing up all jobs in the platform, or gig, economy, Lawrence Mishel of the Economic Policy Institute calculates that they comprise a fraction of one percent of the nation's full-time equivalent jobs.[43] Most gig workers perform their gig jobs part-time, for part of the year. The vast majority of workers continue to hold traditional, non-gig jobs. As Mishel concludes, "the nature of work hasn't fundamentally changed."[44] Nonetheless, gig workers need greater power, and our nation's labor standards should be updated to protect them and be prepared should the much-ballyhooed explosion of gig work actually occur.

Wage and standards boards provide an excellent vehicle to empower workers in those occupations in which organizing campaigns are exceptionally difficult. Unionizing a workplace of one, where the workplace is the employer's home, isn't an option, as a bargaining unit by definition must involve at least two workers. Similarly, so long as many gig economy workers are classified as independent contractors, and do their work largely in isolation from others—such as driving for a ride-hailing service like Uber or Lyft—a traditional organizing campaign is a legal and logistical slog. But uniting, say, ride share workers under a wage board allows for elected worker representatives to bargain with gig economy employers to establish basic floors for pay and working conditions that would govern the entire rideshare industry. It's a model that has a long history in other countries such as France where industry representatives from unions, employers, and the state bargain over pay, benefits, and workplace standards. The resulting agreements establish standards across the industry, regardless of whether employees in particular workplaces are unionized or not. This model explains why France has a unionization rate lower than in the United States, yet nearly all French workers are covered by a collective bargaining agreement.[45]

Australia provides another promising model to follow. Similar to the United States, unionization rates have declined significantly in recent decades. Between 1976 and 2016, unionization in the Land Down Under fell from 51 percent to just 14 percent; a million unionized jobs vanished during the period.[46] But unlike in the United States, inequality didn't skyrocket as a result. Today, the 90 / 10 ratio in Australia—a measure capturing the spread of household incomes between those in the ninetieth percentile of the distribution and those in the tenth—is nearly 50 percent lower than in the United States.[47] Growth in the median wage in Australia has tracked growth in the mean, whereas the two have largely diverged in the United States as income gains flowed disproportionately to those at the top.[48] Partly the difference between the countries stems from greater collective bargaining coverage in Australia. Similar to France, collectively bargained contracts extend to a sizable fraction of the nonunion workforce. But nearly a quarter of Australian workers benefit from another institution: the "Modern Awards" system. Established by a national wage and standards board, these awards set pay standards for industries and occupations, helping to compress pay within and between types of jobs, and ensure that those at the bottom of the pay spectrum don't fall to far behind.[49]

Wage and standards boards aren't completely foreign to the United States. During World War II and the Korean War, tripartite organizations featuring business and labor leaders and government representatives monitored wage patterns in key industries, and instituted pay standards in an attempt to narrow discrepancies between firms.[50] More recently, the State of New York convened a wage board to study and recommend pay standards for fast-food workers, eventually coalescing around the implementation of a $15 per hour minimum rate.[51] Expanding the number of states that have such mechanisms, and the number of industries covered by them, is a crucial step to ensure that otherwise unrepresented workers have some say and power over the conditions and pay of their jobs.[52] Greatly expanding the scope and use of wage boards would also help to realign firms' incentives regarding a key dynamic of the modern firm: fissuring. If, due to a mandated high pay floor, there are few cost savings to be had through outsourcing low-rung occupations, companies may decide it's simply more efficient to keep those workers in-house.

EXPAND THE MIDDLE!

Raising pay floors actually helps increase the wages of workers paid above the minimum wage. Research indicates these "spillover" effects may extend up to workers earning 115 percent of the new minimum, and account for a sizable portion of the overall wage gains that result from minimum wage increases.[53] Much of this stems from equity effects: as we learned back in Chapter 1, workers find it unfair if a new hire suddenly earns as much as a long-time employee as a result of a change in the minimum wage. As a result, workers earning a bit above the old minimum benefit when a new floor is established.

But there are millions of working- and middle-class Americans who won't benefit directly from a minimum wage increase but also deserve a raise, and a wage or salary that comports with basic understandings of fairness. What remedies exist for them? As with efforts to help those at the bottom of the income distribution, any strategy to lift the wages and salaries of those in the middle and ensure their share is equitable must alter the pay-setting process where it occurs: in our workplaces. As we learned in the last chapter, one of the key insights emerging from the growing literature on the importance of workplaces in determining earnings is the enormous variability in pay for workers with similar skill sets. As John Abowd, Kevin McKinney, and Nellie Zheo conclude, "There are large gains from working at a top-paying firm for all skill types."[54] There are "good firms" out there that pay well.[55] The question is, how do we create more of them?

A greatly expanded pay floor is a start, not only through the positive spillover effects it has on workers earning just above the new minimum wage. Raising the floor significantly helps "take wages out of competition," in trade union parlance, thus indirectly helping workers throughout the firm. Forcing every firm to pay, at minimum, a much-increased minimum wage to every worker means that undercutting the competition through rock-bottom pay is no longer an option. Instead, firms' competitive advantages must come from other sources, such as product quality, efficiencies in product or service design, and other innovations. Once "wage chiseling" is out, and firms reorient to compete on these other dimensions, workers throughout the firm's pay distribution should benefit. After all, competing on innovation and quality requires a dedicated, experienced, and skilled set of workers.

Dedication and experience come with working for an extended period at the same organization, in part because you feel valued by management and adequately rewarded for your efforts. Internal labor markets can be a vehicle to foster such a workforce, when combined with modern management practices such as greater transparency around organizational pay plans and finances.[56] The implicit contract in firms that value loyalty and expect you to stick around for a while is that in return you'll receive training, some participation in managerial matters (or at least the information required to offer an informed perspective), and decent pay. Internal labor markets have declined in recent decades.[57] But they provide the stability and, quite often, generous compensation to those workers lucky enough to be employed by an organization that retains such a structure.

A clear-cut policy intervention to mandate the creation of internal labor markets is unavailable, alas. As a start, policymakers could reward firms that pay average workers well. There is recent precedent for such action. Executive Order 13658, implemented by the Obama Administration, established a minimum wage firms contracting with the federal government had to pay.[58] Executive Order 13673, the Fair Pay and Safe Workplaces Executive Order, was another Obama-era rule, mandating that federal contract applications disclose any past labor law violations.[59] Not only could policymakers nudge potential contractors into paying a decent minimum wage, they could go further by, for example, requiring contractors to submit their pay distribution as part of the application process. Companies with a low CEO-to-median pay ratio could be given preference. The hope here is that enough organizations change their pay practices as a direct result of state or federal incentives, and that this leads others to follow suit, including those that don't do business with the government. Over time, as more and more firms mimic one another, these pay standards become institutionalized as inertia sets in and higher floors and a more generous middle become taken-for-granted aspects of the modern labor market, much as they were in many core industries in the decades after the Second World War.

Finally, a fundamental change to pay-setting within workplaces that benefits average workers requires empowering them directly. The key institution that provides workers with the means to shift wage-setting dynamics in their favor in workplace negotiations is the labor union. It's time unions were strengthened significantly in the United States. Plans to do so abound, and nearly all include a radical rewriting of the nation's labor laws, which have mutated into little more than tools of union suppression.[60] This isn't the place for a thorough assessment of the particulars, but the broad message is that any strategy to empower workers vis-à-vis employers in the pay-setting process must include strengthening organized labor, as the core institution for representing workers' interests at the bargaining table.

A strengthened labor movement could help resurrect internal labor markets within firms. The structure of collective bargaining in the United States ties unions to workers in an organization. High turnover at a firm, therefore, means that the union has to convince new entrants that the value of its representation is worth the cost. Failing to make that case often enough could leave the union facing a decertification campaign. Indeed, employers frequently take advantage of high turnover to thwart organization in the first place. For these and other reasons, unions should prefer a stable workforce in organizations they are targeting or have already successfully unionized. Of course, a core purpose of union representation is to raise the pay of members. But that's not the only way unions intervene in pay-determination. The development of internal labor markets coincided with the rise of organized labor in the United States, and in many firms the impetus for instituting an internal labor market came from union pressure.[61] One component of internal labor markets that unions pushed for was seniority-based pay structures, which stripped managers of some of their power to play favorites and discriminate against certain workers. Added to that was pay tied to job classification, not to the individual, which again constrained capricious managers from allocating pay unfairly. Tying pay to seniority and job classification become two pieces central to the internal labor market system.

These strategies have fallen out of favor in the business literature and mainstream press. Seniority-based pay, in particular, is a term often used sneeringly in contemporary education debates, as if the very idea is preposterous on its face. But it emerged as a way to ensure some semblance of equal pay for equal work, given the inherent difficulty in measuring exactly what "equal work" is. And it emerged to inhibit powerful bosses from rewarding friends when setting pay, and to prevent discrimination on the basis of ascriptive characteristics such as race and gender.[62] Gender and racial discrimination remain persistent problems despite decades of anti-discrimination legislation. Emilio Castilla's research finds that managers exhibit "performance reward bias," paying men and white workers more than women and minorities even when no differences exist in their performance evaluations.[63] Experimental research reveals that when left to their personal determination, managers discriminate against women and minorities in pay, especially in organizations in which "meritocracy" is a core value.[64] Seniority-based pay can help mitigate these effects.

Seniority-based pay is often juxtaposed with performance-based pay. But seniority-based pay is a variant of performance-based pay—one that assumes workers' performance improves with experience. Is it a perfect measure? Of course not. But as noted in Chapter 4, perfect measures don't exist. Obviously there are exceptions, but most of us do get better at our jobs with experience. These types of pay structures have another added virtue: seniority-based pay aligns well with major transitions in our lives. Take my own situation: with a toddler in the house, I require more money than I did fifteen years ago when the only dependent was a cat who intermittently stopped by, looking for food. I'm also better at my job now. What's true for me is true for the vast majority of workers: with on-the-job experience, we become better at what we do. Seniority-based pay ensures we're paid for our improvement. Internal labor markets institutionalized a version of seniority-based pay aligned with the general contours of one's working life.

There is no clear way to mandate seniority-based pay schemes, nor should one try. Organizational actors know the internal dynamics of their workplaces better than distant bureaucrats. But a reinvigorated labor movement is likely to push firms in the direction of disassociating pay from the individual, and reattaching it to jobs and seniority. That's okay. In fact, it's quite preferable to many alternatives—and, when combined with strong norms of equity that compress the organization's entire pay distribution—it would go a long way toward reducing inequality within and between organizations.

There are downsides to tying *all* of a worker's pay to seniority or job title. We learned in Chapter 2 that American workers and pay-setters overwhelmingly support connecting pay to performance. We learned in Chapter 4 just how difficult it is to set pay according to individual performance, due to disagreements over what defines performance, difficulties in measuring it, and the problems that arise in hypercompetitive workplaces, where employees often work to game the system to their own advantage. But broader performance measures are, generally, more readily available, especially at the organizational-level. Encouraging organizations to link a portion of wages and salaries to organizational revenue would have at least two

salutary effects on our economy. First, it would align the organization's goals with those of the workers. The disconnect between
rising productivity and workers' wages is a well-established fact of
our modern economy. Between 1948 and 1973, productivity grew by
96 percent, while median real wages for private sector non-supervisory
workers grew by 91 percent. Since then, the trends have diverged:
productivity has increased by 77 percent; average hourly compensation by only 12 percent.[65] The fruits of increased productivity
have been redistributed upward, toward the executive class and
shareholders. Binding some fraction of revenue increases to fatter
paychecks for workers ensures that everyone benefits from organizational success. And second, it would establish a precedent that,
over time, could become an ingrained expectation for workers, who
have grown far too used to "we're all in this together" rhetoric ema-
nating from corporate headquarters without out any tangible evidence that the sentiment is true. If anything, the gargantuan sizes of
recent stock buybacks prove the opposite. Sharing in the surplus
means the rhetoric isn't empty.

Given the diversity of organizational forms that collectively make
up our economic landscape, there isn't a single pay-setting system that
should be implemented everywhere. I've warned of the problems that
accompany paying for individual performance, and I've defended
pay-setting practices common to internal labor markets as fundamentally fairer. But if a firm allocates some portion of pay based on a
metric of individual, group, or (preferably) organizational-level performance, and the workers have bought into the system, with managers completely transparent about the rationale behind it, then I
wouldn't argue for overhauling it completely. After all, recall from
Chapter 2 how workers believe pay should be based on a number of
factors, which could include individual performance. That's defen-
sible, as long as everyone is clear about the actual underpinnings of

pay-setting—which means coming to terms with the choices involved in deciding on what aspect of performance will be rewarded, and being cognizant of the potential downsides of such incentive-based pay schemes.

Pegging pay to organizational or individual performance is no panacea for wage stagnation and rising inequality, of course. Back in 2001, Enron employees' retirement savings were heavily tied to a measure of company performance—namely, its stock price. They saw those savings vanish almost overnight as the firm collapsed amidst evidence of massive fraud. The company exacerbated the problem by preventing workers from altering their plans as the stock price plunged.[66] Year-end bonuses are fairly common, but handing workers a one-time lump sum of a size unknown in advance introduces too much uncertainly for families trying to budget expenses over the long term. Better for organizations to bank a certain fraction of their increased revenue in advance, and then distribute it over a specified period of time, as mutually agreed upon by the employer and workers. It's true that research finds that paying for organizational performance avoids the disequalizing effects of paying for individual performance.[67] But such a system runs the risk of widening between-firm inequality. Workers lucky enough to be employed by the Googles of the world would reap sizable gains while their counterparts working at Microsoft's Bing division wouldn't, increasing pay gaps between otherwise similar workers at different firms. Best, then, to combine workplace incentives of this sort with a core compensation system based on experience and job title.

These prescriptions will not work in isolation. Seniority-based pay in a custodial contracting firm with slim profit margins that competes on low labor costs solves almost nothing. But it can be combined with a greatly expanded pay floor, governmental preferences for firms that pay non-supervisory workers decently, and an empowered workforce. Such a system would help raise pay for average workers while ensuring their wages and salaries are fairly determined.

LOWER THE CEILING!

Addressing the United Nations General Assembly late in his second term, President Barack Obama noted proudly that "After the recession, the top one percent of Americans were capturing more than 90 percent of income growth. But today, that's down to about half."[68] Boasting that the top one percent of earners are only capturing half of all income gains is what constitutes progress in combatting inequality during our present Gilded Age. We can do better, and the American people are demanding it. Nearly two-thirds of Americans believe the economy unfairly favors the powerful.[69] They're right, and today even corporate leaders are listening. A group of 181 CEOs recently called for a return to a system of corporate governance that balances the needs of shareholders with a "fundamental commitment to all of our stakeholders."[70] But such a rebalancing will require more than public statements. Any solution to rising inequality must contend with the exponential growth of top-end incomes. This means reducing the share of organizational revenue going to executives and shareholders.

The first rather obvious step would be to raise top-end tax rates, including the capital gains rate. In a recent poll, nearly 60 percent of registered voters—and 45 percent of registered Republicans—supported a top marginal rate of 70 percent on incomes over $10 million.[71] Such support is longstanding: Gallup polls going back a quarter century indicate majority support for raising taxes on the rich.[72] Crucially, higher top-end tax rates won't just affect posttax inequality. Research by Thomas Piketty, Emmanuel Saez, and Stefanie Stantcheva finds that higher marginal rates are associated with lower pretax earnings.[73] How come? High earners' incentive to bargain for more is reduced when they know much of the resulting gains will go to the government.

Another increasingly popular idea is to ensure worker representation on corporate boards, a practice common in other countries, such as in Germany. The Reward Work Act, originally sponsored by Senator Tammy Baldwin of Wisconsin, subsequently gained the support of 2020 Presidential hopefuls Elizabeth Warren, Kamala Harris, and Bernie Sanders. Section 2 of the Act requires that a third of publicly traded corporate board seats be directly elected by the firm's employees.[74] And lest the sponsors be accused of promoting an unpopular, un-American plan, a recent poll found majority support for the idea. Over a third of Republicans approve, as do over two-thirds of Democrats.[75]

Recent evidence suggest the practice doesn't have deleterious economic consequences for firms. Simon Jäger, Benjamin Schoefer, and Jörg Heining compare German firms with and without worker board representation, and find that firms with worker representatives engage in more capital formation and aren't less profitable than firms solely controlled by management.[76] The authors suggest worker presence on corporate boards facilitates cooperation and leads to more long-term decision-making than found in companies focused on quarterly returns. As one Siemens worker board representative stated, "shared governance per se opposes short-term shareholder interests. The focus is on the long-term security of the company through investments and innovations involving the employees."[77]

If this sort of shared governance does stand against "short-term shareholder interests," then worker board representation could also stem the tide of share buybacks, now standard practice throughout corporate America. The real value of buybacks has exploded since the mid-1990s.[78] Defenders of the practice claim it's simply a reflection of a firm that "cannot efficiently utilize . . . all its cash"[79] and thus a prudent business decision. Such a justification ignores the enormous power shareholders wield over publicly traded firms. Shareholders have grown used to demanding increasing portions of organizational revenue and punishing firms who choose to utilize its cash in other ways—say, by paying its workers more. Giving workers a formal voice in financial decision-making would help redirect revenue away from Wall Street and toward the people who helped produce the revenue in the first place.

We should go further. Another provision of the Reward Work Act overturns the SEC's 10b-18 rule—the one granting "safe harbor" against stock manipulation charges, thereby opening the floodgates for firms to purchase their own stock.[80] While some form of repurchases would still be allowed, the Act would reduce the frequency of this practice that rewards shareholders at the direct expense of workers. As we learned in Chapter 5, the idea that corporations have a fiduciary duty to maximize profits and investor returns is a fiction. But it's a powerful one that is now taken as truth by many CEOs, corporate attorneys, and business journalists. A legal change that explicitly held corporate boards accountable to a range of stakeholders—including the firm's employees—would help dispel this pernicious belief.[81]

Like the sponsors of the Reward Work Act, powerful policymakers back ideas to move us away from the current narrow conception of a firm's fiduciary duty. Of late, a few of these have emerged from unlikely quarters. A recent report on the deleterious effects shareholder capitalism has had on our economy noted that:

Shareholder primacy theory has tilted business decision-making toward delivering returns quickly and predict-

ably to investors, rather than building long-term capabilities
through investment and production . . . and has resulted in
a diminished understanding of the role workers play and the
risk they undertake in the value creation process.[82]

That's from Senator Marco Rubio, Republican of Florida and
former contender for his party's presidential nomination. Rubio released a report in 2019 detailing the problems with shareholder primacy theory, arguing that corporations should embrace more of a
stakeholder model. He advocates changes to our tax laws that would
end incentives for firms that engage in short-term, profit-maximizing
strategies.[83] The plan doesn't go as far as to inscribe in the law a
broader understanding of fiduciary duty, but it's a start, and indicative of a growing coalition of policymakers fed up with the current
economic arrangement.

"MONEY IS NEVER JUST about money," notes Ben Fountain, a writer
of both fiction and narrative nonfiction. "It's about dignity, autonomy,
the saving grace of self-respect."[84] Obviously what we get paid has
significant material consequences for our lives. This is especially
true in a country such as ours where many necessities aren't provided by the government. That raise you didn't receive but were
expecting could mean the difference between being able to afford
your healthcare premiums or not. Or being able to pay for your
daughter's college tuition without saddling her with thousands of
dollars of student debt.

But what we get paid has significant moral consequences as well.
A decent, stable paycheck brings dignity, security, and helps combat
the pervasive cynicism so common in today's civic life. It's hard to
attach yourself to political causes when you're scrambling to put food

on the table. And it's hard to see any point in doing so when nobody has done much of anything to improve your economic plight. In the years surrounding the 2016 presidential election, Jennifer Silva embedded herself in a working-class community in Pennsylvania, interviewing over a hundred people about their political identities. The vast majority of those interviewed didn't bother to vote: "They knew the election was happening but they viewed political participation as pointless. They thought of it as a joke. And they said, 'Look at what's happened in my lifetime, it doesn't really matter who's been president.'" Among her subjects, "there was a fierce distrust and hatred of politicians, a suspicion that politicians and big business were basically working together to take away the American Dream. Everyone was very critical of inequality."[85] What fueled their disenchantment? Poorly paid jobs—for those who were working—in what once was a community knit together by a range of vibrant institutions all undergirded by a stable economic foundation.

For many of us, our sense of self, of our moral value, is wrapped up in our wage or salary, contributing to the deep resistance we feel about disclosing that number on our paycheck. The idea that the size of our salary reflects at some core level our worthiness in this world—and often the world beyond—has a long lineage in the United States. It's time we question it. Reframing our pay not as some reflection of our individual performance, or a natural outcome of our occupation, but as dependent "as much on social forces and political power" as on "simple supply and demand," to quote the Nobel Laureate Paul Krugman,[86] helps free us from feelings of inadequacy, embarrassment, or, for the lucky among us, smugness and moral superiority.

More importantly, an understanding of pay that is rooted in power dynamics, accounts for equity concerns between workers, is cognizant of how pay levels stick with us and to the jobs we occupy, and is aware of how organizations copy one another when it comes to setting pay, should raise some fundamental questions about the current pay distribution. It should raise a question about the outsized gains at the top, with corporate titans and top money managers now earning many times the amount anyone could hope to spend in a hundred lifetimes. No anger need be directed at the recipients; that should be reserved for a system that's distorted enough to reward anyone so much while many others get so little. This understanding of pay should also raise the question of why millions at the bottom who work hard, performing vital jobs, receive such meager wages for their efforts. Finally, for American workers, whose lot has not improved in decades despite working in the richest economy the world has ever known, it should raise a very basic question: Why. Why not a raise? It's past time, and we can afford it.

EPILOGUE
WHAT FOOT SOLDIERS DESERVE

I SENT THE FINAL VERSION of this manuscript to my publisher on February 28, 2020. Within a week, the world had changed. The global pandemic arrived in the United States earlier that winter, but exploded across the nation as spring approached. By the end of March, major sectors of the economy had shuttered, and thousands of lives had been lost. By the end of April, the official death count in the United States approached sixty thousand, and over twenty million Americans had filed for unemployment. Millions more had tried but couldn't access a system straining under unprecedented demand.[1] Never mind getting paid what they're worth, a huge number of American workers suddenly found themselves not getting paid for working at all.

Many still are getting paid, especially those deemed essential workers during the nationwide quarantine. As I write, the direction the pandemic takes us as a nation, in terms of our public health infrastructure, political arrangements, and economic foundations remains unknown. But early as it is in the battle against the virus, our current response has reinforced a key conclusion of this book: in recent decades the fundamental forces that shape our wages and salaries have resulted in far too many hardworking Americans earning far too little for their efforts. Since the epidemic began, corporate leaders, elected officials, and pundits have urged us to applaud workers fighting on the front lines against the virus. Suddenly the home healthcare aide tasked with keeping our elderly engaged, alert, and alive, the grocery worker keeping our pantries full, and the truck driver ensuring the grocery worker has anything to offer us, along with many other employees in essential occupations, are receiving long-deserved recognition.

That's worthy, of course. Any worker forced to choose between a paycheck and a potentially lethal disease deserves our appreciation as well as our sympathy. But these workers deserve a whole lot more—not just short-term hazard pay, but long-term living wages and benefits. As this book demonstrates, we don't have to dream of a world in which workers in bottom-rung occupations—like those currently keeping us cared for, fed, and supplied during the ongoing crisis—are paid well. Many once were. A few still are. And all should be in the future. We are at an historical juncture in which the critical nature of this underpaid and underappreciated workforce is laid bare. As I argue throughout the book, for too long we've assumed these jobs pay poorly due to some inherent feature of the work. As I've documented, the good news is that our own history and current counterexamples suggest otherwise.

For a month now, like millions of other worried relatives across the county, my wife has been unable to visit her father, who is confined to a nursing facility just a few miles from our home. The good news is that he's not alone. He's surrounded, around the clock, by a coterie of caring healthcare professionals—nurses, nurses' assistants, personal care aides—who check his vitals, keep him healthy, and do their best to maintain his spirits. In the best of times, these professionals' work is physically and emotionally exhausting. Right now it's downright deadly. For all their effort and dedication, many of these workers barely make enough to get by. Emily Stewart of *Vox* recently profiled Melanie, a worker at an assisted living center in Colorado who cares for elderly residents with dementia and Alzheimer's. For this vital work, she earns $12 per hour. She doesn't have health insurance.[2] Similar to our treatment of home healthcare aides, long-term care workers deserve more than our applause. They deserve to get paid.

Driving through my city, one sees shuttered business after shuttered business, occasionally happening upon a pizza delivery store or other restaurant offering takeout or curbside delivery during the pandemic. While many of us have discovered the joys of cooking during our extended lockdown, many others haven't had that opportunity because of work or childcare responsibilities, disabilities, or other exigencies. Our food service workers fill this gap—those still lucky enough to be employed. Yet the good fortune that comes with remaining on payroll rarely carries over to actual pay. Wages are typically less than $12 per hour for restaurant workers and food deliverers. They should be higher.

Those of us cooking at home rely on our grocery stores to ensure we've got all the right ingredients (not to mention toilet paper and hand sanitizer). Stocking the shelves, cleaning the store, ringing up purchases—all of it is essential work that millions depend on. Right now it's work that can kill you. Eighteen Walmart workers have already succumbed to Covid-19; one in ten of the giant retailer's workforce is currently on leave.[3] And the work pays poorly. Like so many other essential employees, cashiers typically make less than $11 per hour. Costco and cross-national comparisons make clear that Walmart and other retailers' treatment of frontline workers does not stem from some inherent feature of the retail industry.

The president of the United States recently called truck drivers "the foot soldiers that are carrying us to victory" against Covid-19 and the "lifeblood of our economy." Once upon a time, we matched such flattery with a middle-class salary and decent benefits. Those days are long gone. Deregulation and the subsequent destruction of industrywide wage and benefit standards eroded the living standards of our country's millions of short- and long-haul truck drivers. We paid these foot soldiers well once before. It's past time we did again.

Let's continue to applaud our essential workers for their critical efforts during this ongoing emergency. But let's go further, by supporting policies and organizing efforts to ensure living wages, robust benefits, and safe working conditions. These are what all workers deserve now and for when we emerge from the crisis. Profit margins for some firms might be a bit lower. The amount returned to shareholders may fall. If the present crisis has taught us anything, these are the costs that any just society should be willing to bear.

NOTES

CHAPTER 1: WHAT DOES DETERMINE OUR PAY?

1. J. T. Genter, "United Employees Are Venting Their Fury at Management Over New Bonus Lottery," *The Points Guy* (blog), March 5, 2018, https://thepointsguy.com/2018/03/united-employees-venting-bonus-lottery/.

2. For the original story of the lottery announcement, see Lewis Lazare, "United Airlines Cans Unpopular Lottery Bonus Plan," *Chicago Business Journal,* April 10, 2018. For the aftermath, see Christina Caron, "United Airlines Pauses Lottery for Bonuses after Employees Rebel Online," *New York Times,* March 5, 2018.

3. E. Scott Reckard, "Wells Fargo's Pressure-Cooker Sales Culture Comes at a Cost," *Los Angeles Times,* December 21, 2013.

4. Reckard, "Wells Fargo's Pressure-Cooker Sales Culture."

5. James Rufus Koren, "Wells Fargo Overhauls Pay Plan for Branch Employees Following Fake-Accounts Scandal," *Los Angeles Times,* January 10, 2017.

6. Jim Puzzanghera, "Wells Fargo CEO Tim Sloan Steps Down as Bank Struggles to Get Past Scandals," *Los Angeles Times,* March 28, 2019.

7. Koren, "Wells Fargo Overhauls Pay Plan." The number reflects CEO Tim Sloan's compensation of $17 million in 2017, $18 million in 2018, and a net $1.5 million in 2019 after a substantial clawback. See Kate Berry, "Wells Fargo Cancels $15 Million Bonus to Former CEO Tim Sloan," *American Banker*, March 17, 2020.

8. Barack Obama, "Remarks by the President on Economic Mobility," Washington, DC, December 4, 2013, https://obamawhitehouse.archives.gov/the-press-office/2013/12/04/remarks-president-economic-mobility.

9. Dustin Avent-Holt and Donald Tomaskovic-Devey, "A Relational Theory of Earnings Inequality," *American Behavioral Scientist* 58 (2014): 379–399.

10. See Steven Lukes, *Power: A Radical View* (New York: Palgrave, 1974), especially 23–24.

11. For a formal theory of organizational inertia, see Michael T. Hannan and John Freeman, "Structural Inertia and Organizational Change," *American Sociological Review* 49 (1984): 149–164; for an examination into organizations' responses to changes in their environment, see Dawn Kelly and Terry L. Amburgey, "Organizational Inertia and Momentum: A Dynamic Model of Strategic Change," *Academy of Management Journal* 34 (1991): 591–612.

12. PayScale, "2020 Compensation Best Practices Report," Payscale Research Report, March 11, 2020, 20, https://www.payscale.com/content/report/2020-Compensation-Best-Practices-Report.pdf.

13. Robert E. Hall and Alan B. Krueger, "Evidence on the Incidence of Wage Posting, Wage Bargaining, and On-the-Job Search," *American Economic Journal: Macroeconomics* 4 (2012): 56–67.

14. Kristin Wong, "Don't Ask Me about My Salary History," *New York Times,* October 22, 2019.

15. Joseph F. Porac, James B. Wade, and Timothy G. Pollock, "Industry Categories and the Politics of the Comparable Firm in CEO Compensation," *Administrative Science Quarterly* 44 (1999): 112–144.

16. J. Stacy Adams, "Toward an Understanding of Inequity," *Journal of Abnormal and Social Psychology* 67 (1963): 422–436.

17. For the leaked messages, see Genter, "United Employees Are Venting Their Fury."

18. Quoted in Jim Salter, "St. Louis Businesses Pressured to Keep $10 Minimum Wage," *Associated Press,* July 13, 2017.

19. Quoted in David A. Graham, "How St. Louis Workers Won and Then Lost a Minimum-Wage Hike," *The Atlantic,* August 29, 2017.

20. Truman F. Bewley, *Why Wages Don't Fall During a Recession* (Cambridge, MA: Harvard University Press, 1999), 175.

21. Bewley, *Why Wages Don't Fall,* 175.

22. PayScale, "2017 Compensation Best Practices Report," 40.

23. Quoted in Aimee Picchi, "Why Walmart's Pay Raise Is Backfiring," *CBS News,* August 7, 2015.

24. Rachel Feintzeig and Lauren Weber, "Push for $15 Raises Pay—and Tensions; As Higher Minimum Wages Go into Effect, Some Veteran Employees Are Unhappy about Earning the Same Wage as Less Experienced Hires," *Wall Street Journal,* May 6, 2016.

25. Quoted in Patricia Cohen, "A Company Copes with Backlash against the Raise That Roared," *New York Times,* July 31, 2015.

26. Quoted in Cohen, "A Company Copes with Backlash."

27. Michel Tremblay, Sylvie St.-Onge, and Jean-Marie Toulouse, "Determinants of Salary Referents Relevance: A Field Study of Managers," *Journal of Business and Psychology* 11 (1997): 463–484.

28. See Nina Gupta, Samantha A. Conroy, and John E. Delery, "The Many Faces of Pay Variation," *Human Resource Management Review* 22 (2012), 100–115, 107. For a related analysis of managers in Canada see Tremblay, St.-Onge, and Toulouse, "Determinants of Salary Referents Relevance"; and, for a recent examination of German workers, Carsten Saur and Meike J. May, "Determinants of Just Earnings: The Importance of Comparisons with Similar Others and Social Relations with Supervisors and Co-workers in Organizations," *Research in Social Stratification and Mobility* 47 (2017): 45–54.

29. Arindrajit Dube, Laura Giuliano, and Jonathan S. Leonard, "Fairness and Frictions: The Impact of Unequal Raises on Quit Behavior," *American Economic Review* 109 (2018): 620–663.

30. Paul D. Sweeney and Dean B. McFarlin, "Wage Comparisons with Similar and Dissimilar Others," *Journal of Occupational and Organizational Psychology* 78 (2005): 113–131.

31. Esra Ho Burak, "Is the Sky the Limit? Fair Executive Pay as Performance Rises," *Social Problems* 65 (2018): 211–230, 223.

32. Lawrence Mishel and Jessica Schieder, "CEO Pay Remains High Relative to the Pay of Typical Workers and High-Wage Earners," Economic Policy Institute Report, July 20, 2017.

33. David F. Larcker, Nicholas E. Donatiello, and Brian Tayan, "Americans and CEO Pay: 2016 Public Perception Survey on CEO Compensation," CGRI Survey Series, February 2016.

34. James B. Wade, Charles A. O'Reilly III, and Timothy G. Pollock, "Overpaid CEOs and Underpaid Managers: Fairness and Executive Compensation," *Organization Science* 17 (2006): 527–544.

35. Bewley, *Why Wages Don't Fall,* 173.

36. Wong, "Don't Ask Me about My Salary History."

37. Daniel Kahneman and Amos Tversky, "Prospect Theory: An Analysis of Decision Under Risk," *Econometrica* 47 (1979): 263–291, 279.

38. David I. Levine, "What Do Wages Buy?" *Administrative Science Quarterly* 38 (1993): 462–483, 479.

39. Paul Krugman, "Broken Windows and American Oligarchy," *New York Times,* May 15, 2015; see also Bruce Western and Jake Rosenfeld, "Unions, Norms, and the Rise in U.S. Wage Inequality," *American Sociological Review* 76 (2011): 513–537.

40. The dynamics created by the interplay of these four elements help explain ongoing gender, racial, and ethnic-based disparities in pay. While not a primary focus of this book, other recent research tackles these types of pay discrimination in contemporary labor markets from a perspective aligned with the one I present here. See especially Emilio J. Castilla, "Gender, Race, and the New (Merit-Based) Employment Relationship," *Industrial Relations* 51 (2012): 528–562; Emilio J. Castilla and Stephen Benard, "The Paradox of Meritocracy in Organizations," *Administrative Science Quarterly* 55 (2010): 543–576; Donald Tomaskovic-Devey and Dustin Avent-Holt, *Relational Inequalities: An Organizational Approach* (Oxford: Oxford University Press, 2019), ch. 4; Adia Harvey Wingfield, *Flatlining: Race, Work, and Health Care in the New Economy* (Berkeley: University of California Press, 2019).

41. For a classic statement, see Gary Becker, *Human Capital: A Theoretical and Empirical Analysis, with Special Reference to Education* (Chicago: University of Chicago Press, 1964). For a contemporary critique, see Tomaskovic-Devey and Avent-Holt, *Relational Inequalities.*

42. See Avent-Holt and Tomaskovic-Devey, "A Relational Theory of Earnings Inequality"; and Tomaskovic-Devey and Avent-Holt, *Relational Inequalities* for overviews.

43. For one recent example, see Jae Song, David J. Price, Fatih Guvenen, Nicholas Bloom, and Till von Wachter, "Firming Up Inequality," *Quarterly*

Journal of Economics 134 (2019): 1–50. For a lively critique of the human capital model of pay determination, see James Kwak, *Economism: Bad Economics and the Rise of Inequality* (New York: Pantheon Books, 2017), especially ch. 4.

44. Alan Manning, *Monopsony in Motion: Imperfect Competition in Labor Markets* (Princeton: Princeton University Press, 2003). For recent empirical investigations, see Dube, Giuliano, and Leonard, "Fairness and Frictions"; and Arindrajit Dube, Jeff Jacobs, Suresh Naidu, and Siddharth Suri, "Monopsony in Online Labor Markets," *American Economic Review: Insights,* forthcoming. For a theoretical overview and a summary of related research, see Suresh Naidu, Eric A. Posner, and E. Glen Weyl, "Antitrust Remedies for Labor Market Power," *Harvard Law Review* 132 (2018): 537–601, especially 549–569.

45. For a classic statement see Arthur L. Stinchcome, "Social Structure and Organizations," in *Handbook of Organizations,* ed. James G. March, 142–193 (New York: Rand McNally, 1965), 155–160. For a more recent empirical application, see Paula England, Paul Allison, and Yuxiao Wu, "Does Bad Pay Cause Occupations to Feminize, Does Feminization Reduce Pay, and How Can We Tell with Longitudinal Data?" *Social Science Research* 36 (2007): 1237–1256.

46. The canonical statement is provided by Paul J. DiMaggio and Walter W. Powell, "The Iron Cage Revisited: Institutional Isomorphism and Collective Rationality in Organizational Fields," *American Sociological Review* 48 (1983): 147–160.

47. For a prominent example, see Ernst Fehr, Georg Kirchsteiger, and Arno Riedl, "Does Fairness Prevent Market Clearing? An Experimental Investigation," *Quarterly Journal of Economics* 108 (1993): 437–459.

48. I do not subscribe to doomsday scenarios about the coming jobs apocalypse resulting from the roboticization of wide swaths of the workforce. Automation is an inherent feature of all capitalist economies. That's a good thing, too, as it is a key contributor to productivity. But there remains little evidence that technological changes of the present will result in too few total jobs in the future, although particular industries (similar to auto production in past decades) may be disproportionately affected. See Lawrence Mishel and Heidi Shierholz, "Robots, or Automation, Are Not the Problem," Economic Policy Institute Economic Snapshot, February 21, 2017; and Organisation for Economic Cooperation and Development, OECD Employment

Outlook 2019: The Future of Work (Paris, France: OECD Publishing, 2019). The question is how to make the jobs of the present and future pay fairly.

49. David Brooks, "The Bernie Sanders Fallacy," *New York Times,* January 16, 2020.

50. Larcker, Donatiello, and Tayan, "Americans and CEO Pay." See also Ruth Igielnik and Kim Parker, "Most Americans Say the Current Economy Is Helping the Rich, Hurting the Poor and Middle Class," Pew Research Center Report, December 2019.

CHAPTER 2: WHAT DO WE THINK DETERMINES OUR PAY?

1. Steven Pearlstein, "The $786 Million Question: Does Steve Schwarzman—Or Anyone—Deserve to Make That Much?" *Washington Post*, January 4, 2019. We'll examine private equity in detail in Chapter 5.

2. Jonathan Alter, "Schwarzman: 'It's a War' between Obama, Wall St," *Newsweek,* August 15, 2010.

3. Tyler Cowen, *Big Business: A Love Letter to an American Anti-Hero* (New York: St. Martin's Press, 2019), 44.

4. N. Gregory Mankiw, "Yes, the Wealthy Can Be Deserving," *New York Times,* February 15, 2014.

5. Dylan Scott, "Lamar Alexander, Pillar of Washington's Old Guard, Is Retiring from the Senate," *Vox,* December 17, 2018.

6. Dave Jamieson, "Lamar Alexander Says Minimum Wage Should Be Abolished," *Huffpost,* June 25, 2013.

7. Arthur Delaney and David Jamieson, "Amazon Called for Raising the Minimum Wage, Republicans Say It's Fine as It Is, Thanks," *HuffPost,* October 5, 2018.

8. Dustin Avent-Holt and Donald Tomaskovic-Devey, "A Relational Theory of Earnings Inequality," *American Behavioral Scientist* 58 (2014): 379–399, 380–381.

9. For a non-academic, concise overview of the theory, see Noah Smith, "It Looks Like Lots of Workers Aren't Paid What They're Worth," *Bloomberg,* February 1, 2019.

10. For an overview of these debates, see Russell Coff and Joseph Raffiee, "Toward a Theory of Perceived Firm-Specific Human Capital," *Academy of Management Perspectives* 29 (2015): 326–341. For an earlier statement, see

Masanori Hashimoto, "Firm-Specific Human Capital as a Shared Investment," *American Economic Review* 71 (1981): 475–482.

11. J. R. Hicks, *The Theory of Wages* (New York: Macmillan, 1963 [1932]), 1. Also see Robert F. Frank, "Are Workers Paid Their Marginal Products?," *American Economic Review* 74 (1984): 549–570.

12. Truman F. Bewley, *Why Wages Don't Fall during a Recession* (Cambridge, MA: Harvard University Press, 1999).

13. For a classic statement see George A. Akerlof, "Labor Contracts as Partial Gift Exchange," *Quarterly Journal of Economics* 97 (1982): 543–569.

14. For an overview of the variants of efficiency wage theories, see Lawrence F. Katz, "Efficiency Wage Theories: A Partial Evaluation," *NBER Macroeconomics Annual* 1 (1986): 235–276.

15. David G. Blanchflower, Andrew J. Oswald, and Mario D. Garrett, "Insider Power in Wage Determination," *Economica* 57 (1990): 143–170, 143–144.

16. Manning reframes labor markets as inherently monopsonistic, a perspective recently advanced by a range of empirical and theoretical treatments: Alan Manning, *Monopsony in Motion: Imperfect Competition in Labor Markets* (Princeton: Princeton University Press, 2003). For a statement and summary of this research agenda, see Suresh Naidu, Eric A. Posner, and E. Glen Weyl, "Antitrust Remedies for Labor Market Power," *Harvard Law Review* 132 (2018): 537–601.

17. Richard B. Freeman, "A Tale of Two Clones," Third Way Report, September 27, 2016.

18. Smith, "It Looks Like Lots of Workers Aren't Paid What They're Worth."

19. Mark Thoma, "Marginal Productivity Theory and the Mainstream," *Economist's View* (blog), June 7, 2007, https://economistsview.typepad.com /economistsview/2007/06/marginal_produc.html.

20. Beth Red Bird and David Grusky, "Rent, Rent-Seeking, and Social Inequality," (2015) in *Emerging Trends in the Social and Behavioral Sciences,* ed. Robert A. Scott and Stephen Kosslyn (Hoboken, NJ: John Wiley and Sons, 2015–).

21. For an example see Blanchflower, Oswald, and Garrett, "Insider Power in Wage Determination."

22. Council of Economic Advisors, "Economic Report of the President," Council of Economic Advisors Annual Report, February 2016, 38–44.

23. Jonathan Rothwell, *Republic of Equals: A Manifesto for a Just Society* (Princeton, NJ: Princeton University Press, 2019), ch. 3.

24. Quoted in Asher Schechter, "Nobel Laureates: Eliminating Rent Seeking and Tougher Antitrust Enforcement Are Critical to Reducing Inequality," *Pro-Market,* January 10, 2017.

25. Tyler Cowen, "The Measured Working Man," *MIT Technology Review,* September 28, 2015.

26. Daniel Markovits, *The Meritocracy Trap: How America's Foundational Myth Feeds Inequality, Dismantles the Middle Class, and Devours the Elite* (New York: Penguin Press, 2019).

27. Noam Scheiber, "Are You Getting Paid What You're Worth?" *Pacific Standard,* May 19, 2015.

28. Quoted in Ron Suskind, *Confidence Men: Wall Street, Washington, and the Education of a President* (New York: Harper, 2011), 197. For recent research on loss of worker power and rising inequality, see Anna Stansbury and Lawrence H. Summers, "The Declining Worker Power Hypothesis: An Explanation for the Recent Evolution of the American Economy," NBER Working Paper 27193, 2020.

29. For a definitive statement see Kim A. Weeden, "Why Do Some Occupations Pay More Than Others? Social Closure and Earnings Inequality in the United States," *American Journal of Sociology* 108 (2002): 55–101.

30. Council of Economic Advisors, "Occupational Licensing: A Framework for Policymakers," Council of Economic Advisors Report, July 2015, 3.

31. Morris M. Kleiner and Alan B. Krueger, "The Prevalence and Effects of Occupational Licensing," *British Journal of Industrial Relations* 48 (2010): 676–687.

32. Red Bird and Grusky, "Rent, Rent-Seeking, and Social Inequality," 5.

33. David A. Farenthold, "How Rand Paul Tried to Lead an Eye Doctors' Rebellion," *Washington Post,* February 1, 2015.

34. Cheryl Clark, "Cosmetic, Plastic Surgeons Squabble over 'Board Certified' Label," *MedPage Today,* January 4, 2019.

35. Kim A. Weeden and David B. Grusky, "The Case for a New Class Map," *American Journal of Sociology* 111 (2005): 141–212, 154.

36. Nina Gupta, Samantha A. Conroy, and John E. Delery, "The Many Faces of Pay Variation," *Human Resource Management Review* 22 (2012): 100–115, 105.

37. For a classic study see Donald J. Treiman, *Occupational Prestige in Comparative Perspective* (New York: Academic Press, 1977). For more updated analyses, see Carl Le Grand and Michael Tåhlin, "Class, Occupation, Wages, and Skills: The Iron Law of Labor Market Inequality," *Class and Stratification Analysis* 30 (2013): 3–46.

38. James N. Baron and Jeffrey Pfeffer, "The Social Psychology of Organizations and Inequality," *Social Psychology Quarterly* 57 (1994): 190–209, 197–198.

39. "Employee Job Satisfaction and Engagement: Revitalizing a Changing Workforce," Society for Human Resource Management, April 2016.

40. Jonathan Rothwell and Steve Crabtree, "Not Just a Job: New Evidence on the Quality of Work in the United States," Gallup, 2019, 20.

41. In 2018, for example, only 2 percent said they earned "much more than they deserve." See the GSS data explorer (https://gssdataexplorer.norc.org/) for more, and for details on the pay fairness question see "How Fair Is What Respondent Earns on the Job": https://gssdataexplorer.norc.org/trends/Quality%20of%20Working%20Life?measure=fairearn.

42. Carsten Sauer and Meike J. May, "Determinants of Just Earnings: The Importance of Comparisons with Similar Others and Social Relations with Supervisors and Coworkers in Organizations," *Research in Social Stratification and Mobility* 47 (2017): 45–54, 46.

43. For some examples on US factory workers, see Karyn A. Loscocco and Glenna Spitze, "The Organizational Context of Women's and Men's Pay Satisfaction," *Social Science Quarterly* 72 (1991): 3–19; on German workers, Sauer and May, "Determinants of Just Earnings"; and, on a sample of US workers from various industries, Paul D. Sweeney, Dean B. McFarlin, and Edward J. Inderrieden, "Using Relative Deprivation Theory to Explain Satisfaction with Income and Pay Level: A Multistudy Examination," *Academy of Management Journal* 33 (1990): 423–436.

44. Robert C. Liden, Sandy J. Wayne, Renata A. Jaworski, and Nathan Bennett, "Social Loafing: A Field Investigation," *Journal of Management* 30 (2004): 285–304.

45. David I. Levine, "What Do Wages Buy?" *Administrative Science Quarterly* 38 (1993): 462–483.

46. Christina Lee, Alexander Alonso, Evren Esen, Joseph Coombs, and Yan Dong, "Employee Job Satisfaction and Engagement: The Road to Recovery," Society for Human Resource Management, May 2014.

47. Totals do not quite total 100 percent due to a small fraction that indicated "not applicable." An analysis that excluded the portion of the sample who were self-employed produced similar results.

48. Aside from "individual negotiation" and "cost of living," another factor on the questionnaire not shown in the figures is "your contract is negotiated by a union or other staff association." Unsurprisingly, given the small fraction of the workforce represented by unions today, few respondents suggested this was a very important determinant of their pay.

49. Philip Oreopoulos, Till von Wachter, and Andrew Heisz, "The Short-and-Long-Term Career Effects of Graduating in a Recession," *American Economic Journal: Applied Economics* 4 (2012): 1–29.

50. Although note that the size of the Earned Income Tax Credit (EITC) does vary by number of children.

51. Bewley, *Why Wages Don't Fall During a Recession,* 17.

52. Bewley, *Why Wages Don't Fall During a Recession,* 16.

53. Carl Campbell III and Kunal S. Kamlani, "The Reasons for Wage Rigidity: Evidence from a Survey of Firms," *Quarterly Journal of Economics* 112 (1997): 759–789, 785.

54. "The Great Divide: How a Lack of Trust Is Driving HR & Managers Apart," PayScale Research Report, February 12, 2018.

55. Bewley, *Why Wages Don't Fall During a Recession,* 19.

56. The resulting dataset is not representative of the universe of pay-setters working full-time. Given the difficulties in sampling upper-level management, I instead chose to prioritize a sample spread across a range of industries with a mix of job titles and variation in demographic characteristics.

57. For evidence of this particular form of American exceptionalism, see Victor Tan Chen, *Cut Loose: Jobless and Hopeless in an Unfair Economy* (Berkeley: University of California Press, 2015);and Ofer Sharone, *Flawed System / Flawed Self: Job Searching and Unemployment Experiences* (Chicago: University of Chicago Press, 2013).

CHAPTER 3: EMPLOYERS AGAINST THE FREE MARKET

1. Aly Weisman, "Charlize Theron Reportedly Negotiated a $10 Million Paycheck after Sony Hack Revealed Unequal Pay," *Business Insider,* January 9, 2015.

2. Jeffrey Hayes and Heidi Hartmann, "Women and Men Living on the Edge: Economic Insecurity after the Great Recession," Institute for Women's Policy Research Report, September 30, 2011. See also Jake Rosenfeld, Patrick Denice, and Shengwei Sun, "Pay Secrecy and Gender Inequality in the Workplace," paper presented at the American Sociological Association Annual Meeting, August 2019.

3. Alan Manning, *Monopsony in Motion: Imperfect Competition in Labor Markets* (Princeton: Princeton University Press, 2003), 360.

4. A recent meta-analysis of the academic literature of monopsony finds "strong evidence for monopsonistic competition and implies sizable markdowns in wages." Anna Sokolova and Todd Sorensen, "Monopsony in Labor Markets: A Meta-Analysis," Working Paper, Washington Center for Equitable Growth, February 2020, 31.

5. Jeffrey Pfeffer, "Six Dangerous Myths about Pay," *Harvard Business Review,* May / June, 1998, 95.

6. For the complete transcript, see Michel Martin, "Lilly Ledbetter and the Fight for Gender Equality," NPR News, February 11, 2009, https://www.npr.org/templates/story/story.php?storyId=100557186.

7. White House, "Remarks of President Barack Obama on the Lilly Ledbetter Fair Pay Restoration Act Bill Signing," Washington, DC, January 9, 2009, https://obamawhitehouse.archives.gov/the-press-office/remarks-president-barack-obama-lilly-ledbetter-fair-pay-restoration-act-bill-signin.

8. Hayes and Hartmann, "Women and Men Living on the Edge." See also Jake Rosenfeld, "Don't Ask or Tell: Pay Secrecy Policies in U.S. Workplaces," *Social Science Research* 65 (2017): 1–16, Figure 1.

9. Rafael Gely and Leonard Bierman, "Pay Secrecy / Confidentiality Rules and the National Labor Relations Act," *University of Pennsylvania Journal of Labor and Employment Law* 6 (2003): 121–156, 127.

10. Brian O'Neill, "Pay Confidentiality: A Remaining Obstacle to Equal Pay after Ledbetter," *Seton Hall Law Review* 40 (2011): 1217–1256, 1246.

11. Tom Dreisbach, "'Pay Secrecy' Policies at Work: Often Illegal, and Misunderstood," *NPR,* April 13, 2014.

12. Wesley Lowery, "Senate Falls Six Votes Short of Passing Paycheck Fairness Act," *Washington Post,* April 9, 2014.

13. The latest iteration passed the House of Representatives in early spring 2019, but GOP leadership in the Senate shows no sign of taking up the bill. See Ella Nilsen, "The House Just Passed a Bill to Close the Gender Pay Gap," *Vox,* March 27, 2019.

14. Dreisbach, "'Pay Secrecy' Policies at Work."

15. Thanks to Shengwei Sun for producing the figure.

16. For information on these state laws, see US Department of Labor, "Pay Transparency and Equal Pay Protections," https://www.dol.gov/agencies /wb/equal-pay-protections.

17. See Rosenfeld, Denice, and Sen, "Pay Secrecy and Gender Inequality in the Workplace" for further details of the survey results.

18. These gender pay discrimination scandals aren't limited to the United States. For the British controversy stemming from the BBC's pay disclosure, see Graham Ruddick, "BBC Pay: Key Questions Behind the Disclosures," *Guardian,* July 19, 2017.

19. Rosenfeld, "Don't Ask or Tell," 3.

20. Rosenfeld, Denice, and Sen, "Pay Secrecy and Gender Inequality in the Workplace."

21. Cynthia L. Estlund, "Just the Facts: The Case for Workplace Transparency," *Stanford Law Review* 63 (2011): 351–407, 372.

22. See the discussion in Jake Rosenfeld and Patrick Denice, "The Power of Transparency: Evidence from a British Workplace Survey," *American Sociological Review* 80 (2015): 1045–1068, 1047; and, for more, in Edward J. Lawler, "Power Processes in Bargaining," *Sociological Quarterly* 33 (1992): 17–34, 20.

23. Marlene Kim, "Pay Secrecy and the Gender Wage Gap in the United States," *Industrial Relations* 54 (2015): 648–667.

24. Mari Rege and Ingeborg F. Solli, "Lagging behind the Joneses: The Impact of Relative Earnings on Job Separation," unpublished manuscript, 2014.

25. Lars Bevanger, "Norway: The Country Where No Salaries Are Secret," *BBC News,* July 22, 2017.

26. Rege and Solli, "Lagging behind the Joneses," 7.

27. Rege and Solli, "Lagging behind the Joneses," 1.

28. Michael Baker, Yosh Halberstam, Kory Kroft, Alexandre Mas, and Derek Messacar, "Pay Transparency and the Gender Gap," NBER Working Paper 25834, 2019, 16.

29. Morris M. Kleiner and Marvin L. Bouillon, "Providing Business Information to Production Workers: Correlates of Compensation and Profitability," *ILR Review* 41 (1988): 605–617.

30. Morris M. Kleiner and Marvin L. Bouillon, "Information Sharing of Sensitive Business Data with Employees," *Industrial Relations* 30 (1991): 480–491.

31. Kleiner and Bouillon, "Information Sharing of Sensitive Business Data with Employees," Table 1.

32. Kleiner and Bouillon, "Providing Business Information to Production Workers, 611.

33. Kleiner and Bouillon, "Providing Business Information to Production Workers, Table 2.

34. Kleiner and Bouillon, "Information Sharing of Sensitive Business Data with Employees," Table 2.

35. Rosenfeld and Denice, "The Power of Transparency."

36. Rosenfeld and Denice, "The Power of Transparency," 1047–1048.

37. George A. Akerlof and Janet L. Yellen, "The Fair Wage-Effort Hypothesis and Unemployment," *Quarterly Journal of Economics* 105 (1990): 255–283.

38. Agis Salpukas, "Two-Tier Wage System: For Many It Leads to a Second-Class Status," *New York Times,* July 21, 1987.

39. David Card, Alexandre Mas, Enrico Moretti, and Emmanuel Saez, "Inequality at Work: The Effect of Peer Salaries on Job Satisfaction," *American Economic Review* 102 (2012): 2981–3003.

40. For the origins of the mythical Minnesota town, see Garrison Keillor and Richard Olsenius, "In Search of Lake Wobegon," *National Geographic,* December 2000.

41. Herbert H. Meyer, "The Pay-for-Performance Dilemma," *Organizational Dynamics* 3 (1975): 39–50, 42–43.

42. Alison Griswold, "Here's Why Whole Foods Lets Employees Look Up Each Other's Salaries," *Business Insider,* March 3, 2014.

43. For a first-person account of the change, see Nick Rahaim, "Thank God I Don't Work at Whole Foods Anymore," *Vox,* June 21, 2017.

44. "Buffer's Transparent Salary Calculator," Buffer website, https://buffer.com/salary/product-designer-3/average/.

45. Matthew A. Edwards, "The Law and Social Norms of Pay Secrecy," *Berkeley Journal of Employment & Labor Law* 26 (2005): 41–63, 41–42.

46. George J. Borjas, "The Wage Structure and the Sorting of Workers into the Public Sector," NBER Working Paper 9313, 2002.

47. Paul W. Miller, "The Gender Pay Gap in the US: Does Sector Make a Difference?" *Journal of Labor Research* 30 (2009): 52–74.

48. William J. Carrington, Kristin McCue, and Brooks Pierce, "Black / White Wage Convergence: The Role of Public Sector Wages and Employment," *ILR Review* 49 (1996): 456–471.

49. Rosenfeld, Denice, and Sen, "Pay Secrecy and Gender Inequality in the Workplace."

50. Jena McGregor, "Why Is It Still So Taboo to Talk About What We Make?" *Washington Post,* May 5, 2015.

51. Daniel Wiessner, "Jimmy John's Settles Illinois Lawsuit over Non-compete Agreements," Reuters, December 7, 2016. Jimmy John's eventually removed their noncompete clause after various states sued the company. They remain in place in numerous other brand-name firms.

52. Oliver Darcy, "Independent Journal Review Asks Employees to Sign New Noncompete as Top Talent Continues to Leave," *CNN,* June 14, 2017.

53. Cora Lewis and Steven Perlberg, "Now This Forbids Staff from Taking Jobs at Other News Outlets," *Buzzfeed News,* June 9, 2017.

54. Alvin Chang, "Sinclair's Takeover of Local News, in One Striking Map," *Vox,* April 6, 2018.

55. Quoted in Jordyn Holman, Rebecca Greenfield, and Gerry Smith, "Sinclair Employees Say Their Contracts Make It Too Expensive to Quit," *Bloomberg,* April 3, 2018.

56. Stephanie Russell-Kraft, "I Learned the Hard Way Why Non-Competes Are Bad for Journalists," *Columbia Journalism Review,* June 16, 2017.

57. Evan Starr, J. J. Prescott, and Norman Bishara, "Noncompetes in the U.S. Labor Force," University of Michigan Law & Economics Research Paper No. 18-013, July 3, 2019.

58. Matt Marx, "The Firm Strikes Back: Non-compete Agreements and the Mobility of Technical Professionals," *American Sociological Review* 76 (2011): 695–712, 705.

59. Marx, "The Firm Strikes Back," 705.

60. Matissa N. Hollister and Kristin E. Smith, "Unmasking the Conflicting Trends in Job Tenure by Gender in the United States, 1983–2008," *American Sociological Review* 79 (2014): 159–181.

61. Steven Greenhouse, "Noncompete Clauses Increasingly Pop Up in Array of Jobs," *New York Times,* June 9, 2014.

62. Starr, Prescott, and Bishara, "Noncompetes in the U.S. Labor Force," Figure 2.

63. Quoted in Koby Levin, "As Noncompete Agreements Proliferate, So Do Lawsuits," *Joplin Globe,* March 17, 2018.

64. Levin, "As Noncompete Agreements Proliferate."

65. White House, "Non-Compete Agreements: Analysis of the Usage, Potential Issues, and State Responses," White House brief, Washington, DC, May 2016, 5. See also Starr, Prescott, and Bishara, "Noncompetes in the U.S. Labor Force."

66. White House, "Non-Compete Agreements."

67. Natarajan Balasubramanian, Jin Woo Chang, Mariko Sakakibara, Jagadeesh Sivadasan, and Evan Starr, "Locked In? The Enforceability of Covenants Not to Compete and the Careers of High-Tech Workers," US Census Bureau Center for Economic Studies Paper No. CES-WP-17-09, 2018.

68. Balasubramanian et al., "Locked In?"

69. Quoted in Marx, "The Firm Strikes Back," 706.

70. David Streitfeld, "Engineers Allege Hiring Collusion in Silicon Valley," *New York Times,* February 28, 2014.

71. Streitfeld, "Engineers Allege Hiring Collusion in Silicon Valley."

72. Dan Levine, "U.S. Judge Approves $415 Mln Settlement in Tech Worker Lawsuit," Reuters, September 2, 2015.

73. Rachel Abrams, "Why Aren't Paychecks Growing? A Burger-Joint Clause Offers a Clue," *New York Times,* September 27, 2017. See also Alan B. Krueger and Orley Ashenfelter, "Theory and Evidence on Employer Collusion in the Franchise Sector," NBER Working Paper 24831, 2018.

74. Krueger and Ashenfelter, "Theory and Evidence on Employer Collusion," Table 1b.

75. Rachel Abrams, "7 Fast Food Chains to End 'No Poach' Deals That Lock Down Low-Wage Workers," *New York Times,* July 12, 2018.

76. Abrams, "Why Aren't Paychecks Growing?"

77. Krueger and Ashenfelter, "Theory and Evidence on Employer Collusion," 21.

78. Wallace C. Murchison, "Significance of the American Tobacco Company Case," *North Carolina Law Review* 26 (1948): 130–172, 314.

79. Robert F. Durden, *The Dukes of Durham, 1865–1929* (Durham, NC: Duke University Press, 1975), 71.

80. Patrick G. Porter, "Origins of the American Tobacco Company," *Business History Review* 43 (1969): 59–76, 59–60.

81. To an extent, anyway. What had been a monopoly evolved into an oligopoly in which the few major firms dominating the tobacco market were still insulated from much competition. See Murchison, "Significance of the American Tobacco Company Case."

82. Quoted in Bryce Covert, "Does Monopoly Power Explain Workers' Stagnant Wages?" *The Nation,* February 15, 2018.

83. Covert, "Does Monopoly Power Explain Workers' Stagnant Wages?"

84. For an overview, see Suresh Naidu, Eric Posner, and Glen Weyl, "More and More Companies Have Monopoly Power over Workers' Wages. That's Killing the Economy," *Vox,* April 6, 2018.

85. Efraim Benmelech, Nittai Bergman, and Hyunseob Kim, "Strong Employers and Weak Employees: How Does Employer Concentration Affect Wages?" NBER Working Paper 24307, 2018.

86. José Azar, Ioana Marinescu, and Marshall I. Steinbaum, "Labor Market Concentration," NBER Working Paper 24147, 2017.

87. For a general discussion of the phenomenon, see Nathan Wilmers, "The Links between Stagnating Wages and Buyer Power in U.S. Supply Chains," Washington Center for Equitable Growth Report, May 22, 2018; and for technical details, see Nathan Wilmers, "Wage Stagnation and Buyer Power: How Buyer-Supplier Relations Affect Workers' Wages, 1978 to 2014," *American Sociological Review* 83 (2018): 213–242.

88. Murchison, "Significance of the American Tobacco Company Case."

89. Thomas J. Donohue, "Free Enterprise Is Key to Prosperity," In Your Corner blog, US Chamber of Commerce, August 10, 2015.

90. Alan B. Krueger, "The Rigged Labor Market," *Milken Institute Review*, April 28, 2017.

CHAPTER 4: MISMEASURING PERFORMANCE AND THE PITFALLS OF PAYING FOR MERIT

1. This discussion of Countrywide and its CEO draws extensively on Bruck's excellent 2009 profile. Connie Bruck, "Angelo's Ashes," *New Yorker,* June 29, 2009.

2. Alex Dobuzinskis, "Angelo Mozilo: From Housing Hero to Subprime Foe," Reuters, October 15, 2010.

3. "Past Executive Leadership Award Honorees," Innovate@UCLA (formerly IS Associates), https://isassociates.ucla.edu/pages/past-executive-leadership-award-honorees.

4. Mozilo's complete remarks were printed for distribution on the day: Angelo R. Mozilo, "The American Dream of Homeownership: From Cliché to Mission," Joint Center for Housing Studies, Harvard University, February 4, 2003, https://www.jchs.harvard.edu/sites/default/files/mo3-1_mozilo.pdf.

5. For complete details of the settlement, see Securities and Exchange Commission, "Former Countrywide CEO Angelo Mozilo to Pay SEC's Largest-Ever

Financial Penalty against a Public Company's Senior Executive," press release, October 15, 2010, https://www.sec.gov/news/press/2010/2010-197.htm.

6. Bruck, "Angelo's Ashes."

7. Quoted in Gretchen Morgenson, "Inside the Countrywide Lending Spree," *New York Times,* August 26, 2007.

8. In 2010, the Federal Trade Commission (FTC) levied a \$108 million fine on Countrywide for misleading homeowners and charging excessive fees. For details of the settlement, see Federal Trade Commission, "Countrywide Will Pay \$108 Million for Overcharging Struggling Homeowners; Loan Servicer Inflated Fees, Mishandled Loans of Borrowers in Bankruptcy," press release, June 7, 2010, https://www.ftc.gov/news-events/press-releases/2010/06/countrywide-will-pay-108-million-overcharging-struggling.

9. Amanda M. Fairbanks, "College Professor Rankings in Texas Spark National Debate," *Huffington Post,* April 7, 2011.

10. Fairbanks, "College Professor Rankings."

11. Matthew Bidwell, Forest Briscoe, Isabel Fernandez-Mateo, and Adina Sterling, "The Employment Relationship and Inequality: How and Why Changes in Employment Practices Are Reshaping Rewards in Organizations," *Academy of Management Annals* 7 (2013): 61–121, 68.

12. Maury Gittleman and Brooks Pierce, "How Prevalent is Performance-Related Pay in the United States? Current Incidence and Recent Trends," *National Institute Economic Review* 226 (2013): R4–R16.

13. Thomas Lemieux, W. Bentley MacLeod, and Daniel Parent, "Performance Pay and Wage Inequality," *Quarterly Journal of Economics* 124 (2009): 1–49, Table 1.

14. For the distributions in the years in which the GSS included the item, see "Eligible for Performance Based Pay," GSS Data Explorer, https://gssdataexplorer.norc.org/variables/2855/vshow.

15. My 2019 survey of pay-setters included a question about whether "performance is measured and rewarded at the individual level." The vast majority of respondents said yes, in contrast to the results found in the pay secrecy survey. How the pay-setters I interviewed interpreted this question and what fraction of worker compensation they based on individual performance re-

mains unclear. Given the small sample size and the preponderance of the academic evidence, including evidence from my much larger pay-secrecy survey, I interpret this result with caution.

16. Scott J. Adams, John S. Heywood, and Richard Rothstein, "Teachers, Performance Pay, and Accountability," Economic Policy Institute Series on Alternative Teacher Compensation Systems, No. 1, 2009, 14.

17. Adams, Heywood, and Rothstein, "Teachers, Performance Pay, and Accountability," 57.

18. Hamilton Nolan, "Time Inc. Rates Writers on How 'Beneficial' They Are to Advertisers," *Gawker,* August 18, 2014.

19. Mathew Ingram, "The Hiring Spreadsheet and the Clash at The Markup," *Columbia Journalism Review,* April 30, 2019.

20. In 2016, the outlet was forced into bankruptcy after a jury awarded $140 million in damages to Hulk Hogan after *Gawker* published a video of the ex-wrestler having sex. For the bizarre and lurid details see Timothy L. Lee, "Why Gawker is Shutting Down Next Week," *Vox,* August 18, 2016.

21. Quoted in Jonathan Mahler, "Gawker's Moment of Truth," *New York Times,* June 12, 2015.

22. Jerry Z. Muller, *The Tyranny of Metrics* (Princeton, NJ: Princeton University Press, 2018), 3.

23. Stephen Kerr, "On the Folly of Rewarding A, While Hoping for B," *Academic of Management Journal* 18 (1975): 769–783, 769.

24. Matt McGee, "Facebook's $5 Billion IPO, By the Numbers," *Marketing Land,* February 1, 2012. Also see Mariel Soto Reyes, "Scandals and Teen Dropoff Weren't Enough to Stop Facebook's Growth," *Business Insider,* April 26, 2019, for annual user data.

25. Jason Abbruzzese, "Facebook Hits 2.27 Billion Monthly Active Users as Earnings Stabilize," *NBC News,* October 30, 2018.

26. Nicholas Thompson and Fred Vogelstein, "15 Months of Fresh Hell Inside Facebook," *Wired,* April 16, 2019.

27. Quoted in Michael Lev-Ram, "Facebook's Employee Bonuses Now Hinge on 'Social' Progress," *Fortune,* February 5, 2019.

28. Clarence E. Ridley and Herbert A. Simon, *Measuring Municipal Activities: A Survey of Suggested Criteria and Reporting Forms for Appraising Administration* (Chicago: International City Manager's Association, 1938), ch. 1.

29. Rebecca Goldstein, Michael W. Sances, and Hye Young You, "Exploitative Revenues, Law Enforcement, and the Quality of Government Service," *Urban Affairs Review* 56 (2020): 5–31.

30. Executive Order 13688, "Federal Support for Local Law Enforcement Equipment Acquisition," was signed by President Obama on January 16, 2015

31. President's Task Force on 21st Century Policing, *Final Report of the President's Task Force on 21st Century Policing* (Washington, DC: Office of Community Oriented Policing Services, 2015), https://cops.usdoj.gov/pdf/taskforce /taskforce_finalreport.pdf.

32. Richard Rosenfeld, Thaddeus L. Johnson, and Richard Wright, "Are College-Educated Police Officers Different? A Study of Stops, Searches, and Arrests," *Criminal Justice Policy Review* 31 (2020): 206–236, 227.

33. Rosenfeld, Johnson, and Wright, "Are College-Educated Police Officers Different?," 206.

34. Rosenfeld, Johnson, and Wright, "Are College-Educated Police Officers Different?," 230.

35. Congressional Budget Office, "A Review of the Department of Defense's National Security Personnel System," CBO Paper, November 2008, Table 3-2.

36. John Stein Monroe, "Pay for Performance Haunted by NSPS Failure," *FCW,* October 29, 2009.

37. Quoted in Ezra Klein, "Work as Identity, Burnout as Lifestyle," *Ezra Klein Show* (podcast), April 22, 2019, https://podcasts.apple.com/us/podcast/work -as-identity-burnout-as-lifestyle/id1081584611?i=1000436045971.

38. Ferris Jabr, "The Truth about Dentistry," *The Atlantic,* May 2019.

39. Jeffrey Camm, "MyView: Creative Diagnosis," *ASA News,* October 21, 2013.

40. Robert Watts and Laura Donnelly, "Don't Leave Patients in Ambulances to Hit A&E Targets, Hospitals Told," *The Telegraph,* October 27, 2012.

41. Martin Roland and Frede Olesen, "Can Pay for Performance Improve the Quality of Primary Care?" *BMJ,* August 4, 2016.

42. Andreea Voinea-Griffin, D. Brad Rindal, Jeffrey L. Fellows, Andrei Barasch, Gregg H. Gilbert, and Monika M. Safford, "Pay-for-Performance in Dentistry: What We Know," *Journal for Healthcare Quality* 32 (2010): 51–58, 52.

43. Stephen B. Soumerai and Ross Koppel, "Paying Doctors Bonuses for Better Health Outcomes Makes Sense in Theory. But It Doesn't Work," *Vox,* January 25, 2017.

44. Chad Aldeman, "The Teacher Evaluation Revamp, in Hindsight," *Education Next* 17 (2017): 60–68, 62–63.

45. National Council on Teacher Quality, "2015 State Teacher Policy Yearbook National Summary," National Council on Teacher Quality Report, 2015, Figure F.

46. Daniel Weisberg, Susan Sexton, Jennifer Mulhern, and David Keeling, "The Widget Effect: Our National Failure to Acknowledge and Act on Differences in Teacher Effectiveness," The New Teacher Project Report, June 2009, 6.

47. Matthew A. Kraft and Allison F. Gilmour, "Revisiting *The Widget Effect:* Teacher Evaluation Reforms and the Distribution of Teacher Effectiveness," *Educational Researcher* 46 (2017): 234–249, 234.

48. United States Government Accountability Office, "K-12 Education: States' Test Security Policies and Procedures Varied," GAO 13-495R, May 16, 2013.

49. Jenny Jarvie, "Atlanta School Cheating Trial Has Teachers Facing Prison," *Los Angeles Times,* September 6, 2014.

50. Lisa Stark, "Prison Time Begins for Atlanta Educators Convicted in Cheating Scandal," *Education Week,* October 10, 2018.

51. Donald T. Campbell, "Assessing the Impact of Planned Social Change," *Evaluation and Program Planning* 2 (1979): 67–90, 85.

52. Muller, *The Tyranny of Metrics,* 19.

53. Quoted in Rachel Aviv, "Wrong Answer," *New Yorker,* July 14, 2014.

54. Quoted in Aviv, "Wrong Answer."

55. Quoted in Michele Martin, "Former Teacher Blames Education Policy-makers for Atlanta Cheating Scandal," *NPR,* February 16, 2016.

56. Ridley and Simon, *Measuring Municipal Activities,* 43.

57. Ridley and Simon, *Measuring Municipal Activities,* 45.

58. Ridley and Simon, *Measuring Municipal Activities,* 45.

59. Susanna Loeb and Christopher A. Candelaria, "How Stable Are Value-Added Estimates across Years, Subjects, and Student Groups?" Carnegie Foundation for the Advancement of Teaching Report, 2012; Richard J. Shavelson, Robert L. Linn, Eva L. Baker, Helen F. Ladd, Linda Darling-Hammond, Lorrie A. Shepard, Paul E. Barton, Edward Haertel, Diane Ravitch, and Richard Rothstein, "Problems with the Use of Student Test Scores to Evaluate Teachers," Economic Policy Institute Briefing Paper #278, August 27, 2010.

60. Jesse Rothstein, "Don't Be Too Quick to Embrace 'Value-Added' Assessments," *New York Times' Room for Debate,* January 13, 2012.

61. Raj Chetty and John N. Friedman, "The Value of Data in Teacher Evaluations," *New York Times' Room for Debate,* January 17, 2012.

62. Adam Grant and Jitendra Singh, "The Problem with Financial Incentives—and What to Do about It," *Knowledge@Wharton,* March 30, 2011.

63. Lauren A. Rivera and András Tilcsik, "Scaling Down Inequality: Rating Scales, Gender Bias, and the Architecture of Evaluation," *American Sociological Review* 84 (2019): 248–274, 248.

64. Rivera and Tilcsik, "Scaling Down Inequality."

65. Anne Bowers and Matteo Prato, "The Structural Origins of Unearned Status: How Arbitrary Changes in Categories Affect Status Position and Market Impact," *Administrative Science Quarterly* 63 (2018): 668–699.

66. Boris Groysberg, Paul M. Healy, and David A. Maber, "What Drives Sell-Side Analyst Compensation at High-Status Investment Banks?" *Journal of Accounting Research* 49 (2011): 969–1000.

67. For an overview, see Kevin Hallock, *Pay: Why People Earn What They Earn and What You Can Do Now to Make More* (Cambridge: Cambridge University Press, 2012), 117–118.

68. Kurt Eichenwald, "Microsoft's Lost Decade," *Vanity Fair,* August 2012.

69. Shira Ovide and Rachel Feintzeig, "Microsoft Abandons 'Stack Ranking' of Employees," *Wall Street Journal,* November 12, 2013.

70. For example, see Jonah E. Rockoff and Cecilia Speroni, "Subjective and Objective Evaluations of Teacher Effectiveness: Evidence from New York City," *Labour Economics* 18 (2011): 687–696.

71. Donald Tomaskovic-Devey and Dustin Avent-Holt, *Organizational Inequalities: A Relational Approach* (Oxford: Oxford University Press, 2019), 9.

72. Adams, Heywood, and Rothstein, "Teachers, Performance Pay, and Accountability," Table 12.

73. Vanessa O'Connell, "Retailers Reprogram Workers in Efficiency Push," *Wall Street Journal,* September 10, 2008.

74. O'Connell, "Retailers Reprogram Workers in Efficiency Push."

75. Quoted in Lydia DePillis, "The Under-the-Radar Profit-Maximizing Scheduling Practice That Can Put Workers in a 'Downward' Spiral," *Washington Post,* January 8, 2016.

76. Quoted in DePillis, "The Under-the-Radar Profit-Maximizing Scheduling Practice."

77. Noam Scheiber, "The Last Days of Big Law," *New Republic,* July 21, 2013.

78. Herbert H. Meyer, "The Pay-for-Performance Dilemma," *Organizational Dynamics* 3 (1975): 39–50, 45.

79. Scheiber, "The Last Days of Big Law."

80. Alexandre Mas and Enrico Moretti, "Peers at Work," *American Economic Review* 99 (2009): 112–145, 141.

81. Jeffrey Pfeffer, *The Human Equation: Building Profits by Putting People First* (Boston: Harvard Business School Press, 1998).

82. For evidence of managerial effects on subordinates' output, see Edward P. Lazear, Kathryn L. Shaw, and Christopher T. Stanton, "The Value of Bosses," *Journal of Labor Economics* 33 (2015): 823–861.

83. Michael B. Dorff, *Indispensible and Other Myths: Why the CEO Pay Experiment Failed and How to Fix It* (Berkeley: University of California Press, 2014), 126.

84. Charlie O. Trevor, Greg Reilly, and Barry Gerhart, "Reconsidering Pay Dispersion's Effect on the Performance of Interdependent Work: Reconciling Sorting and Pay Inequality," *Academy of Management Journal* 55 (2012): 585–610.

85. Edward P. Lazear, "Performance Pay and Productivity," *American Economic Review* 90 (2000): 1346–1361.

86. Jason D. Shaw, "Pay Dispersion," *Annual Review of Organizational Psychology and Organizational Behavior* 1 (2014): 521–544, 537.

87. Jed DeVaro and John S. Heywood, "Performance Pay and Work-Related Health Problems: A Longitudinal Study of Establishments," *ILR Review* 70 (2017): 670–703.

88. Jed DeVaro and John Pencavel, "Working Hours, Health and Absenteeism, and Performance Pay," paper presented at the Allied Social Sciences Association Annual Meeting, January 2020.

89. Benjamin Artz, Colin P. Green, and John S. Heywood, "Does Performance Pay Increase Alcohol and Drug Use?" paper presented at the Allied Social Sciences Association Annual Meeting, January 2020.

CHAPTER 5: THE BOSSES' BOSS

1. Nelson Lichtenstein, *The Retail Revolution: How Wal-Mart Created a Brave New World of Business* (New York: New Press, 2006; New York: Picador, 2010), 117–119.

2. Arindrajit Dube, T. William Lester, and Barry Eidlin, "Firm Entry and Wages: Impact of Wal-Mart Growth on Earnings throughout the Retail Sector," Institute of Industrial Relations Working Paper No. iirwps-126-05, 2007.

3. Charles Fishman, "The Wal-Mart You Don't Know," *Fast Company,* December 1, 2003.

4. Hedrick Smith and Rick Young, "Is Wal-Mart Good for America? Interview with Gary Gereffi," *Frontline*, September 9, 2004.

5. Abigail Goldman and Nancy Cleeland, "An Empire Built on Bargains Remakes the Working World," *Los Angeles Times,* November 23, 2003.

6. Nandita Bose, "Exclusive: Wal-Mart Launches New Front in U.S. Price War, Targets Aldi in Grocery Aisle," Reuters, February 26, 2017.

7. Nandita Bose, "Exclusive: Target Increases Minimum Wage to $10 an Hour," *Reuters*, April 18, 2016.

8. Sruthi Ramakrishnan and Nathan Layne, "Wal-Mart, Under Pressure, Boosts Minimum U.S. Wage to $9 an Hour," Reuters, February 19, 2015.

9. Matthew Yglesias, "American Airlines Gave Its Workers a Raise. Wall Street Freaked Out," *Vox,* April 29, 2017.

10. Mary Schlangenstein, "Airline Stocks Plunge after American's 'Worrying Precedent' on Pay," *Bloomberg,* April 27, 2017; "American Airlines Announces Pay Raises, and Investors Balk," *Associated Press*, April 27, 2017.

11. Steven Pearlstein, "When Shareholder Capitalism Came to Town," *American Prospect,* April 19, 2014. Given this chapter's focus on shareholder value, it should be noted that about a third of US (non-farm) private sector workers are employed by publicly-traded firms. See David R. Francis, "Changing Business Volatility," National Bureau of Economic Research Digest, April 2007. Private companies may also imitate pay-setting practices of publicly-traded firms.

12. For an illuminating exploration of the connections between financial capitalism and rising inequality, see Ken-Hou Lin and Megan Tobias Neely, *Divested: Inequality in the Age of Finance* (Oxford: Oxford University Press, 2020).

13. Ann Zimmerman, "Costco's Dilemma: Be Kind to Its Workers, or Wall Street?" *Wall Street Journal,* March 26, 2004.

14. Steven Greenhouse, "How Costco Became the Anti-Wal-Mart," *New York Times,* July 17, 2005.

15. Rosemary Batt and Eileen Appelbaum, "Investors as Managers: How Private Equity Firms Manage Labor and Employment Relations," in *Inequality, Uncertainty, and Opportunity: The Varied and Growing Role of Finance in Labor Relations,* ed. Christian E. Weller (Champaign, IL: Labor and Employment Relations Association, 2015), 199; see also Lynn Stout, *The Shareholder Value Myth* (San Francisco: Berrett-Koehler, 2012).

16. James C. Worthy, *Shaping an American Institution: Robert E. Wood and Sears, Roebuck* (Champaign: University of Illinois Press, 1984), 64.

17. Milton Friedman, "The Social Responsibility of Business Is to Increase Its Profits," *New York Times Magazine,* September 13, 1970.

18. Steven Pearlstein, "When Shareholder Capitalism Came to Town."

19. Nelson D. Schwartz, "How Wall Street Bent Steel," *New York Times,* December 7, 2014.

20. Quoted in Mark Wilming, "Hostile Takeovers Are the Dark Side of Capitalism," *Risk Magazine,* March 28, 2017. Other CEOs at firms ranging from meat packager Tyson to device maker Perceptron also saw their tenures cut short after missing estimates. See "Tyson Foods Says CEO Will Step Down at End of Year," *Associated Press*, November 21, 2016, and Dustin Walsh, "Perceptron Inc. CEO Resigns," *Crain's Detroit Business*, November 12, 2019.

21. David Dayen, "Unfriendly Skies," *American Prospect,* Fall 2017.

22. Often in name only, as many firms grew fat and mean with bloated managerial staff overseeing a shrunken non-managerial workforce suffering through wage and benefit cuts. See Adam Goldstein, "Revenge of the Managers: Labor Cost-Cutting and the Paradoxical Resurgence of Managerialism in the Shareholder Value Era, 1984 to 2001," *American Sociological Review* 77 (2012): 268–294; David M. Gordon, *Fat and Mean: The Corporate Squeeze of Working Americans and the Myth of Managerial "Downsizing"* (New York: Free Press, 1996).

23. For the definitive treatment on fissuring in US firms, see David Weil, *The Fissured Workplace: Why Work Became So Bad for So Many and What Can Be Done to Improve It* (Cambridge, MA: Harvard University Press, 2014).

24. Weil, *The Fissured Workplace,* 74–75.

25. Much of the following discussion about Timken Company is drawn from Nelson Schwartz's 2014 investigation of the firm.

26. Quoted in Schwartz, "How Wall Street Bent Steel," 2014.

27. Quoted in Carleton English, "What is Happening at TimkenSteel?" *TheStreet,* January 12, 2016.

28. Quoted in Schwartz, "How Wall Street Bent Steel." For more on the cross-pressures many Americans now face in their roles as workers and investors, see Michael McCarthy, *Dismantling Solidarity: Capitalist Politics and American Pensions since the New Deal* (Ithaca, NY: Cornell University Press, 2017).

29. Quoted in "Remember When Companies Actually Created Products?" editorial, *Wall Street Journal,* September 18, 1997.

30. Pearlstein, "When Shareholder Capitalism Came to Town."

31. Stout, *The Shareholder Value Myth,* 4.

32. Business Roundtable, "Business Roundtable Redefines the Purpose of a Corporation to Promote 'An Economy That Serves All Americans,'" press release, August 19, 2019, https://www.businessroundtable.org/business -roundtable-redefines-the-purpose-of-a-corporation-to-promote-an -economy-that-serves-all-americans.

33. Rick Wartzman, interview and email with author, April 2, 2018, and March 3, 2020.

34. Quoted in Faye Rice, Stratford P. Sherman, Brian O'Reilly, Brian Dumaine, Sarah Smith, and Patricia Sellers, "Leaders of the Most Admired," *Fortune,* January 29, 1990.

35. Quoted in Schwartz, "How Wall Street Bent Steel."

36. Constance L. Hays, *The Real Thing: Truth and Power at the Coca-Cola Company* (New York: Random House, 2005), 67.

37. Frank Dobbin and Jiwook Jung, "The Misapplication of Mr. Michael Jensen: How Agency Theory Brought Down the Economy and Why It Might Again," *Research in the Sociology of Organizations* 30B (2010): 29–64, 30.

38. With some notable exceptions, such as Division I NCAA basketball and football coaches, who can earn multiples more than their titular boss, the university president.

39. Rick Wartzman, *The End of Loyalty* (New York: Public Affairs, 2017), 275.

40. Lawrence Mishel and Jessica Schieder, "CEO Pay Remains High Relative to the Pay of Typical Workers and High-Wage Earners," Economic Policy Institute Report, July 20, 2017, Figure B.

41. Nikole Hannah-Jones, "Living Apart: How the Government Betrayed a Landmark Civil Rights Law," *ProPublica,* October 29, 2012.

42. T. George Harris, *Romney's Way: A Man and an Idea* (New York: Prentice-Hall, 1968), 186.

43. David Leonhardt, "When the Rich Said No to Getting Richer," *New York Times,* September 4, 2017.

44. Harris, *Romney's Way,* 186.

45. Batt and Appelbaum, "Investors as Managers," 198–199.

46. Robert Gavin and Sacha Pfeiffer, "The Making of Mitt Romney: Reaping Profit in Study, Sweat," *Boston Globe,* June 26, 2007.

47. Gavin and Pfeiffer, "The Making of Mitt Romney," 2007.

48. Matt Viser, "Romney Worth between $190m and $250m, Campaign Says," *Boston Globe,* August 13, 2011.

49. Sorapop Kiatpongsan and Michael I. Norton, "How Much (More) Should CEOs Make? A Universal Desire for More Equal Pay," *Perspectives on Psychological Science* 9 (2014): 587–593, 587.

50. David F. Larcker, Nicholas E. Donatiello, and Brian Tayan, "Americans and CEO Pay: 2016 Public Perception Survey on CEO Compensation," CGRI Survey Series, February 2016.

51. Quoted in Rebecca Kaplan, "Donald Trump on CEO Pay: It's a 'Complete Joke,'" *CBS News,* September 13, 2015.

52. Natascha Van der Zwan, "Making Sense of Financialization," *Socio-Economic Review* 12 (2014): 99–129, 109. Lower top marginal tax rates also contributed to higher pretax earnings for CEOs, an issue we'll explore in Chapter 9. See Thomas Piketty, Emmanuel Saez, and Stephanie Stantcheva, "Optimal Taxation of Top Labor Incomes: A Tale of Three Elasticities," *American Economic Journal: Economy Policy* 6 (2014): 230–271.

53. Zoe Chase, "How Mitt Romney's Firm Tried—And Failed—To Build a Paper Empire," *NPR,* February 23, 2012; Benjamin Wallace-Wells, "The Romney Economy," *New York Magazine,* October 23, 2011.

54. Quoted in Robert Gavin, "As Bain Slashed Jobs, Romney Stayed to Side," *Boston Globe,* January 27, 2008.

55. Peer C. Fiss, Mark T. Kennedy, and Gerald F. Davis, "How Golden Parachutes Unfolded: Diffusion and Variation of a Controversial Practice," *Organization Science* 23 (2012): 1077–1099.

56. Laura M. Holson, "Ruling Upholds Disney's Payment in Firing of Ovitz," *New York Times,* August 10, 2005.

57. Steven J. Davis, John Haltiwanger, Kyle Handley, Ron Jarmin, Josh Lerner, and Javier Miranda, "Private Equity, Jobs, and Productivity," *American Economic Review* 104 (2014): 3956–3990, 3958.

58. Marianne Bertrand and Sendhil Mullainathan, "Enjoying the Quiet Life? Corporate Governance and Managerial Preferences," *Journal of Political Economy* 111 (2003): 1043–1075; see also J. Adam Cobb, "How Firms Shape Income Inequality: Stakeholder Power, Executive Decision Making, and the Structuring of Employment Relationships," *Academy of Management Review* 41 (2016): 324–348.

59. Robert J. Shapiro and Nam D. Pham, "American Jobs and the Impact of Private Equity Transactions," Sonecon, January 2008, 1.

60. Private Equity Growth Capital Council, "2013 Annual Report," Private Equity Growth Capital Council Report, January 31, 2014.

61. Donald Tomaskovic-Devey and Dustin Avent-Holt, *Organizational Inequalities: A Relational Approach* (Oxford: Oxford University Press, 2019), 216.

62. Ken-Hou Lin and Donald Tomaskovic-Devey, "Financialization and U.S. Income Inequality, 1970–2008," *American Journal of Sociology* 118 (2013): 1284–1329, 1286.

63. Lin and Tomaskovic-Devey, "Financialization and U.S. Income Inequality," 1313.

64. Neil Fligstein and Taekjin Shin, "Shareholder Value and the Transformation of the U.S. Economy, 1984–2000," *Sociological Forum* 22 (2007): 399–424.

65. Fligstein and Shin, "Shareholder Value and the Transformation of the U.S. Economy," 416–417.

66. Fligstein and Shin, "Shareholder Value and the Transformation of the U.S. Economy," 420.

67. David Dayen, "Unfriendly Skies."

68. For competing estimates, see David B. Richards, "Did Passenger Fare Savings Occur after Airline Deregulation?" *Transportation Research Forum* 46 (2007): 73–93; and Derek Thompson, "How Airline Ticket Prices Fell 50% in 30 Years (and Why Nobody Noticed)," *The Atlantic,* February 28, 2013.

69. Pierre-Eves Cremieux, "The Effect of Deregulation on Employee Earnings: Pilots, Flight Attendants and Mechanics, 1959–1992," *ILR Review* 49 (1996): 223–242.

70. Dayen, "Unfriendly Skies."

71. Dayen, "Unfriendly Skies."

72. For the complete note, see Goldman Sachs, "Does Consolidation Create Value?" Tactical Research report, February 12, 2014, https://www.document cloud.org/documents/3124001-Goldman-merger-analysis.html.

73. Bryce Covert, "Does Monopoly Power Explain Workers' Stagnant Wages?" *The Nation,* February 15, 2018.

74. E. M. Beck and Lee Watson, "Oligopoly Capitalism, Labor Organization, and Wages of Workers in American Manufacturing Industries," *Sociological Quarterly* 29 (1988): 83–95.

75. Dan Merica, "Trump Signs Tax Bill before Leaving for Mar-A-Largo," *CNN.com,* December 22, 2017.

76. Matt Phillips, "Trump's Tax Cuts in Hand, Companies Spend More on Themselves Than on Wages," *New York Times,* February 27, 2018.

77. Nick Wells, Helen Zhao, and Fred Imbert, "These Companies Are Paying Bonuses with Their Tax Savings," *CNBC.com,* January 26, 2018.

78. It is also a decision American Airlines didn't make quickly, waiting until after competitor Southwest Airlines announced its bonuses before moving. Parker's entire letter is contained in American Airlines, "American Airlines to Distribute $1,000 to Each Team Member," news release, January 2, 2018, http://s21.q4cdn.com/616071541/files/doc_news/American-Airlines -to-distribute-1000-to-each-team-member.pdf.

79. Rick Wartzman and William Lazonick, "Don't Let Pay Increases Coming Out of Tax Reform Fool You," *Washington Post,* February 6, 2018.

80. William Lazonick, "To Boost Investment, End S.E.C. Rule That Spurs Stock Buybacks," *New York Times,* March 6, 2015.

81. Edward T. Zajac and James D. Westphal, "The Social Construction of Market Value: Institutionalization and Learning Perspectives on Stock Market Re-actions," *American Sociological Review* 69 (2004): 433–457, Figure 1.

82. Zajac and Westphal, "The Social Construction of Market Value."

83. William Lazonick and Mary O'Sullivan, "Maximizing Shareholder Value: A New Ideology for Corporate Governance," *Economy and Society* 29 (2000): 13–35, Figure 4.

84. Josh Eidelson, "Unions Squeeze Companies to Divulge Plans for Tax Bill Windfall," *Bloomberg,* April 4, 2018.

85. Zachs Equity Research, "American Airlines (AAL) Surges 22% in 6 Months: Here's Why," *Nasdaw.com,* March 15, 2018.

86. Phillips, "Trump's Tax Cuts in Hand."

87. "Well-Heeled Investors Reap the Republican Tax Cut Bonanza," editorial, *New York Times,* February 25, 2018.

88. Hayley Peterson, "Sears' CEO Blames the Media for Company's Decline— But His Obsession with Wall Street Set It Up for Failure," *Business Insider,* May 21, 2017.

89. Peterson, "Sears' CEO Blames the Media."

90. Peterson, "Sears' CEO Blames the Media."

91. Andria Cheng, "Walmart's Fight against Amazon Is Picking Up Steam," *Forbes,* November 15, 2018.

92. For Walmart's 2018 revenues, see Walmart 2018 Annual Report, https://s2 .q4cdn.com/056532643/files/doc_financials/2018/annual/WMT-2018 _Annual-Report.pdf. For country GDP figures, see "World Economic Outlook: Challenges to Steady Growth," International Monetary Fund, Washington, DC, October 2018.

CHAPTER 6: WHEN GOOD JOBS GO BAD

1. See Drew DeSilver, "The Polarized Congress of Today Has Its Roots in the 1970s," Pew Research Center, June 12, 2014.

2. John Kerry, "Kerry: We Are Here to Make America Stronger," transcript of July 30, 2004 speech,https://www.cnn.com/2004/ALLPOLITICS/07/30 /dems.kerry.transcript.4/index.html.

3. John McCain, "Remarks on Day Two of the 'Time for Action Tour' at Youngstown State University, in Youngstown, Ohio," April 22, 2008, available at Gerhard Peters and John T. Woolley, *The American Presidency Project,* University of California Santa Barbara, http://www.presidency.ucsb.edu/ws /index.php?pid=77138..

4. Barack Obama, "Remarks by the President in the State of the Union Address," February 12, 2013, https://obamawhitehouse.archives.gov/the-press -office/2013/02/12/remarks-president-state-union-address.

5. Donald Trump, "Remarks Introducing Governor Mike Pence as the 2016 Republican Vice Presidential Nominee in New York City," July 16, 2016, The American Presidency Project https://www.presidency.ucsb.edu/documents /remarks-introducing-governor-mike-pence-the-2016-republican-vice -presidential-nominee-new.

6. Donald Trump, "Remarks by President Trump in Meeting with Manufacturing CEOs," February 23, 2017, https://www.whitehouse.gov/briefings -statements/remarks-president-trump-meeting-manufacturing-ceos/.

7. Craig A. Giffi and Jennifer McNelly, "Leadership Wanted: U.S. Public Opinions on Manufacturing," Deloitte Development LLC and the Manufacturing Institute, 2012.

8. "Why Old-Fashioned Manufacturing Jobs Won't Return to the West," *Economist,* January 20, 2017.

9. Thomas Sugrue, "From Motor City to Motor Metropolis: How the Automobile Industry Reshaped Urban America," *Automobile in American Life and Society* (Detroit: Henry Ford Museum and University of Michigan, 2005).

10. Paul Lewis, "Pain, Anger, and Fear: US Voters Deprived of a Serious Presidential Election," *The Guardian,* November 4, 2016.

11. Employment trends provided by the Current Employment Statistics: https://www.bls.gov/ces/. For mining employment totals, see series CES102120000. For coal mining, see series CES102121000.

12. Current Employment Statistics, series CES3133100006.

13. Leonard S. Silk, "Economic Analysis: Blue-Collar Blues," *New York Times,* September 9, 1970.

14. Agis Salpukas, "Workers Increasingly Rebel against Boredom on Assembly Line," *New York Times,* April 2, 1972.

15. Campbell Gibson and Kay Jung, "Historical Census Statistics on Population Totals by Race, 1790 to 1990, and by Hispanic Origin, 1970 to 1990, for Large Cities and Other Urban Places in the United States," US Census Bureau Population Division Working Paper No. 76, February, 2005, Table 23.

16. Catherine Ruckelshaus and Sarah Leberstein, "Manufacturing Low Pay: Declining Wages in the Jobs That Built America's Middle Class," National Employment Law Project Report, 2014, 9–10.

17. Lawrence Mishel, "Yes, Manufacturing Still Provides a Pay Advantage, but Staffing Firm Outsourcing Is Eroding It," Economic Policy Institute Report, March 12, 2018, Table 3.

18. Paul S. Davies, "Factors Influencing Employment in the U.S. Automobile Industry," *Park Place Economist* 1 (1993): 41–57, Figure 1.

19. Christopher J. Singleton, "Auto Industry Jobs in the 1980's: A Decade of Transition," *Monthly Labor Review,* February 1992, Table 1.

20. Robert E, Scott, "The Status of the Steel Industry and U.S. Manufacturing," Testimony before the Congressional Steel Caucus, June 16, 2009, Figure 2.

21. For more, see Federal Reserve Bank of St. Louis, Economic Research, "Manufacturing Sector: Real Output," https://fred.stlouisfed.org/series/OUTMS#0.

22. For goods-producing employment numbers, see Current Employment Statistics series CES0600000001. For total nonfarm employment numbers, see Current Employment Statistics series CES0000000001.

23. David H. Autor, David Dorn, Gordon H. Hanson, and Jae Song, "Trade Adjustment: Worker-Level Evidence," *Quarterly Journal of Economics* 129 (2014): 1799–1860.

24. Claire Cain Miller, "The Long-Term Jobs Killer Is Not China. It's Automation," *New York Times,* December 21, 2016.

25. Michael J. Hicks and Srikant Devaraj, "The Myth and the Reality of Manufacturing in America," Center for Business and Economic Research, Ball State University, June 2015.

26. Allan Collard-Wexler and Jan De Loecker, "Reallocation and Technology: Evidence from the US Steel Industry," *American Economic Review* 105 (2015): 131–171.

27. Paul Wiseman, "As Trump Weighs Tariff, US Steelmakers Enjoy Rising Profits," Associated Press, March 13, 2018.

28. Quoted in Miller, "The Long-Term Jobs Killer Is Not China."

29. Nelson Lichtenstein, *State of the Union: A Century of American Labor* (Princeton, NJ: Princeton University Press, 2002), 79.

30. Alisa Priddle, "Ford Adding 850 Jobs at Dearborn F-150 Plant," *Detroit Free Press,* October 13, 2014.

31. Bureau of Labor Statistics (BLS) State and Area Employment, Hours, and Earnings Series SMU26000003133610001.

32. Justin Fox, "Farewell to the Blue-Collar Elite," *Bloomberg,* April 6, 2015.

33. Barack Obama, "Remarks of President Barack Obama—State of the Union Address as Delivered," January 13, 2016, https://obamawhitehouse.archives .gov/the-press-office/2016/01/12/remarks-president-barack-obama -%E2%80%93-prepared-delivery-state-union-address.

34. Donald Trump, "Remarks by President Trump, Vice President Pence, Members of Congress, and Members of the Cabinet in Meeting on Trade," February 13, 2018, https://www.whitehouse.gov/briefings-statements/remarks -president-trump-vice-president-pence-members-congress-members -cabinet-meeting-trade/.

35. Eric D. Lawrence, "GM Moving Jobs from Korea to Detroit? Trump's Claims Don't Hold Up," *Detroit Free Press,* February 14, 2018.

36. Michael B. Sauter and Samuel Stebbins, "Manufacturers Bringing the Most Jobs Back to America," *USA Today,* April 23, 2016.

37. Autor et al., "Trade Adjustment: Worker-Level Evidence."

38. Brad Plumer, "Is U.S. Manufacturing Making a Comeback—Or Is It Just Hype?" *Washington Post,* May 1, 2013.

39. Steve Johnson, "Chinese Wages Now Higher Than in Brazil, Argentina and Mexico," *Financial Times,* February 26, 2017.

40. Plumer, "Is U.S. Manufacturing Making a Comeback."

41. Boston Consulting Group, "Made in America, Again: Fourth Annual Survey of U.S.-Based Manufacturing Executives," Boston Consulting Group, December, 2015.

42. Timothy Aeppel, "Where Manufacturing Jobs Are Plentiful, Trump's Supporters Want Better," *Reuters,* June 20, 2017.

43. Aeppel, "Where Manufacturing Jobs Are Plentiful."

44. Quoted in Aeppel, "Where Manufacturing Jobs Are Plentiful."

45. Quoted in Aeppel, "Where Manufacturing Jobs Are Plentiful."

46. Joyce Shaw Peterson, "Auto Workers and Their Work, 1900–1933," *Labor History* 22 (1981), 213–236 228.

47. Peterson, "Auto Workers and Their Work," 229.

48. Lizabeth Cohen, *Making a New Deal: Industrial Workers in Chicago, 1919–1939,* 2nd ed. (Cambridge: Cambridge University Press, 2014), 317.

49. Ruckelshaus and Leberstein, "Manufacturing Low Pay."

50. Peter Waldman, "Inside Alabama's Auto Jobs Boom: Cheap Wages, Little Training, Crushed Limbs," *Bloomberg Businessweek,* March 23, 2017. The following discussion of Matsu and Reco Allen draws from Waldman's detailed exposé.

51. Waldman, "Inside Alabama's Auto Jobs Boom."

52. Waldman, "Inside Alabama's Auto Jobs Boom."

53. Waldman, "Inside Alabama's Auto Jobs Boom."

54. Athens Banner-Herald Editorial Board, "Nakanishi in Athens Expanding, Adding Jobs," *Athens Banner-Herald,* February 6, 2016.

55. Ken Jacobs, Zohar Perla, Ian Perry, and Dave Graham-Squire, "Producing Poverty: The Public Cost of Low-Wage Production Jobs in Manufacturing," UC Berkeley Center for Labor Research and Education Research Brief, May 2016, 1.

56. Jacobs et al., "Producing Poverty," 9.

57. For an exploration of how reclassification is changing the nature of work, see Danny Vinik, "The Real Future of Work," *Politico Magazine,* January / February 2018; for the academic underpinnings of this process, see David Weil, *The Fissured Workplace: Why Work Became So Bad for So Many and What Can Be Done to Improve It* (Cambridge, MA: Harvard University Press, 2014).

58. Zach Parolin, "Organized Labor and the Employment Trajectories of Workers in Routine Jobs: Evidence from U.S. Panel Data," Brookings Institution Report, January 2020.

59. Peter S. Goodman, "A City as a Basic-Income Test Lab," *New York Times,* June 3, 2018.

60. Quoted in Dale Kasler and Mark Glover, "Tesla Bringing Plant to Central Valley, but It's Not the Big One," *Sacramento Bee,* April 22, 2014.

61. Quoted in Nathan Donato-Weinstein, "Tesla to Open Facility in Central Valley and Evidence Points to Manufacturing Hub," *Silicon Valley Business Journal,* April 22, 2014.

62. Quoted in Pui-Wing Tam, "Idle Fremont Plant Gears Up for Tesla," *Wall Street Journal,* October 21, 2010.

63. For more details on the facility, see "Tesla Factory," Tesla website, https://www.tesla.com/factory.

64. David Dayen, "Charge Time: Electric Car Workers Accuse Tesla of Low Pay and Intimidation," *American Prospect,* April 10, 2017.

65. Sergei Klebnikov, "8 Innovative Ways Elon Musk Made Money before He Was a Billionaire," *Money,* August 8, 2017.

66. For the full breakdown of greenhouse gas emission sources, see United States Environmental Protection Agency, "Sources of Greenhouse Gas Emissions," EPA website,https://www.epa.gov/ghgemissions/sources -greenhouse-gas-emissions.

67. Elon Musk, "Making Humans a Multi-Planetary Species," *New Space* 5 (2017): 46–61.

68. Samantha Masunaga, "A Quick Guide to Elon Musk's New Brain-Implant Company Neuralink," *Los Angeles Times,* April 21, 2017.

69. Salvador Rodriguez, "Worker Testifies That Tesla Stopped Him from Organizing Union," Reuters, June 11, 2018.

70. Ryan Felton, "Elon Musk Told Workers Tesla 'Would Allow' Them To Unionize If He Couldn't Make Them Safe: NLRB," *Jalopnik,* July 12, 2018.

71. For the complete email, see Caroline O'Donovan, "Elon Musk Slams Tesla Union Drive, Promises Workers Free Frozen Yogurt," *BuzzFeed News,* February 24, 2017. Musk has argued that Tesla's lower wages should be considered alongside the stock it grants to employees, but it is hard to assess "How much stock is meted out, to whom, and after how many years of employment." Bryan Menegus, "Elon Musk Responds to Claims of Low Pay, Injuries, and Anti-Union Policies at Tesla Plant," *Gizmodo,* February 9, 2017.

72. For a canonical statement, see Richard B. Freeman and James L. Medoff, *What Do Unions Do?* (New York: Basic Books, 1984). For an updated investigation into the consequences of union decline for our economy and polity, see Jake Rosenfeld, *What Unions No Longer Do* (Cambridge, MA: Harvard University Press, 2014).

73. For an overview of explanations for union decline in the United States, see Rosenfeld, *What Unions No Longer Do,* ch. 1.

74. Mark Barenberg, "Widening the Scope of Worker Organizing: Legal Reforms to Facilitate Multi-Employer Organizing, Bargaining, and Striking," Roosevelt Institute Report, October 7, 2015.

75. Henry S. Farber, Daniel Herbst, Ilyana Kuziemko, and Suresh Naidu, "Unions and Inequality over the Twentieth Century: New Evidence from Survey Data," NBER Working Paper 24587, 2018.

76. John Raisian, "Union Dues and Wage Premiums," *Journal of Labor Research* 4 (1983): 1–18; Leo Troy, "American Unions and Their Wealth," *Industrial Relations* 14 (1975): 134–144, 141.

77. Patrick Denice and Jake Rosenfeld, "Unions and Nonunion Pay in the United States, 1977–2015," *Sociological Science* 5 (2018): 541–561; Nicole M. Fortin, Thomas Lemieux, and Neil Lloyd, "Labor Market Institutions and the Distribution of Wages: The Role of Spillover Effects," paper presented at the University of Michigan, September 2018; Jake Rosenfeld, Patrick Denice, and Jennifer Laird, "Union Decline Lowers Wages of Nonunion Workers," Economic Policy Institute Report, August 30, 2016.

78. Rich Yeselson, "Not with a Bang, but a Whimper: The Long, Slow Death Spiral of America's Labor Movement," *The New Republic,* June 6, 2012.

79. This section draws from the depiction of temp workers at the Georgetown, Kentucky, Toyota plant: Jonathan Weisman, "Permanent Job Proves an Elusive Dream," *Washington Post,* October 11, 2004.

80. Erin Hatton, "The Making of the Kelly Girl: Gender and the Origins of the Temp Industry in Postwar America," *Journal of Historical Sociology* 21 (2008): 1–29, 7.

81. Erin Hatton, *The Temp Economy: From Kelly Girls to Permatemps in Postwar America* (Philadelphia: Temple University Press, 2011), 21.

82. Hatton, *The Temp Economy,* 7.

83. "Manpower, Inc., Stresses Brawn," *New York Times,* September 20, 1962.

84. Matthew Dey, Susan H. Houseman, and Anne E. Polivka, "Manufacturers' Outsourcing to Staffing Services," *ILR Review* 65 (2012): 533–559, 536.

85. Dey, Houseman, and Polivka, "Manufacturers' Outsourcing to Staffing Services," 548–549.

86. Sarah Jaffe, "Forever Temp?" *In These Times,* January 6, 2014.

87. Quoted in Janice Castro, "Disposable Workers," *Time Magazine,* March 29, 1993.

88. Hatton, *The Temp Economy,* 9.

89. Quoted in Weisman, "Permanent Job Proves an Elusive Dream."

90. Weil, *The Fissured Workplace,* 90.

91. Quoted in Kate Bronfenbrenner, "We'll Close! Plant Closings, Plant-Closing Threats, Union Organizing and NAFTA," *Multinational Monitor* 18 (1997): 8–14, 9–10.

92. Bronfenbrenner, "We'll Close!" 12.

93. Quoted in Trip Gabriel, "Alone on the Open Road: Truckers Feel Like 'Throwaway People,'" *New York Times,* May 22, 2017.

94. Steve Viscelli, *The Big Rig: Trucking and the Decline of the American Dream* (Berkeley: University of California Press, 2016).

95. Charles R. Perry, *Deregulation and the Decline of the Unionized Trucking Industry* (Philadelphia: Industrial Research Unit, Wharton School, University of Pennsylvania, 1986), Table V-1.

96. See Ifeoma Ajunwa, Kate Crawford, and Jason Schultz, "Limitless Worker Surveillance," *California Law Review* 105 (2017): 735–776.

97. Ajunwa, Crawford, and Shultz, "Limitless Worker Surveillance," 735.

98. Dale E. Belman and Kristen A. Monaco, "The Effects of Deregulation, De-Unionization, Technology, and Human Capital on the Work and Work Lives of Truck Drivers," *ILR Review* 54 (2001): 502–524.

99. Rachel Premack, "Truck Drivers' Salaries are Experiencing an 'Unprecedented' Jump, But It's Not Enough to End the Driver Shortage That's Making Everything More Expensive," *Business Insider,* August 4, 2018.

100. Viscelli, *The Big Rig,* 210.

101. Steve Viscelli, email to author, June 1, 2018.

102. Steve Viscelli, email, June 1, 2018.

103. Steve Viscelli, email, June 1, 2018.

104. Ruth Milkman, "Putting Wages Back into Competition: Deunionization and Degradation in Place-Bound Industries," in *The Gloves-Off Economy: Problems and Possibilities at the Bottom of America's Labor Market,* ed. Annette

Bernhardt, Heather Boushey, Laura Dresser, and Chris Tilly (Champaign: Labor and Employment Relations Association, University of Illinois, 2008), 67.

105. Carole Shifrin, "Bill to Deregulate Trucks Proposed," *Washington Post,* January 23, 1979.

106. Motor Carrier Act of 1980, *Jimmy Carter: 1980–81,* Book 2, Public Papers of the Presidents of the United States, 1265, https://quod.lib.umich.edu/p/ppotpus/4732203.1980.002/315?rgn=full+text;view=image.

107. Viscelli *The Big Rig,* 20–21.

108. Barry T. Hirsch, "Trucking Deregulation and Labor Earnings: Is the Union Premium a Compensating Differential?" *Journal of Labor Economics* 11 (1993): 279–301.

109. Steve Viscelli, email, June 1, 2018.

110. Viscelli, *The Big Rig,* 33.

111. Viscelli, *The Big Rig,* 121.

112. Lydia DePillis, "Deregulation Created an Industry Full of Independent Contractors, Who Have Freedom on a Shoestring," *Washington Post,* April 28, 2014.

113. Quoted in DePillis, "Deregulation Created an Industry Full of Independent Contractors."

114. DePillis, "Deregulation Created an Industry Full of Independent Contractors."

115. Author's calculations using Current Population Survey (CPS) data. See also Nicholas Kristof, "The Cost of a Decline in Unions," *New York Times,* February 19, 2015.

116. For employment projections among detailed occupations, see "Employment by Detailed Occupation," US Bureau of Labor Statistics, https://www.bls.gov/emp/tables/emp-by-detailed-occupation.htm.

117. Milkman, "Putting Wages Back into Competition," 68.

118. Steven G. Allen, "Unit Costs, Legal Shocks, and Unionization in Construction," *Journal of Labor Research* 16 (1995): 367–377.

119. For updated estimates, see Barry T. Hirsch and David A. Macpherson, "Union Membership and Coverage Database from the Current Population Survey: Note," *ILR Review* 56 (2003): 349–354; and Barry T. Hirsch and

David A. Macpherson, "Union Membership and Coverage Database," at www.unionstats.com.

120. Quoted in Milkman, "Putting Wages Back into Competition," 70.

121. For historical tables on housing and rental costs, see United States Census, "Housing Characteristics in the U.S.–Tables," https://www.census.gov/hhes /www/housing/census/histcensushsg.html.

122. Edward L. Glaeser, Joseph Gyourko, and Raven E. Saks, "Why Have Housing Prices Gone Up?" *American Economic Review* 95 (2005): 329–333.

123. Kevin Duncan and Russell Ormiston, "What Does the Research Tell Us about Prevailing Wage Laws?" *Labor Studies Journal* 44 (2019): 139–160.

CHAPTER 7: BAD JOBS CAN BE GOOD

1. For age breakdowns of various occupations, see "Labor Force Statistics from the Current Population Survey," US Bureau of Labor Statistics, https://www .bls.gov/cps/cpsaat11b.htm. "Retail salespersons" is the detailed occupation with a median age of thirty-six and "Combined food preparation and serving workers, including fast food" is the detailed occupation with a median age of twenty-six.

2. See "Employment Projections," US Bureau of Labor Statistics, https://data .bls.gov/projections/occupationProj.

3. As of May 2018, there were nearly 232,000 "Meat, poultry, and fish cutters and trimmers" and "Slaughterers and meat packers."

4. Françoise Carré and Chris Tilly, *Where Bad Jobs Are Better: Retail Jobs across Countries and Companies* (New York: Russell Sage Foundation, 2017), 1.

5. Hayley Peterson, "Wal-Mart Asks Workers to Donate Food to Its Needy Employees," *Business Insider,* November 20, 2014.

6. Quoted in Olivera Perkins, "Is Walmart's Request of Associates to Help Provide Thanksgiving Dinner for Co-Workers Proof of Low Wages?" *Cleveland Plain-Dealer,* November 18, 2013.

7. Carré and Tilly, *Where Bad Jobs Are Better,* 192.

8. Lucia Lo, Lu Wang, and Wei Li, "Consuming Wal-Mart: A Case Study in Shenzen," in *Wal-Mart World: The World's Biggest Corporation in the Global Economy,* ed. Stanley Brunn (New York: Routledge / Taylor & Francis, 2006).

9. Carré and Tilly, *Where Bad Jobs Are Better,* 194.

10. Wayne F. Cascio, "The High Cost of Low Wages," *Harvard Business Review,* December 2006.

11. "Costco Wholesale Corporation's (COST) Q3 2018 Results—Earnings Call Transcript," *Seeking Alpha,* June 1, 2018, https://seekingalpha.com/article /4178716-costco-wholesale-corporations-cost-q3-2018-results-earnings -call-transcript?part=single.

12. James Sinegal, "Costco: How Our Ethic Evolved over the First 30 Years," Raytheon Lectureship in Business Ethics, Bentley University, March 26, 2015.

13. Kate Taylor, "Costco Exec Says the Company Still Pays Better Than Any Rival Following Amazon's Move to Raise Wages to \$15 per Hour," *Business Insider,* October 5, 2018.

14. Quoted in Steven Greenhouse, *The Big Squeeze: Tough Times for the American Worker* (New York: Alfred Knopf, 2008), 156.

15. Daniel Aaronson, "Price Pass-Through and the Minimum Wage," *Review of Economics and Statistics* 83 (2001): 158–169

16. Sara Lemos, "A Survey of the Effects of the Minimum Wage on Prices," *Journal of Economic Surveys* 22 (2008): 187–212, Table 1.

17. Lemos, "A Survey of the Effects of the Minimum Wage on Prices," 208.

18. Louis Uchitelle, "Wages May Be Heading Up, but Prices Hold Their Own," *New York Times,* April 11, 1997. For historical data on the Consumer Price Index, see Federal Reserve Bank of Minneapolis, "Consumer Price Index, 1913–," https://www.minneapolisfed.org/community/financial-and -economic-education/cpi-calculator-information/consumer-price-index -and-inflation-rates-1913.

19. Carré and Tilly, *Where Bad Jobs Are Better,* 16.

20. Leslie Kaufman, "As Biggest Business, Wal-Mart Propels Changes Else-where," *New York Times,* October 22, 2000.

21. For the full text of the letter DeLauro co-signed, see "DeLauro Helps Kick Off 'Love Mom, Not Wal-Mart Campaign,'" press release, April 26, 2005, https://www.powervoter.us/Rosa_DeLauro/DeLauro_Helps_Kick_Off _Love_Mom__Not_Wal_Mart_Campaign.

22. For details, see "Economic News Release: Table B-1. Employees on Non-farm Payrolls by Industry Sector and Selected Industry Detail," US Bureau of Labor Statistics, https://www.bls.gov/news.release/empsit.t17.htm#ces_table1.f.phttps://www.bls.gov/news.release/empsit.t17.htm#ces_table1.f.p.

23. Rachel Abrams and Robert Gebeloff, "A Fast Food Problem: Where Have All the Teenagers Gone?" *New York Times,* May 3, 2018.

24. For the fraction of Americans who consume fast food daily, see Cheryl D. Fryar, Jeffrey P. Hughes, Kirsten A. Herrick, and Namanjeet Ahluwalia, "Fast Food Consumption among Adults in the United States, 2013–2016," National Center for Health Statistics Brief 322, October 2018. For the number of fast food establishments in the United States, see United States Department of Agriculture Economic Research Service, "Chain Outlets Make Up a Smaller Share of Restaurants in the Northeast and Pacific Northwest," https://www.ers.usda.gov/data-products/chart-gallery/gallery/chart-detail/?chartId=95156.

25. "Pizza Sets New Delivery Record," *BBC News,* May 22, 2001.

26. Julian Ryall, "Domino's Plans Pizza on the Moon," *The Telegraph,* September 1, 2011.

27. "2002 Economic Census: Industry Series," United States Census Bureau, August 2006, Table 21.

28. David Leonhardt, "$73 an Hour: Adding It Up," *New York Times,* December 9, 2008.

29. Rachel Premack, "Here's How Much CEOs at Amazon, McDonald's, and 13 Other Lucrative Brands Earn Compared to the Typical Worker," *Business Insider,* December 10, 2018.

30. For the average cost of a Big Mac, see "The Big Mac Index," *Economist,* https://www.economist.com/news/2020/07/15/the-big-mac-index, accessed July 15, 2020.

31. Catherine Ruetschlin, "Fast Food Failure: How CEO-to-Worker Pay Disparity Undermines the Industry and the Overall Economy," Demos Report, April 22, 2014.

32. For a video of her remarks, see "Hillary Clinton: 'I Want to Be the Small Business President,'" *NBC News,* May 22, 2015, https://www.nbcnews.com/video/hillary-clinton-i-want-to-be-the-small-business-president-449339971601.

33. "President Donald J. Trump's State of the Union Address," White House, January 30, 2018, https://www.whitehouse.gov/briefings-statements/president-donald-j-trumps-state-union-address/.

34. Although one might quibble with how the government determines what counts as a "small" business, it defines this as a firm employing fewer than five hundred workers. US Small Business Administration, Office of Advocacy, "2018 Small Business Profile," https://www.sba.gov/sites/default/files/advocacy/2018-Small-Business-Profiles-US.pdf.

35. Robert D. Atkinson and Michael Lind, *Big Is Beautiful: Debunking the Myth of Small Business* (Cambridge, MA: MIT Press, 2018), 64–66.

36. For a comparative perspective, see John Gibson and Steven Stillman, "Why Do Big Firms Pay Higher Wages? Evidence from an International Database," *Review of Economics and Statistics* 91 (2009): 213–218. For an examination of the decline in the firm size wage effect in the United States in recent decades (though it remains sizable), see Matissa N. Hollister, "Does Firm Size Matter Anymore? The New Economy and Firm Size Wage Effects," *American Sociological Review* 69 (2004): 659–676.

37. J. Adam Cobb and Ken-Hou Lin, "Growing Apart: The Changing Firm-Size Wage Premium and Its Inequality Consequences," *Organization Science* 28 (2017), 429–446.

38. Samuel Berlinski, "Wages and Contracting Out: Does the Law of One Price Hold?" *British Journal of Industrial Relations* 46 (2008): 59–75; Arindrajit Dube and Ethan Kaplan, "Does Outsourcing Reduce Wages in the Low-Wage Service Occupations? Evidence from Janitors and Guards," *ILR Review* 63 (2010): 287–306.

39. Cobb and Lin, "Growing Apart," 431–432.

40. David Weil, *The Fissured Workplace: Why Work Became So Bad for So Many and What Can Be Done to Improve It* (Cambridge, MA: Harvard University Press, 2014), 87.

41. Atkinson and Lind, *Big is Beautiful,* 66.

42. For the company's financial performance and how it compares to its industry and sector, see "Mcdonald's Corp MCD.N," Reuters, https://www.reuters.com/finance/stocks/financial-highlights/MCD.N.

43. See the discussion in Weil, *The Fissured Workplace,* 126–129.

44. Quoted in Liz Alderman and Steven Greenhouse, "Living Wages, Rarity for U.S. Fast Food Workers, Served Up in Denmark," *New York Times,* October 27, 2014.

45. Abrams and Gebeloff, "A Fast Food Problem."

46. Alderman and Greenhouse, "Living Wages, Rarity for U.S. Fast Food Workers."

47. Alderman and Greenhouse, "Living Wages, Rarity for U.S. Fast Food Workers."

48. See US Bureau of Labor Statistics, "Occupational Employment and Wages, May 2017: 35-3021 Combined Food Preparation and Serving Workers, Including Fast Food," https://www.bls.gov/oes/2017/may/oes353021.htm.

49. Quoted in Alderman and Greenhouse, "Living Wages, Rarity for U.S. Fast Food Workers."

50. Alex Dobuzinskis, "California City Plans $16 Minimum Wage by 2019, Highest in U.S.," *Reuters,* May 6, 2015.

51. Matthew Desmond, "The $15 Minimum Wage Doesn't Just Improve Lives. It Saves Them," *New York Times Magazine,* February 24, 2019.

52. For a recent example, see Doruk Cengiz, Arindrajit Dube, Attila Lindner, and Ben Zipperer, "The Effect of Minimum Wages on Low-Wage Jobs," *Quarterly Journal of Economics* 134 (2019): 1405–1454.

53. For California county and city unemployment data, updated monthly, see State of California Employment Development Department, "Labor Force and Unemployment Rate for Cities and Census Designated Places," https://www.labormarketinfo.edd.ca.gov/data/labor-force-and-unemployment-for-cities-and-census-areas.html.

54. Eduardo Porter, "Retail Jobs Don't Need to Be Bad. Here's Proof," *New York Times,* November 28, 2017.

55. Kiera Feldman, "Trashed: Inside the Deadly World of Private Garbage Collection," *ProPublica,* January 4, 2018. Accounts here of severed fingers and other dangers of New York City's sanitation industry draw heavily on Feldman's extraordinary account.

56. US Bureau of Labor Statistics, "National Census of Fatal Occupational Injuries in 2018," https://www.bls.gov/news.release/pdf/cfoi.pdf; Cole Rosen-

gren, "BLS: Collection Worker Fatalities Up Dramatically in 2018," *Waste Dive*, December 19, 2019.

57. Rosengren, "BLS."

58. Safety and Health Magazine, "SWANA Calls for Renewed Focus on Safety amid 'Unacceptable' Surge in Sanitation Worker Deaths," *Safety and Health Magazine,* January 30, 2019.

59. In the labor economics literature, "compensating differentials" can also refer to wage premia attached to jobs in undesirable locations and premia for other "disagreeable" job characteristics beyond dangerousness. For a review, see Robert S. Smith, "Compensating Wage Differentials and Public Policy: A Review," *ILR Review* 32 (1979): 339–352. In this chapter, I focus only on the ways in which the theory is applied to dangerous jobs.

60. Carl Zimring, "The Brutal Life of a Sanitation Worker," *New York Times,* February 9, 2018.

61. US Bureau of Labor Statistics, "Occupational Employment and Wages, May 2017: 53-7081 Refuse and Recyclable Material Collectors," https://www .bls.gov/oes/2017/may/oes537081.htm.

62. David M. Newman, "Dirty and Dangerous: Worker Safety and Health in New York City's Scofflaw Commercial Waste Industry," New York Committee for Occupational Safety and Health Report, May 2016, 47.

63. David Cooper and Teresa Kroeger, "Employers Steal Billions from Workers' Paychecks Each Year," Economic Policy Institute Report, May 10, 2017.

64. Abha Bhattarai, "The Whopping Fine Carl's Jr. Was Ordered to Pay for Allegedly Shortchanging Workers," *Washington Post,* June 30, 2017. On efforts at the state- and city-level to combat wage theft, see Daniel J. Galvin, "Combating Wage Theft under Donald Trump," *American Prospect,* December 22, 2016.

65. Simon Deakin, David Gindis, Geoffrey M. Hodgson, Kainan Huang, and Katharina Pistor, "Legal Institutionalism: Capitalism and the Constitutive Role of Law," *Journal of Comparative Economics* 45 (2017): 188–200, 189.

66. US Securities and Exchange Commission, "SeaWorld and Former CEO to Pay More Than $5 Million to Settle Fraud Charges," press release, September 18, 2018, https://www.sec.gov/news/press-release/2018-198.

67. Lawrence Hurley, "Court Upholds Ruling against SeaWorld over Trainer Safety," Reuters, April 11, 2014.

68. Feldman, "Trashed."

69. For a chart detailing OSHA's maximum penalties, see United States Department of Labor, "OSHA Penalties," https://www.osha.gov/penalties/.

70. Ben Geier, "Fired SeaWorld CEO is Getting a Splashy Severance Payment," *Fortune,* January 6, 2015.

71. Andrew Strom, "How We Value Investors and Workers," *OnLabor,* September 25, 2018.

72. Weil, *The Fissured Workplace,* Figure 9.2.

73. Feldman, "Trashed."

74. Newman, "Dirty and Dangerous," 2.

75. For details, see City of New York Department of Citywide Administrative Services, "Notice of Examination: Sanitation Worker, Exam No. 5001," https://www1.nyc.gov/assets/dcas/downloads/pdf/noes/201505001000.pdf.

76. Feldman, "Trashed."

77. Feldman, "Trashed."

78. See Keith Bender and John Heywood, "Out of Balance? Comparing Public and Private Sector Compensation over 20 Years," Center for State and Local Government Excellence and National Institute for Retirement Security, 2010; and Jeffrey Keefe, "Public-Sector Workers Are Paid Less Than Their Private-Sector Counterparts—and the Penalty Is Larger in Right-to-Work States," Economic Policy Institute Economic Snapshot, January 14, 2016.

79. Kevin Purse, "Work-Related Fatality Risks and Neoclassical Compensating Wage Differentials," *Cambridge Journal of Economics* 28 (2004): 597–617, 614.

80. Steve Tobak, "The Gender Pay Gap Is a Complete Myth," *CBS News,* April 17, 2011.

81. Upton Sinclair, *The Jungle* (New York: Doubleday, 1906), 126.

82. For a full list of the FMIA's provisions, see United States Department of Agriculture, "Federal Meat Inspection Act," https://www.fsis.usda.gov/wps/portal/fsis/topics/rulemaking/federal-meat-inspection-act.

83. H. Templeton Brown, "The First 50 Years under the Federal Meat Inspection Act of 1906," *Food Drug Cosmetic Law Journal* 11 (1956): 127–132, 127. Some of this discussion of meatpacking history was first published in Jake Rosenfeld, "Unsanitized: Welcome to the Jungle, Again," *American Prospect*, May 17, 2020.

84. Sinclair rarely ate meat, and was unsympathetic to those who consumed tainted beef: "any man who takes into his stomach food which has been prepared under the direction of unscrupulous commercial pirates . . . deserves all the poisoning he gets." Upton Sinclair, "What Life Means to Me," *Cosmopolitan,* October, 1906.

85. Daniel Calamuci, "Return to the Jungle: The Rise and Fall of Meatpacking Work," *New Labor Forum* 17 (2008): 67–77, 69.

86. For details, see US Bureau of Labor Statistics, Occupational Employment and Wages, May 2018: 51-3022 Meat, Poultry, and Fish Cutters and Trimmers, https://www.bls.gov/oes/2018/may/oes513022.htm.

87. In 2017, mean hourly earnings for retail salespersons was \$13.20 per hour. See the US Bureau of Labor Statistics Occupational Employment and Wage series 51-3023 for slaughterhouse workers and 41-2013 for retail salespersons.

88. Andrew Wasley, Christopher D. Cook, and Natalie Jones, "Two Amputations a Week: The Cost of Working in a US Meat Plant," *Guardian,* July 5, 2018.

89. Jessica G. Ramsey, Kristin Musolin, and Charles Mueller, "Evaluation of Carpal Tunnel Syndrome and Other Musculoskeletal Disorders among Employees at a Poultry Processing Plant," HHE Report No. 2014-0040–3232, June 2015.

90. Kennith Culp, Mary Brooks, Kerri Rupe, and Craig Zwerling, "Traumatic Injury Rates in Meatpacking Plant Workers," *Journal of Agromedicine* 13 (2008): 7–16.

91. United States Government Accountability Office, "Additional Data Needed to Address Continued Hazards in the Meat and Poultry Industry," GAO Report to Congressional Requesters, April 2016.

92. Georgeanne Artz, Rebecca Jackson, and Peter F. Orazem, "Is It a Jungle Out There? Meat Packing, Immigrants, and Rural Communities," *Journal of Agricultural and Resource Economics* 35 (2010): 299–315, 299–300.

93. Kulp et al., "Traumatic Injury Rates."

94. For a more recent example, see Eric Schlosser, *Fast Food Nation: The Dark Side of the All-American Meal* (New York: Houghton Mifflin, 2001).

95. Quoted in Peggy Lowe, "Working 'The Chain,' Slaughterhouse Workers Face Lifelong Injuries," *NPR,* August 11, 2016.

96. Lowe, "Working the Chain."

97. John Brueggemann and Cliff Brown, "The Decline of Industrial Unionism in the Meatpacking Industry: Event-Structure Analyses of Labor Unrest, 1946–1987," *Work and Occupations* 30 (2003) 327–360, 328.

98. Calamuci, "Return to the Jungle," 68.

99. John R. Commons, "Introduction," in *History of Labor in the United States, 1896–1932,* vols. 3 and 4, ed. Elizabeth Brandeis and Don D. Lescohier, ix–xxx (New York: Macmillan, 1935), xxv.

100. William Glaberson, "Misery on the Meatpacking Line," *New York Times,* June 14, 1987.

101. Brueggemann and Brown, "Decline of Industrial Unionism": Figure 2.

102. Karen Olsson, "The Shame of Meatpacking," *The Nation,* August 29, 2002.

103. Olsson, "The Shame of Meatpacking."

104. Peter Waldman and Kartikay Mehrotra, "America's Worst Graveyard Shift Is Grinding Up Workers," *Bloomberg Businessweek,* December 29, 2017.

105. Quoted in Waldman and Mehrotra, "America's Worst Graveyard Shift."

106. Mildred Haley, "Livestock, Dairy, and Poultry Outlook," United States Department of Agriculture Outlook Report, January 19, 2018, 21.

107. Megan Durisin and Shruti Singh, "Americans Will Eat a Record Amount of Meat in 2018," *Bloomberg,* January 2, 2018.

108. Paul Osterman, *Who Will Care for Us? Long-Term Care and the Long-Term Workforce* (New York: Russell Sage Foundation, 2017), 22.

109. Kezia Scales, "Staffing in Long-Term Care Is a National Crisis," *PHI,* June 8, 2018.

110. Paraprofessional Healthcare Institute, "U.S. Home Care Workers: Key Facts," PHI Report, September 1, 2016, 5.

111. Osterman, *Who Will Care for Us?* Table 4.1.

112. Quoted in Paula Span, "Wages for Home Care Aides Lag and Demand Grows," *New York Times,* September 23, 2016.

113. Quoted in Kalena Thomhave, "Who Cares for the Care Workers?" *American Prospect,* December 21, 2018.

114. Span, "Wages for Home Care Aides Lag."

115. Eileen Boris and Jennifer Klein, *Caring for America: Home Health Workers in the Shadow of the Welfare State* (Oxford: Oxford University Press, 2015), 227.

116. Eduardo Porter, "Home Health Care: Shouldn't It Be Work Worth Doing?" *New York Times,* August 29, 2017.

117. Osterman, *Who Will Care for Us?* Table 1.1.

118. Emilio J. Castilla, "Gender, Race, and Meritocracy in Organizational Careers," *American Journal of Sociology* 113 (2008): 1479–1526.

119. Candace Howes, "Living Wages and Retention of Homecare Workers in San Francisco," *Industrial Relations* 44 (2005): 139–163.

120. Kenneth E. Thorpe, "Building Evidence-Based Interventions to Avert Disease and Reduce Health Care Spending," Working Paper, November 2011.

121. Howes, "Living Wages and Retention of Homecare Workers," 139.

122. Barack Obama, "Remarks by the President on Minimum Wage and Overtime Protections for In-Home Care Workers, White House, December 15, 2011, https://obamawhitehouse.archives.gov/the-press-office/2011/12/15/remarks -president-minimum-wage-and-overtime-protections-home-care-worker.

CHAPTER 8: RETHINKING INEQUALITY

1. Elise Gould, "Decades of Rising Economic Inequality in the U.S.," Testimony before the US House of Representatives Ways and Means Committee, March 27, 2019, Figure E.

2. David Wessel, "The Typical Male U.S. Worker Earned Less in 2014 Than in 1973," *Wall Street Journal,* September 18, 2015.

3. See Lawrence Mishel and Julia Wolfe, "Top 1.0 Percent Reaches Highest Wages Ever—Up 157 Percent aince 1979," Working Economics Blog, Economic Policy Institute, October 18, 2018, for the estimates. All comparisons are in inflation-adjusted dollars.

4. Mishel and Wolfe, "Top 1.0 Percent Reaches Highest Wages Ever," Figure A.

5. Thomas Piketty, Emmanuel Saez, and Gabriel Zucman, "Distributional National Accounts: Methods and Estimates for the United States," NBER Working Paper 22945, 2016.

6. This book's focus is on pretax earnings—what your employer decides to pay you before the government takes away some of your money through taxes and returns some through benefits. But it's important to note that the trend in posttax inequality is similar. Dial back a half-century, and the bottom fifty percent of earners paid less than a fifth of their income in taxes. Those in the top one percent, meanwhile, paid 44 percent, and those at the very top—those lucky enough to earn more than 999 out of every 1,000 Americans—paid over half their income in local, state, and federal taxes. Today, the bottom fifty percent pays nearly a quarter of what they receive from their employer in taxes, and those in the top one percent pay less than a third. And the luckiest among us in terms of pretax earnings are growing increasingly lucky in terms of posttax obligations, paying just a third of their market income in taxes. Our nation's tax system is currently progressive in name only. For the tax figures, see "State and Local Taxes Worsen Inequality," editorial, _New York Times,_ July 21, 2019; and for the methodology, see Piketty, Saez, and Zucman, "Distributional National Accounts."

7. Erling Barth, Alex Bryson, James C. Davis, and Richard B. Freeman, "It's Where You Work: Increases in the Dispersion of Earnings across Establishments and Individuals in the United States," _Journal of Labor Economics_ 34 (2016): S67–S97, S68.

8. Barth et al., "It's Where You Work," S90.

9. Barack Obama, "Remarks by the President on Economic Mobility," White House, December 04, 2013, https://obamawhitehouse.archives.gov/the-press-office/2013/12/04/remarks-president-economic-mobility for a full transcript of the remarks.

10. Jan Tinbergen, "My Life Philosophy," _American Economist_ 28 (1984): 5–8, 5.

11. For an example, see Floyd Norris, "Solving for $," _New York Times,_ January 6, 2013.

12. Samuel Stebbins, "These CEOs Make 1,000 Times More Than Their Employees," _USA Today,_ April 19, 2019.

13. This comparatively low ratio masks the enormous amounts that J. B. Hunt's CEO, John Roberts, made in the years prior to the disclosure. For more on why low ratios are often misleading, see Bob Lord, "About Those Low CEO-to-Worker Pay Ratios," *Inequality.org,* August 10, 2018.

14. Broer Akkerboom, "The Tinbergen Standard Does Not Exist," *Me Judice,* May 15, 2015.

15. Jan Tinbergen, "Misunderstandings Concerning Income Distribution Policies," *De Economist* 129 (1981): 8–20, 12.

16. Claudia Goldin and Lawrence F. Katz, *The Race Between Education and Technology* (Cambridge, MA: Belknap Press of Harvard University Press, 2008), 473.

17. Timothy Noah, *The Great Divergence: America's Growing Inequality Crisis and What We Can Do about It* (London: Bloomsbury Press, 2012), 80.

18. For the occupation's job outlook, see US Bureau of Labor Statistics, "Occupational Outlook Handbook: Tellers," https://www.bls.gov/ooh/office-and-administrative-support/tellers.htm#tab-6.

19. George Bush, "President Bush Delivers State of the Economy Report," speech, Federal Hall, New York, January 31, 2007, https://georgewbush-whitehouse.archives.gov/news/releases/2007/01/20070131-1.html.

20. Ben S. Bernanke, "The Level and Distribution of Economic Well-Being: Remarks before the Greater Omaha Chamber of Commerce," Omaha, NE, February 6, 2007, https://fraser.stlouisfed.org/title/453/item/8952.

21. Barack Obama, "Remarks by the President in State of the Union Address," White House, January 20, 2015, https://obamawhitehouse.archives.gov/the-press-office/2015/01/20/remarks-president-state-union-address-January-20-2015.

22. For updated analyses, see Elise Gould, "Higher Returns on Education Can't Explain Growing Wage Inequality," Working Economics Blog, Economic Policy Institute, March 15, 2019.

23. Richard B. Freeman, *The Overeducated American* (New York: Academic Press, 1976).

24. For updated estimates of the college wage premium, see Federal Reserve Bank of St. Louis, "Is College Still Worth It?" FRED blog, July 19, 2018, https://fredblog.stlouisfed.org/2018/07/is-college-still-worth-it/.

25. Goldin and Katz, *The Race between Education and Technology,* Figure 8.3.

26. For details, see The Hamilton Project, "The Education Wage Premium Contributes to Wage Inequality," Brookings Institution, https://www.hamiltonproject.org/charts/the_education_wage_premium_contributes_to_wage_inequality.

27. Nader Habibi, "America Has an Overeducation Problem," *New Republic,* December 2, 2015.

28. Lydia DePillis, "Why Not Having a College Degree Is a Bigger Barrier Than It Used to Be," *Washington Post,* September 11, 2014.

29. While my students are obvious exceptions, Richard Arum and Josipa Roksa find that nearly half of undergraduates they surveyed demonstrate no significant improvements in basic analytical skills and writing ability during their first two years in college. See Richard Arum and Josipa Roksa, *Academically Adrift: Limited Learning on College Campuses* (Chicago: University of Chicago Press, 2010).

30. For two reviews, see Richard B. Freeman and James L. Medoff, *What Do Unions Do?* (New York: Basic Books, 1984); and Jake Rosenfeld, 2014, *What Unions No Longer Do* (Cambridge, MA: Harvard University Press, 2014).

31. Jake Rosenfeld, Patrick Denice, and Jennifer Laird, "Union Decline Lowers Wages of Nonunion Workers," Economic Policy Institute Report, August 30, 2016;; Patrick Denice and Jake Rosenfeld, "Unions and Nonunion Pay in the United States, 1977–2015," *Sociological Science* 5 (2018): 541–561.

32. Ben Zipperer, "The Erosion of the Federal Minimum Wage Has Increased Poverty, Especially for Black and Hispanic Families," Economic Snapshot, Economic Policy Institute, June 13, 2018.

33. Bernanke, "The Level and Distribution of Economic Well-Being," 11–12, https://fraser.stlouisfed.org/title/453/item/8952.

34. Jennifer Hunt and Ryan Nunn, "Is Employment Polarization Informative about Wage Inequality and Is Employment Really Polarizing?" NBER Working Paper 26064, 2019.

35. See Patrick Sisson, "Construction Industry, Mid Boom, Can't Find Enough Skilled Workers," *Curbed,* January 23, 2018.

36. Quoted in Asher Schechter, "Angus Deaton on the Under-Discussed Driver of Inequality in America: 'It's Easier for Rent-Seekers to Affect Policy Here Than in Much of Europe,'" *Pro-Market,* February 8, 2018.

37. For example, see Ian Dew-Becker and Robert J. Gordon, "The Rise in American Inequality," *Vox CEPR Policy Portal,* June 19, 2008.

38. For a summary of the evidence, see Josh Bivens and Lawrence Mishel, "The Pay of Corporate Executives and Financial Professionals as Evidence of Rents in Top 1 Percent Incomes," *Journal of Economic Perspectives* 27 (2013): 57–78.

39. For recent trends in licensing and government certification requirements, see Morris M. Kleiner and Alan B. Krueger, "Analyzing the Extent and Influence of Occupational Licensing on the Labor Market," *Journal of Labor Economics* 31 (2013): S173–S202.

40. For more on uneven patterns of rent creation and destruction and their relationships to inequality, see Kim A. Weeden and David B. Grusky, "Inequality and Market Failure," *American Behavioral Scientist* 58 (2014): 473–491; Beth Red Bird and David Grusky, "Rent, Rent-Seeking, and Social Inequality," (2015) in *Emerging Trends in the Social and Behavioral Sciences,* ed. Stephen Kosslyn and Robert Scott (Hoboken, NJ: John Wiley and Sons, 2015–).

41. Alan B. Krueger, "Do You Need a License to Earn a Living? You Might Be Surprised at the Answer," *New York Times,* March 2, 2006.

42. For estimates of 2018 median weekly earnings for detailed occupations, see United States Bureau of Labor Statistics, "Labor Force Statistics from the Current Population Survey," https://www.bls.gov/cps/cpsaat39.htm. For comparable figures for 1988, see Federal Reserve Bank of St. Louis, "Median Weekly Earnings of Full-Time Wage and Salary Workers by Detailed Occupation and Sex," https://fraser.stlouisfed.org/title/60/item/19841/toc/149643.

43. Yu Xie, Alexandra Killewald, and Christopher Near, "Between- and Within-Occupation Inequality: The Case of High-Status Positions," *Annals of the American Academy of Political Science* 663 (2016): 53–79, Figure 2C.

44. Caroline Hanley, "Investigating the Organizational Sources of High-Wage Earnings Growth and Rising Inequality," *Social Science Research* 40 (2011): 902–916, 908.

45. Anders Akerman, Elhanan Helpman, Oleg Itskhoki, Marc-Andreas Muendler, and Stephen Redding, "Sources of Wage Inequality," *American Economic Review: Papers & Proceedings* 103 (2013): 214–219.

46. Xie, Killewald, and Near, "Between- and Within-Occupation Inequality," Figure 4A.

47. Ted Mouw and Arne L. Kalleberg, "Occupations and the Structure of Wage Inequality in the United States, 1980s to 2000s," *American Sociological Review* 75 (2010): 402–431.

48. One study estimates that 45 percent of janitors worked for a contracting firm by 2000. Matthew Dey, Susan N. Houseman, and Anne E. Polivka, "What Do We Know about Contracting Out in the United States? Evidence from Household and Establishment Surveys," W. E. Upjohn Institute for Employment Research Working Paper 09-157, 2009, Figure 7. Another study, using a different data set, suggest the percentage is lower. Arindrajit Dube and Ethan Kaplan, "Does Outsourcing Reduce Wages in the Low-Wage Service Occupations? Evidence from Janitors and Guards," *ILR Review* 63 (2010): 287–306.

49. Dube and Kaplan, "Does Outsourcing Reduce Wages in the Low-Wage Service Occupations?"

50. J. Adam Cobb and Ken-Hou Lin, "Growing Apart: The Changing Firm-Size Wage Premium and Its Inequality Consequences," *Organization Science* 28 (2017): 429–446.

51. Cobb and Lin, "Growing Apart," 443.

52. Thomas Lemieux, W. Bentley MacLeod, and Daniel Parent, "Performance Pay and Wage Inequality," *Quarterly Journal of Economics* 124 (2009): 1–49, Figure IV.

53. Lemieux, MacLeod, and Parent, "Performance Pay and Wage Inequality," Figure V.

54. Hanley, "Investigating the Organizational Sources."

55. Lemieux, MacLeod, and Parent, "Performance Pay and Wage Inequality," 38.

56. Jae Song, David J. Price, Fatih Guvenen, Nicholas Bloom, and Till von Wachter, "Firming Up Inequality," *Quarterly Journal of Economics* 134 (2019): 1–50.

57. Edward P. Lazear and Kathryn L. Shaw, "Introduction: Firms and the Distribution of Income: The Roles of Productivity and Luck," *Journal of Labor Economics* 36 (2018): S1–S12, S8–S9.

58. Daisuke Wakabayashi, "Google's Shadow Work Force: Temps Who Outnumber Full-Time Employees," *New York Times,* May 28, 2019.

59. Quoted in Chrystia Freeland, *Plutocrats: The Rise of the New Global Super-Rich and the Fall of Everyone Else* (New York: Penguin Press, 2012), 236.

60. Wakabayashi, "Google's Shadow Work Force."

61. Quoted in Wakabayashi, "Google's Shadow Work Force."

62. For Evans's story, see Neil Irwin, "To Understand Rising Inequality, Consider the Janitors at Two Top Companies, Then and Now," *New York Times,* September 3, 2017.

63. Eileen Appelbaum, "Domestic Outsourcing, Rent Seeking, and Increasing Inequality," *Review of Radical Political Economics* 49 (2017): 513–528, 516.

64. Arindrajit Dube, Laura Giuliano, and Jonathan S. Leonard, "Fairness and Frictions: The Impact of Unequal Raises on Quit Behavior," *American Economic Review* 109 (2018): 620–663, 39.

65. J. Adam Cobb, "How Firms Shape Income Inequality: Stakeholder Power, Executive Decision Making, and the Structuring of Employment Relationships," *Academy of Management Review* 41 (2016): 324–348, 336. See also Peter H. Cappelli, "Assessing the Decline of Internal Labor Markets," in *Sourcebook of Labor Markets: Evolving Structures and Processes,* ed. Ivar Berg and Arne L. Kalleberg, 207–245 (New York: Kluwer Academic / Plenum, 2001).

66. When asked by President Obama what it would take for Apple to produce their phones in the United States, Jobs reportedly replied, "Those jobs aren't coming back." See Charles Duhigg and Keith Bradsher, "How the U.S. Lost Out on iPhone Work," *New York Times,* January 21, 2012.

67. Lawrence F. Katz and Alan B. Krueger, "The Rise and Nature of Alternative Work Arrangements in the United States, 1995–2015," *ILR Review* 72 (2019): 382–416.

68. Katz and Krueger, "The Rise and Nature of Alternative Work Arrangements."

69. For a summary, see Suresh Naidu, Eric Posner, and Glen Weyl, "More and More Companies Have Monopoly Power over Workers' Wages. That's Killing the Economy," *Vox,* April 6, 2018b.

70. Zach Mortice, "What Facebook Can Learn from Company Towns," *Citylab,* July 19, 2017.

71. David Streitfeld, "Welcome to Zucktown, Where Everything Is Just Zucky," *New York Times,* March 21, 2018.

72. For an overview of this growing research field, see Council of Economic Advisors, "Labor Market Monopsony: Trends, Consequences, and Policy Responses," Council of Economic Advisors Issue Brief, October 2016.

73. José Azar, Ioana Marinescu, and Marshall I. Steinbaum, "Labor Market Concentration," NBER Working Paper 24147, 2017.

74. Josh Bivens, Lawrence Mishel, and John Schmitt, "It's Not Just Monopoly and Monopsony," Economic Policy Institute Report, April 25, 2018.

75. Pew Research Center, "2012 American Values Survey," Pew Research Center, June 4, 2012, 9.

76. Pew Research Center, "2012 American Values Survey," 8.

77. Pew Research Center, "2012 American Values Survey," 8.

CHAPTER 9: TOWARD A FAIRER WAGE

1. Political scientist Jacob Hacker, who coined the term, discusses its impact on British politics in Jacob Hacker, "Miliband's Not Talking about 'Predistribution' but He Has Embraced My Big Idea," *New Statesman America,* April 29, 2015.

2. For a primer on marketcraft, see Steven Vogel, "Marketcraft: How Government Can Beat Inequality by Reshaping Markets," *Vox,* July 29, 2019.

3. For analyses of how to reduce CEOs' pretax earnings through the tax system, see Thomas Piketty, Emmanuel Saez, and Stephanie Stantcheva, "Optimal Taxation of Top Labor Incomes: A Tale of Three Elasticities," *American Economic Journal: Economy Policy* 6 (2014): 230–271.

4. Alexia Fernández Campbell, "The House Just Passed a $15 Minimum Wage. It Would Be the First Increase in a Decade," *Vox,* July 18, 2019.

5. McConnell expressed this view in a live interview with Maria Bartiromo, Fox Business Network, July 18, 2019; language here is from his follow-up tweet sharing a clip: @senatemajldr tweet 12:06 PM, July 18, 2019, https://twitter.com/senatemajldr/status/1151885990862237697.

6. Matthew Sheffield, "Poll: Majority of Voters Support $15 Minimum Wage," *The Hill,* January 24, 2019.

7. Lydia DePillis, "Leaked Documents Show Strong Business Support for Raising the Minimum Wage," *Washington Post,* April 4, 2016.

8. Quoted in DePillis, "Leaked Documents Show Strong Business Support."

9. Quoted in Katherine Tully-McManus and Lindsey McPherson, "House Votes to Raise Federal Minimum Wage," *Roll Call,* July 18, 2019.

10. Anna Godøy and Michael Reich, "Minimum Wage Effects in Low-Wage Areas," IRLE Working Paper No. 106–19, Institute for Research on Labor and Employment, July 2019.

11. Doruk Cengiz, Arindrajit Dube, Attila Lindner, and Ben Zipperer, "The Effect of Minimum Wages on Low-Wage Jobs," *Quarterly Journal of Economics* 134 (2019): 1405–1454.

12. Andrew Van Dam, "It's Not Just Paychecks: The Surprising Society-Wide Benefits of Raising the Minimum Wage," *Washington Post,* July 8, 2019.

13. William H. Dow, Anna Godøy, Christopher A. Lowenstein, and Michael Reich, "Can Economic Policies Reduce Deaths of Despair?" NBER Working Paper 25787, 2019.

14. Amanda Y. Agan and Michael D. Makowsky, "The Minimum Wage, EITC, and Criminal Recidivism," NBER Working Paper 25116, 2018.

15. Quoted in Christopher Robbins, "What Happens When Low Wage Workers Suddenly Get a Living Wage?" *Gothamist,* June 5, 2014.

16. Quoted in Robbins, "What Happens When Low Wage Workers Suddenly Get a Living Wage?"

17. Robbins, "What Happens When Low Wage Workers Suddenly Get a Living Wage?"

18. Quoted in Robbins, "What Happens When Low Wage Workers Suddenly Get a Living Wage?"

19. Drew DeSilver, "5 Facts about the Minimum Wage," Pew Research Center, January 4, 2017.

20. Chris Marr, "States with $15 Minimum Wage Laws Doubled This Year," *Bloomberg Law,* May 23, 2019.

21. For an industry and occupational breakdown of the beneficiaries of a raised minimum wage, see DeSilver, "5 Facts about the Minimum Wage."

22. Quoted in Matthew Desmond, "Americans Want to Believe Jobs Are the Solution to Poverty. They're Not," *New York Times Magazine,* September 11, 2018.

23. For more on Vanessa and her family, see Desmond, "Americans Want to Believe."

24. Laura Huizar and Yannet Lathrop, "Fighting Wage Preemption: How Workers Have Lost Billions in Wages and How We Can Restore Local Democracy," NELP Report, National Employment Law Project, July 2019.

25. Huizar and Lathrop, "Fighting Wage Preemption," Figure 1.

26. For basic information about the program's reach, see Internal Revenue Service, "Why EITC Is Important?" https://www.eitc.irs.gov/eitc-central/about -eitc/about-eitc.

27. The conservative Friedman's original idea for the program, which did not have a work requirement, proved too liberal for policymakers. See Robert H. Frank, "The Other Milton Friedman: A Conservative with a Social Welfare Program," *New York Times,* November 23, 2006.

28. For program eligibility rules, see this primer: Center on Budget and Policy Priorities, "Policy Basics: The Earned Income Tax Credit," updated December 10, 2019, https://www.cbpp.org/research/federal-tax/policy-basics -the-earned-income-tax-credit.

29. For an up-to-date list of these states, see Internal Revenue Service, "States and Local Governments with Earned Income Tax Credit," https://www.irs .gov/credits-deductions/individuals/earned-income-tax-credit/states-and -local-governments-with-earned-income-tax-credit.

30. Erica Williams and Samantha Waxman, "States Can Adopt or Expand Earned Income Tax Credits to Build a Stronger Future Economy," Center on Budget and Policy Priorities Report, March 7, 2019.

31. Chris Marr, "Reagan's Actions Made Him a True EITC Champion," Center on Budget and Policy Priorities, August 1, 2014.

32. Quoted in Dave Jamieson, "Lamar Alexander Says Minimum Wage Should Be Abolished," *Huffington Post,* June 25, 2013.

33. Gabrielle Paluch, "Why Wasn't a Tax Cut with Rare Bipartisan Support Part of Tax Overhaul Talks?" Center for Public Integrity, April 17, 2019.

34. Dylan Matthews, "Gavin Newsom's Biggest Accomplishment as Governor Yet: A $1 Billion Cash Plan for the Poor," *Vox,* June 27, 2019.

35. Teresa Ghilarducci and Aida Farmand, "What's Not to Like about the EITC? Plenty, It Turns Out," *American Prospect,* June 28, 2019.

36. Ghilarducci and Farmand, "What's Not to Like about the EITC?".

37. To understand how the two programs complement one another, see Jesse Rothstein and Ben Zipperer, "The EITC and Minimum Wage Work Together to Reduce Poverty and Raise Incomes," Economic Policy Institute Report, January 22, 2020.

38. Lauren Hilgers, "Out of the Shadows," *New York Times Magazine,* February 21, 2019.

39. Linda Burnham and Nik Theodore, "Home Economics: The Invisible and Unregulated World of Domestic Work," National Domestic Workers Alliance and Center for Urban Economic Development, University of Illinois at Chicago Data Center, 2012, xi. See also Figure 2.

40. For a summary of the legislation, see "Summary of National Domestic Workers Bill of Rights," website of Kamala D. Harris, https://www.harris .senate.gov/imo/media/doc/Domestic%20Workers%20Bill%20of%20 Rights%20Summary.pdf. For more on the wage and standards board, see David Madland and Adam Stromme, "A New 'Bill of Rights' for Domestic Workers Will Let Them Finally Bargain Collectively," *Fortune,* July 19, 2019.

41. Ai-jen Poo, "They Look After Your Children. They Deserve Basic Rights," *New York Times,* July 14, 2019.

42. For details, see Bureau of Labor Statistics, "Contingent and Alternative Employment Arrangements—May 2017," Bureau of Labor Statistics News Release, June 7, 2018.

43. For example, a driver for Uber who only drives for three months out of the year counts as one quarter of a "full-time equivalent job," assuming she's driving full-time for those three months. If she's only driving half-time during those three months, then her Uber job is the equivalent of one-sixth

of a full-time job. For methodological details, see Lawrence Mishel, "Uber and the Labor Market," Economic Policy Institute Report, May 15, 2018.

44. Quoted in Robert J. Samuelson, "Is the Gig Economy a Myth?" *Washington Post,* June 17, 2018.

45. Organisation for Economic Co-ordination and Development, "OECD Employment Outlook 2019: The Future of Work," OECD Publishing, 2019.

46. Geoff Gilfillan and Chris McGann, "Trends in Union Membership in Australia," Parliament of Australia Research Paper Series, October 15, 2018.

47. For the latest updates of the OECD's inequality statistics, see "Income Inequality," https://data.oecd.org/inequality/income-inequality.htm for the latest estimates.

48. Arindrajit Dube, "Using Wage Boards to Raise Pay," Economics for Inclusive Prosperity Policy Brief 4, February 2019, Figure 4.

49. For a description of the awards system and an analysis of their impact, see Dube, "Using Wage Boards to Raise Pay."

50. Bruce Western and Jake Rosenfeld, "Unions, Norms, and the Rise in U.S. Wage Inequality," *American Sociological Review* 76 (2011): 513–537, 518.

51. David Madland, "Wage Boards for American Workers," Center for American Progress Report, April 9, 2018.

52. For a blueprint of how to expand tripartite bargaining of this type in the United States, see Kate Andrias, "The New Labor Law," *Yale Law Journal* 126 (2016): 2–100.

53. David Cooper, "Raising the Federal Minimum Wage to $15 by 2024 Would Lift Pay for Nearly 40 Million Workers," Economic Policy Institute Report, February 5, 2019. But on the possibility that measurement error may bias spillover estimates, see David H. Autor, Alan Manning, and Christopher L. Smith, "The Contribution of the Minimum Wage to US Wage Inequality over Three Decades: A Reassessment," *American Economic Journal: Applied Economics* 8 (2016): 58–99.

54. John M. Abowd, Kevin L. McKinney, and Nellie L. Zhao, "Earnings Inequality and Mobility Trends in the United States: Nationally Representative Estimates from Longitudinally Linked Employer-Employee Data," *Journal of Labor Economics* 36 (2018): S183–S300, S183.

55. Edward P. Lazear and Kathryn L. Shaw, "Introduction: Firms and the Distribution of Income: The Roles of Productivity and Luck," *Journal of Labor Economics* 36 (2018): S1–S12, S9.

56. For a discussion of best managerial practices for boosting organizational productivity, see Lazear and Shaw, "Introduction: Firms and the Distribution of Income," S9–S10.

57. For a summary of the evidence, see Matissa N. Hollister, "Employment Stability in the U.S. Labor Market: Rhetoric versus Reality," *Annual Review of Sociology* 37 (2011): 305–324.

58. For details, see US Department of Labor, "Executive Order 13658, Establishing a Minimum Wage for Contractors: Annual Update," https://www.dol.gov/whd/flsa/eo13658/.

59. For the full text, see Barack Obama, "Executive Order—Fair Pay and Safe Workplaces," White House, July 31, 2014, https://obamawhitehouse.archives.gov/the-press-office/2014/07/31/executive-order-fair-pay-and-safe-workplaces. The Trump Administration subsequently overruled the executive order. See Gregory Korte, "Trump Signs Four Bills to Roll Back Obama-era Regulations," *USA Today,* March 27, 2017.

60. For a comprehensive set of ideas, see Sharon Block and Benjamin Sachs, "Clean Slate for Worker Power: Building a Just and Sustainable Democracy," Labor and Worklife Program, Harvard Law School, January 2020. Also see Richard Bales and Charlotte Garden, eds., *The Cambridge Handbook of U.S. Labor Law for the Twenty-First Century* (Cambridge: Cambridge University Press, 2019), especially the contributions in Part 2.

61. Sanford M. Jacoby, "The Development of Internal Labor Markets in American Manufacturing Firms," in *Internal Labor Markets,* ed. Paul Osterman, 23–69 (Cambridge, MA: MIT Press, 1984), 51–53.

62. While effective at preventing pay discrimination between workers hired at the same time, given how much later women and minorities entered many industries, strict seniority rules in pay and hiring and firing often worked to their disadvantage. For the example of the postwar auto industry see Thomas J. Sugrue, *The Origins of the Urban Crisis: Race and Inequality in Postwar Detroit* (Princeton, NJ: Princeton University Press, 1996), chap. 4.

63. Emilio J. Castilla, "Gender, Race, and Meritocracy in Organizational Careers," *American Journal of Sociology* 113 (2008): 1479–1526.

64. Emilio J. Castilla and Stephen Benard, "The Paradox of Meritocracy in Organizations," *Administrative Science Quarterly* 55 (2010): 543–576.

65. Economic Policy Institute, "The Productivity-Pay Gap," Economic Policy Institute, August 2018.

66. Richard A. Oppel Jr., "Employees' Retirement Plan Is a Victim as Enron Tumbles," *New York Times,* November 22, 2001.

67. Erling Barth, Bernt Bratsberg, Torbjørn Hægeland, and Oddbjørn Raaum, "Performance Pay, Union Bargaining and Within-Firm Wage Inequality," *Oxford Bulletin of Economics and Statistics* 74 (2012): 327–362.

68. Barack Obama, "Address by President Obama to the 71st Session of the United Nations General Assembly," September 20, 2016, https://obamawhitehouse .archives.gov/the-press-office/2016/09/20/address-president-obama-71st -session-united-nations-general-assembly.

69. Amina Dunn, "Partisans Are Divided Over the Fairness of the U.S. Economy— and Why People are Rich or Poor," Pew Research Center, October 4, 2018.

70. Business Roundtable, "Our Commitment," https://opportunity.business roundtable.org/ourcommitment/.

71. Matthew Sheffield, "Poll: A Majority of Americans Support Raising the Top Tax Rate to 70 Percent," *The Hill,* January 15, 2019.

72. Frank Newport, "Americans' Long-Standing Interest in Taxing the Rich," *Gallup,* February 22, 2019.

73. Piketty, Saez, and Stantcheva "Optimal Taxation of Top Labor Incomes."

74. The full text of the proposed Reward Work Act is posted on Tammy Baldwin's website: https://www.baldwin.senate.gov/imo/media/doc/Reward%20 Work%20Act%203.21.18.pdf.

75. For the complete poll results, see Dylan Matthews, "Workers Do Not Have Much Say in Corporations. Why Not Give Them Seats on the Board?" *Vox,* April 6, 2018.

76. Simon Jäger, Benjamin Schoefer, and Jörg Heining, "Labor in the Boardroom," IZA Discussion Paper No. 12799, Institute of Labor Economics (IZA), July 2019.

77. Quoted in Jäger, Schoefer, and Heining, "Labor in the Boardroom," 28.

78. Lenore M. Palladino, "Ending Shareholder Primacy in Corporate Governance," Roosevelt Institute Working Paper, February 8, 2019, Figure 1.

79. Jesse M. Fried and Charles C. Y. Wang, "Are Buybacks Really Shortchanging Investment?," *Harvard Business Review,* March–April 2018.

80. For a summary of the act, see "U.S. Senator Tammy Baldwin Introduces Legislation to Rein in Stock Buybacks and Give Workers a Seat at the Table," press release, Senate Office of Tammy Baldwin, March 22, 2018, https://www.baldwin.senate.gov/press-releases/reward-work-act.

81. For more on the idea, see Palladino, "Ending Shareholder Primacy," 25.

82. Marco Rubio, "American Investment in the 21st Century: Project for Strong Labor Markets and National Development," United States Senate, May 15, 2019, 23–33.

83. James Hohmann, "The Daily 202: Marco Rubio Slams CEOs for Bad China Deals, Short-Term Thinking and Not Investing in U.S. Workers," *Washington Post,* May 15, 2019.

84. Ben Fountain, "O Billionaires!" *New York Review of Books,* May 23, 2019.

85. Quoted in Nick Lehr, "Why Do So Many Working Class Americans Feel Politics Is Pointless?," *The Conversation,* August 5, 2019. See also Jennifer M. Silva, *We're Still Here: Pain and Politics in the Heart of America* (New York: Oxford University Press, 2019).

86. Paul Krugman, "Walmart's Visible Hand," *New York Times,* March 2, 2015.

EPILOGUE

1. Sarah Nassauer, "Walmart's Coronavirus Challenge in Just Staying Open," *Wall Street Journal*, April 18, 2020.

2. Emily Stewart, "Essential Workers are Taking Care of America. Are We Taking Care of Them?," *Vox*, April 23, 2020.

3. Ben Zipperer and Elise Gould, "Unemployment Filing Failures," Economic Policy Institute Working Economics Blog, April 28, 2020.

ACKNOWLEDGMENTS

This is the book I've wanted to write ever since I took my first undergraduate sociology course with Jeff Weintraub many, many years ago. Jeff instilled in me a deep curiosity about why certain people receive so much and others so little, along with a healthy skepticism about prevailing explanations of pay determination. That question—who gets what and why—guides this book. Answering that question was a collective affair.

Along the way I've been blessed to work with a remarkable group of young social scientists who contributed to the analyses that helped shape various chapters. Laura Adler's advice on what questions to ask pay-setters was crucial to the development of the survey instrument I present in Chapter 2; so too was her feedback on how to interpret the subsequent answers. Patrick Denice is everything one can hope for in a colleague: reliable, exceedingly careful in all stages of the research process, and extraordinarily smart. He adds a lot of patience and kindness to that already rare mix. He was crucial in the development of the worker survey described in Chapter 2, and in the investigations of the prevalence and consequences of informational asymmetries in the modern workplace presented in Chapter 3. Shengwei Sun arrived on the pay secrecy project as Patrick departed, and quickly proved to be an amazingly skilled data analyst and project coordinator. She was essential to seeing the investigation into pay secrecy policies in the modern workplace through to fruition.

To Patrick and Shengwei: I cannot thank you enough, and now we can work on those journal articles I've long promised.

At Washington University-St. Louis I've been blessed with a pair of undergraduates who helped in various stages of the research process. Gangyi Sun came aboard when I had only an inchoate notion of where the project was heading, which resulted in a series of what must have seemed strange and unrelated tasks. Yet he accomplished them all eagerly, professionally, and his excitement for the various themes of the book served as an early motivator for me to get the thing into shape. Jordan Coley brought some needed efficiency and organization to the project, and always stood ready to take on more assignments, no matter the level of drudgery. Both are well on their way to becoming top-notch researchers, and I'm honored to have worked with them at the beginning stages of their careers.

My undergraduate course, Getting Paid, served as a laboratory to test some of the core ideas of the book. My students' insightful questions and, periodically, outright skepticism helped sharpen my arguments and jettison those that weren't fully formed. As an added bonus, the classroom setting allowed me to assign a range of sources I draw on in the book to check that my students' interpretations of them aligned with my own. So far all of your help, thanks, and for those currently enrolled, now is not the time to let up. The deadline for your research papers is right around the corner.

Diana Finch of the Diana Finch Literary Agency patiently provided me a series of lessons on the ins and outs of the contemporary book-publishing world. Through her efforts I became persuaded that I had chosen the right publisher. It helped that Ian Malcolm at Harvard University Press championed the project from the very beginning, well before it had matured into anything book-length. His enthusiasm convinced me I was onto something. And his deadlines sped the maturation process right along. I toil in an occupation where actual deadlines are exceedingly rare. Confronting them was terrifying, but also ensured the book materialized before my attention wandered to another topic, or, more likely, I was wheeled off to the retirement home. Ian's characteristic cheerfulness, a constant even when presenting the punishing timeline, eased my fears. (A bit.) Julia Kirby of Harvard University Press provided an exceedingly thorough and substantial edit. Her efforts helped produce a cleaner, more consistent final product—and should protect me from any libel lawsuits. I thank the reviewers at Harvard University Press for their probing questions, key insights, and helpful suggestions on an early version of the manuscript. This final one benefited greatly from their collective expertise.

Institutional support of various kinds provided the backbone of the project. Support from the Weidenbaum Center on the Economy, Government, and Public Policy at Washington University–St. Louis partially funded the surveys of workers and pay-setters I describe in Chapter 2. Support from the National Science Foundation (NSF Award #1727350) funded the pay secrecy survey I describe in Chapter 3. Qualtrics and GfK survey research staff were the ones who actually got my surveys into the field, ensured a sufficient response rate, and conducted critical data quality checks. Computing support for this research came from a Eunice Kennedy Shriver National Institute of Child Health and Human Development research infrastructure grant (P2C HD042828) to the Center for Studies in Demography and Ecology (CSDE) at the University of Washington.

Ours remains a family affair, and I'm blessed to be surrounded by loved ones who served as sounding boards, support systems, and provided healthy distractions along the way. On the latter contribution, Ida May really stood out. Decidedly unhelpful in all stages of the process, and steadfastly uninterested in what her father was writing about, she was a constant reminder to let work go and watch this beautiful kid grow. I can only hope that when the day arrives that she does take this book up, we'll have made progress toward a fairer, more equitable country, and the problems I describe here will read as historical relics, not ongoing concerns. First, though, she has to learn to read. Frances Hoffmann once again proved that there was an alternate career path as an excellent editor awaiting her all along. I've been blessed that she didn't take it, giving her the time and enthusiasm to sharpen my language, clarify my arguments, and aim for as broad an audience as possible. Every page bears the imprint of her efforts. The constant encouragement of Alison Allman and Robert McCoole, as well as their devotion and care for Ida May, helped see the book through all of its stages—but especially in the mad dash to the final deadline. I owe you both a hundred dinner outings, and then some. Janet Lauritsen and Richard Rosenfeld were quick to offer a drink, a helping hand, and an excuse to put work aside and have a bit of fun. Finally, some healthy sibling rivalry propelled the project forward. In the time I finished the research for one part of one chapter, the brilliant Erica DeBruin wrote an entire book. And if Sam Rosenfeld hadn't begun work on his second one, there's no telling how many more decades I'd have spent mulling this book over. Nice try, Sam. You're up next.

INDEX

Aaronson, Daniel, 189

Abowd, John, 255

Academic-Industry Research Network, 141

Academics. *See* Education; Scholarship; Universities

Activism, worker, 4

Activist investors, 122–123, 124, 128

Adams, Amy, 57, 58

Adams, J. Stacy, 10

Adobe, 80

Aeppel, Timothy, 155

African Americans: in factory jobs, 150. *See also* Discrimination; Racial/ethnic pay gap

Agency theory, 122, 126, 129. *See also* Shareholder capitalism

Airlines: American Airlines, 15, 118, 141, 142, 302n78; deregulation of, 138; United Airlines, 3, 10, 14

Akerlof, George, 69

Akkerboom, Broer, 224

Alabama, 157–158

Alemeda County, California, 199

Alexander, Lamar, 27, 244, 249

Alienation, worker, 150

Allen, Reco, 157

Alternative work jobs, 239. *See also* Independent contractors; Temp workers / staffing agencies

Amalgamated Meat Cutters (AMC), 211

Amazon, 27, 72, 85

AMC (American Motors Corporation), 16, 131, 140

American Airlines, 15, 118, 141, 142, 302n78

American Board of Cosmetic Surgery, 36

American Board of Ophthalmology, 35–36

American Board of Plastic Surgery, 36

American Motors Corporation (AMC), 16, 131, 140

American Tobacco Company, 82–83

Ampad (American Pad & Paper), 132, 134

Anderson, Howard, 133

Ann Taylor, 110

Anticompetitive arrangements. *See* No-poaching agreements

Appelbaum, Eileen, 132, 239
Apple, 80
Ashenfelter, Orley, 81
Atchison, Jim, 203
Australia, 253
Auto industry: automation and, 153; auto parts suppliers, 157–158; concentration and, 140; global competition and, 151; labor cost in, 192; piece work in, 156; power shifts in, 176; Tesla Motors, 161–165; unions in, 140, 156, 165. *See also* "Good jobs"; Manufacturing
Automation. *See* Technology / automation
Avent-Holt, Dustin, 110
Azar, José, 240

"Bad jobs," 185–217; conditions in, 186; improving, 22, 186, 188, 190, 191, 196–197, 199, 204–206, 216–217, 270; minimum wage and, 247; number of, 185–186, 191; power in, 217. *See also* Fast food industry; Home healthcare; Meatpacking; Retail; Sanitation industry
Bain Capital, 132
Baldwin, Tammy, 263
Bank tellers, 225
Barenberg, Mark, 168
Barger, David, 123–124
Barriers to entry, 33–36, 179
Base salary, focus on, 4
Batt, Rosemary, 132
Baugh, Monica, 78

Benefits: decline in, 165; in fast food industry, 197; in "good jobs," 165; lack of, 197; temp work and, 170, 172. *See also* Healthcare
Berger, Suzanne, 126
Bernanke, Ben, 226–227, 231
Bewley, Truman, 12, 15, 47, 48
Big is Beautiful (Atkinson and Lind), 195
Blackstone Group, 26
Blair, Tony, 101
Blanchflower, David, 30
Bloom, Barrett, 75
Bloomberg, 31, 153
BLS (Bureau of Labor Statistics), 182, 201, 208, 225, 233
Blue-collar occupations. *See* Auto industry; Construction work; "Good jobs"; Manual labor; Manufacturing; Mining work
Boards. *See* Corporate boards
Bonuses, 48, 96, 141, 261, 302n78. *See also* Performance pay
Brin, Sergey, 80
Brooks, David, 24
Brown, Cliff, 210
Brueggemann, John, 210
Buffer, 72
Burak Ho, Esra, 14
Bureau of Labor Statistics (BLS), 181, 201, 208, 225, 233
Bush, George W., 226, 227
G. W. Bush administration, 98
Business Roundtable, 128
Buybacks, 141–142, 143, 260, 263

Caban, Alex, 200, 204

Calamuci, Daniel, 208

California, 70, 78, 79, 161, 198–199, 216–217

California State Teachers' Retirement System (CalSTRS), 126

Calvinism, 129

Campbell, Carl III, 47–48

Campbell, Donald, 105

Care workers. *See* Home healthcare

Carl's Jr., 201

Carrabis, Ron, 176

Carré, Françoise, 187, 188, 190

Carried interest loophole, 26

Carter, Jimmy, 179

Carty, Donald J., 15

Castilla, Emilio, 258

Ceiling, lowering, 243, 262–265. *See also* Executive compensation; Shareholder capitalism; Shareholders

CEO pay. *See* Executive compensation

Certifications, 34–36

Chamber of Commerce, US, 86

Chauhan, Pradeep, 237–238

Chief executive officers (CEOs). *See* Executive compensation; Executives

China: manufacturing in, 154–155; wages in, 156

Choice. *See* Competition; Job options; Labor markets

Claims-making, 18. *See also* Pay; Pay-setting

"Clickbait" approach, 94–95

Clinton, Hillary, 193

Closure theory, 33–36

Coca-Cola Company, 128, 137

Collective action, 33–34. *See also* Unions

Collective bargaining agreements, 253. *See also* Unions

College education, 227, 228. *See also* Education; Skill-biased technological change theory; Universities

Collusion, 80–81, 82, 139, 240

Commissions, 87–89, 91. *See also* Performance pay

Commons, John, 210

Company towns, 240

Compensating differentials, theory of, 200, 206, 208, 317n59

Compensation. *See* Pay; Pay-setting

Competition: in airline industry, 138; assumption of, 28; global, 151, 174; in labor market, 20, 57, 58, 80, 89–90 (*see also* Noncompetes; No-poaching agreements); licensing and, 33–34, 232–233; in manufacturing, 176; relation with pay, 18, 205; restoring, 90; restricting, 20–21, 58, 86, 89–90 (*see also* Concentration; Noncompetes; No-poaching agreements; Secrecy, pay); in sanitation industry, 200; Sherman Antitrust Act, 83; taking wages out of, 255; within workplace, 92, 109, 112. *See also* Job options; Labor markets

Computerization, 225. *See also* Technology / automation

Concentration, 82–85, 138, 139–140, 240. *See also* Mergers; Monopoly; Monopsony

Congress, 244–245, 263. *See also* Government; Labor laws; Minimum-wage legislation

Conroy, Samantha, 37

Consolidation. *See* Concentration

Construction work, 166, 181–183, 231. *See also* "Good jobs"

Contingent employees, 237–239. *See also* Fissuring; Independent contractors; Temp workers / staffing agencies

Cooperation: importance of to pay-setters, 53; performance pay and, 92, 109, 112

Core workers, 52

Coronavirus, 268–271

Corporate boards, 224, 263–264. *See also* Shareholder capitalism

Costco, 119–120, 188, 190, 191, 270

Cost of living, 43, 48

Countrywide Financial Corporation, 87–88, 91, 290n8

Covid-19, 268–271

Cowen, Tyler, 26, 27, 32

Craggs, Tommy, 95

Creative destruction, 135

Credentialism, 229

Criminal record, 204, 246

Custodial work, 234, 238, 326n48. *See also* Fissuring

Danger: injury data, 212; job options and, 206–207; in meatpacking, 207, 208–209; OSHA and, 201–203, 212; pay and, 200, 206; reducing cost and, 212; in sanitation industry, 199–200, 203, 206

Davies, Cassidy, 156

Dayen, David, 139, 164

Dayforce, 111

Death, workplace, 206. *See also* Danger

Deaton, Angus, 231

Defense Department, US, 98–99

DeLauro, Rosa, 190

Delery, John, 37

Denice, Patrick, 68

Denmark, 196–197

Denton, Nick, 95

Denver, Colorado, 197

Deregulation, 138, 179, 180, 270

Desmond, Matthew, 198

Detroit, Michigan, 157

Differentials, relative, 12–15. *See also* Fairness

Disclosure, 68–69. *See also* Secrecy, pay; Transparency

Discrimination, 62, 64, 242, 258. *See also* Equity; Fairness; Gender pay gaps; Inequality / inequity; Pay disparities; Racial / ethnic pay gap; Secrecy, pay

Disparities, 7. *See also* Equity; Fairness; Gender pay gaps; Inequality / inequity; Pay disparities; Racial / ethnic pay gap; Secrecy, pay

Disruption, 103. *See also* Power shifts

Dodd-Frank Act, 223

Domestic workers, 215, 250–252. *See also* Home healthcare

Donohue, Thomas, 86

Double-breasted firms, 182

Douglas, Bettie, 11
Duke, James Buchanan, 82
Duncan, Arne, 103, 105

Earned Income Tax Credit (EITC), 248–250
Easterbrook, Steve, 192, 195
Eastman Kodak, 238
Economic inequality. *See* Inequality / inequity; Pay ratios
Economic Policy Institute, 252
Economics, neoclassical, 28
Economy: in 1970s, 122, 129; fair, 243 (*see also* Ceiling, lowering; Middle, expanding; Pay floor, raising); financialization of, 125, 212 (*see also* Private equity model; Shareholder capitalism); Great Recession, 88–89, 91, 104, 118, 153, 155, 161, 162; oil shocks, 121, 151, 179; recession (early 1980s), 179; small businesses in, 193
Education, 227, 228, 324n29; cheating in schools, 105–107; overeducation, 228–229; performance measurement in, 103–108, 109–110; relation with pay, 67, 225–232; as screening device, 229; standardized tests, 103–108; in workers' perception of pay influencers, 41. *See also* Human capital; Skill-biased technological change theory; Universities
Education, US Department of, 103
Edwards, Matthew, 72
Efficiency wage theory, 19, 30, 188
EITC (Earned Income Tax Credit), 248–250

Elite, economic, 221–222. *See also* Executive compensation; Inequality / inequity; Shareholders
Elkhart, Indiana, 155–156
Elofsson, Hampus, 196, 197, 198, 199
Emeryville, California, 198–199
Employees. *See* Workers
Employers. *See* Executive compensation; Executives; Organizations; Pay-setters
Employment choices. *See* Job options; Labor markets; Occupational model
End of Loyalty, The (Wartzman), 127–128
Energy shocks, 121, 151, 179
Enron, 261
Equality. *See* Discrimination; Equity; Fairness; Gender pay gaps; Inequality / inequity; Pay disparities; Racial / ethnic pay gap; Secrecy, pay
"Equal pay for equal work," 46, 59–60, 234, 258. *See also* Discrimination; Equity; Fairness; Gender pay gaps; Inequality / inequity; Pay disparities; Racial / ethnic pay gap; Secrecy, pay
Equity, 5, 10–16, 19; company size and, 194; efficiency wage theory, 19; "equal pay for equal work," 46, 59–60, 234, 258; in fast food industry, 195, 197; in home healthcare, 216; horizontal, 14; importance of to pay-setting, 47, 51, 53; internal, 235; mimicry and, 10, 16; morale and, 48; outside US, 197; power and, 14, 16; power relations and, 18, 216; relative

Equity (*continued*)
    differentials, 12–15; temp work and,
    173; transparency and, 69–72, 71;
    unions and, 169; vertical, 14–15, 234.
    See also Discrimination; Fairness;
    Gender pay gaps; Inequality / ineq-
    uity; Pay disparities; Racial / ethnic
    pay gap; Secrecy, pay
Equity analysts, ratings systems for, 108
Equity firms. *See* Private equity model
Essential workers, 268–271
Estlund, Cynthia, 65
Evans, Gail, 238
Executive compensation, 4; Ameri-
    cans' attitudes toward, 15; beliefs
    about, 133; determined by board,
    224; disclosure of, 9; in fast food
    industry, 192–193; increase in, 16,
    130–134, 231–232; justifications for,
    9–10; mimicry and, 9–10; pay ratios,
    16, 130–133, 223–224, 256, 323n13;
    productivity and, 223, 232; as reflec-
    tion of performance, 26–27; sever-
    ance packages, 135, 203; shareholder
    capitalism and, 129–130; shareholder
    power and, 232; stock options,
    129–130, 135; vertical comparisons,
    14–15. *See also* Ceiling, lowering;
    Elite, economic; Shareholder
    capitalism
Executives: gender of, 49; obligations
    of, 122, 126, 127–128 (*see also* Share-
    holder capitalism); performance
    of, measuring, 26–27, 232; power
    of, 133–134. *See also* Organizations;
    Pay-setters

Experience, 20, 41, 42–43, 44, 50,
    53, 258–259. *See also* Seniority; Skills

Facebook, 95–96, 240
Factory work. *See* "Good jobs";
    Manufacturing
Faculty. *See* Universities
Fair economy, requirements for, 243.
    See also Ceiling, lowering; Middle,
    expanding; Pay floor, raising
Fairness: cost of living and, 48; "equal
    pay for equal work," 46, 234, 258;
    increasing, 25; minimum-wage
    legislation and, 11; of pay, workers'
    perception of, 38–39; pay cuts and,
    11–12, 30; performance pay and, 111,
    112; temp work and, 173; transpar-
    ency and, 70–72, 73. *See also* Equity
Fama, Eugene, 122
Fannie Mae, 88
Farmand, Aida, 250
Fast food industry, 185, 192–199, 312n1;
    average pay in, 192; no-poaching
    agreements in, 81; outside US,
    196–197, 199; wage theft in, 201.
    See also "Bad jobs"
Fatalities, workplace. *See* Danger
Federal contractors, 256
Federal government workers. *See*
    Public sector
Federal Meat Inspection Act (FMIA),
    207
Feldman, Kiera, 204
Financial crises. *See* Economy
Financial information, workplace. *See*
    Secrecy, pay; Transparency

Financialization of economy, 125, 212.
  See also Private equity model; Shareholder capitalism

Financial performance, prioritizing.
  See Private equity model; Shareholder capitalism

Firms. *See* Organizations

Fissuring, 173–174, 212, 234, 236–239,
  254. *See also* Outsourcing /
  offshoring; Temp workers /
  staffing agencies

Flag Container Services, 203

Fligstein, Neil, 137–138

Floor, pay. *See* Minimum wage; Pay
  floor, raising

FMIA (Federal Meat Inspection Act),
  207

Food. *See* Fast food industry;
  Meatpacking

Food and Drug Administration,
  207

Food service workers, 270. *See also* Fast
  food industry; Meatpacking

Food stamps. *See* Government
  assistance

Founding effects, 19

Fountain, Ben, 265

Fox, Justin, 153

Foxx, Virginia, 245

France, 253

Franchise model, 195–196

Freddie Mac, 88

Freeman, Richard, 228

Fremont, California, 162

Friedman, Milton, 121–122, 126, 248,
  330n27

Frisch, Ragnar, 223

Fromstein, Mitchell, 172

Garbage workers. *See* "Bad jobs";
  Sanitation industry

Garrett, Mario, 30

Gates, Bill, 228

Gawker.com, 94–95

Gender, 108; of executives, 49; in
  home healthcare workforce,
  214, 215–216; median earnings and,
  221; pay secrecy and, 66–67;
  temp workers and, 170–171;
  view of performance pay and,
  51, 53

Gender pay gaps, 57, 333n62; "equal
  pay for equal work" and, 46, 59–60,
  234, 258; Lilly Ledbetter Fair Pay
  Act, 59–60; men's pay and, 68; pay
  secrecy and, 66, 67, 68; perpetuation
  of, 8; in public sector, 72; Sony
  Pictures disclosure and, 61; theory
  of compensating differentials and,
  206; transparency and, 68, 73; unions
  and, 68. *See also* Discrimination;
  Equity; Inequality / inequity; Pay
  disparities; Secrecy, pay

General Electric, 154

General Motors, 154

General Social Survey, 38, 92–93

George, Bill, 128

Germany, 263–264

GfK (Ipsos), 63

Ghilarducci, Teresa, 250

Gift exchange version of efficiency
  wage theory, 30

Gig economy workers, 251–253, 331–332n43

Gittleman, Maury, 92

Globalization, 121, 129; manufacturing and, 150–151, 152, 160–161; NAFTA, 174–175; union decline and, 166. *See also* Outsourcing/offshoring

Going rate. *See* Market rate of pay

Goizueta, Roberto C., 128, 137

Goldin, Claudia, 224

Goldman Sachs, 139

"Good jobs," 147–184; African-Americans in, 150; benefits in, 165; decline in, 149–153; manufacturing conflated with, 148; myth of, 22; politicians and, 147–148; power shifts and, 149–153, 167, 176, 183; reclassification and, 184; returning, 22, 147–149, 153–157; temp work and, 169–174; turned bad, 22–23; unions and, 164–169, 183. *See also* Auto industry; Construction work; Manual labor; Manufacturing; Mining work; Trucking industry

Goodman, Peter, 161

Goods-producing sector. *See* Construction work; "Good jobs"; Manufacturing; Mining work

Goodyear, 59

Google, 80, 237, 238

Gottfried, Oliver, 210

Government: anticompetitive practices and, 86; markets linked with, 243. *See also* Congress

Government Accountability Office, 209

Government assistance, 159, 197, 199, 215, 217

Government sector: California state employees, 70; defining performance in, 96–99; pay disparities in, 72; pay secrecy and, 64; performance as pay influencer in, 41; sanitation industry in, 204–206; workers' views about pay-setting in, 45

Gravity Payments, 13, 15

Great Recession, 104, 118, 153, 155, 161, 162

Green Giant, 107

Grocery workers, 270

Gupta, Nina, 37

Harris, Kamala, 251, 263

Hatton, Erin, 172

Hawaii, 79

Healthcare, 35–36, 165, 246; fee-for-service model, 103; inertia in, 103; performance measurement in, 101–102; under shareholder capitalism, 134; Walmart and, 116. *See also* Benefits; Home healthcare

Heining, Jörg, 263

Hicks, J. R., 29

Hicks, Phillip, 169–170, 172, 173

Hierarchies, 6. *See also* Power relations

Hill, Joe, 6

Hispanics, 209. *See also* Immigrants

Home healthcare, 185, 186, 213–217, 247, 250–252, 269–270. *See also* "Bad jobs"

Homeless, working, 247

Horizontal comparisons, 14

Hostile takeovers, 123

House of Representatives, 244. *See also* Congress

Housing market, 87–89, 91

Human capital: firm-specific, 29. *See also* Education

Human capital model, 17–18, 24, 28, 42, 47, 144, 222; assumptions of, 57–58, 90; bonuses and, 48; inadequacy of, 73; labor market and, 20, 57–58; market failures and, 31–32; price takers in, 58; scholarship on, 28–33; skill-biased technological change theory and, 224–225; usefulness of, 31; workplace consequences of performance pay and, 91–92. *See also* Marginal productivity; Market; Performance pay

Human resource managers: surveys of, 19. *See also* Executives; Pay-setters

J. B. Hunt Transport Services, 224, 323n13

IBP, 211

Identity, occupation and, 34

Ideology: polarization and, 147. *See also* Politics

Imitation, 19. *See also* Mimicry

Immigrants, 204; in home healthcare workforce, 214, 215–216; in meat-packing, 209, 211, 212

Imports, 154, 174. *See also* Competition, global; Globalization

Incentive pay, 3, 98. *See also* Performance measurement; Performance pay

Income distribution, 221–222, 224, 244. *See also* Inequality / inequity; Pay disparities; Pay ratios

Income inequality. *See* Inequality / inequity

Independent contractors, 159, 181, 237–239, 252, 331–332n43. *See also* Fissuring; Reclassification; Temp workers / staffing agencies

Independent Journal Review (IJR), 74–75

Inequality / inequity, 4, 10, 221; collective bargaining agreements and, 253; concentration and, 240; EITC and, 248–250; inertia and, 242; maintaining, 58; minimum wage and, 231; occupational model and, 232–233; within occupations, 233, 236–237 (*see also* Pay disparities; Temp workers / staffing agencies); organizations and, 24, 222, 233–237; pay-setting and, 23–24; performance measurement and, 32–33; performance pay and, 112; power shifts and, 233–237, 241–242; recognition of, 241; remedying, 25, 243 (*see also* Ceiling, lowering; Middle, expanding; Pay floor, raising); rents and, 31, 232; skill-biased technological change theory, 224–232; starting pay and, 70; technology and, 225–232; Tinbergen on, 221; unions and, 169, 231. *See also* Ceiling, lowering; Discrimination; Equity; Gender pay gaps; Pay disparities; Pay ratios; Racial / ethnic pay gap; Secrecy, pay; Wage stagnation

Inertia, 5, 19; common sense and, 7; described, 7; disruption and, 103; expanding middle and, 256; fissuring and, 239; in healthcare, 103; inequality and, 242; market rate and, 43; overcoming, 25; performance measurement and, 103; power and, 16; starting pay and, 8, 43–44, 49; union-negotiated contracts and, 168

Information: about company's finances, 68–69; available online, 67, 72; pay secrecy and, 66; power and, 58, 59, 65–66. *See also* Secrecy, pay; Transparency

Information and communications technology, 225

Information asymmetries, 58, 65, 180, 240

Injury, workplace. *See* Danger

Institute for Women's Policy Research (IWPR), 59–60, 61, 63, 64

Institutional Investor, 108

Integration, vertical, 168

Intel, 80

Internal referents, 14

Investors. *See* Shareholders

Ipsos, 63

Isom, Robert, 141

Isomorphism, 19. *See also* Mimicry

ITT Automotive, 174–175

IWPR (Institute for Women's Policy Research), 59–60, 61, 63, 64

Jäger, Simon, 263

Japanese employees, fairness and, 15

Jayapal, Pramila, 251

Jensen, Michael, 122

JetBlue, 123–124

Jimmy John's, 74, 286n51

Job classification, 258, 259. *See also* Reclassification

Job options: concentration and, 84–85; danger and, 206–207; legal standing and, 204, 206–207; limiting, 74 (*see also* Noncompetes; No-poaching agreements)

Jobs, Steve, 80, 228, 239

Johnson, Kevin, 223

Johnson, Randy, 134, 135

Journalism: "clickbait" approach, 94–95; noncompetes in, 74–76; performance measurement in, 93–94, 100

Jungle, The (Sinclair), 207

Justice, relative, 10. *See also* Equity; Fairness

Kamlani, Kunal, 47–48

Katz, Lawrence, 152, 224

Kavanaugh, Brett, 202

Kennedy, Ted, 179

Kerry, John, 147

Knowledge, 66, 68. *See also* Information

Kohl's, 223

Krauss, Carl, 117

Krueger, Alan, 81

Krugman, Paul, 266

Labor, organized. *See* Unions

Labor, US Department of, 173

Labor cost, 192

Labor force, size of, 152

Labor laws: compliance with, 60–61; in construction work, 183; federal contractors and, 256; Lilly Ledbetter Fair Pay Act, 59–60; NLRA, 60–61; obsolete, 25, 64; OSHA, 158, 201–202, 212; Paycheck Fairness Act, 61; pay secrecy and, 64–65; penalties for violating, 64–65, 168, 201–202; prevailing wage laws, 183; wage and standards boards, 251–254. *See also* Labor standards; Law; Minimum-wage legislation

Labor market reforms, 244

Labor markets: addressing inequalities in, 243; competition in, 20, 57, 58, 88–90; concentration and, 84–85, 240–241; employer power and, 30; fissuring and, 238; free and fair, 20; human capital model and, 20, 57–58; peculiar properties of, 29; rent-generation and, 24–25; restricting, 20–21, 58, 89–90 (*see also* Noncompetes; No-poaching agreements; Secrecy, pay); trucking industry and, 180. *See also* Job options; Market

Labor markets, internal, 238, 239, 256; company size and, 194; decline of, 77; unions and, 257–258

Labor standards, 157–158; in US, 156; wage and standards boards, 251–254. *See also* Labor laws

Labor supply: in construction work, 231; pay and, 226. *See also* Labor markets

Labor unions. *See* Unions

Lakewood Engineering & Manufacturing Co, 117

Lampert, Edward, 143

Langbein, Laura, 99

Law: as expression of economic values, 203; as institutionalized power, 201–202; power relations and, 203. *See also* Labor laws; Minimum wage; Minimum-wage legislation

Law360, 76

Law firms, performance pay in, 111–112

Lawler, Edward, 65

Lawrence, Jennifer, 57, 58

Layoffs, 47, 137–138

Ledbetter, Lilly, 59, 61

Lilly Ledbetter Fair Pay Act, 59–60

Legal standing, 204, 246. *See also* Immigrants

Legislation: pay secrecy policies and, 61–62. *See also* Labor laws; Minimum-wage legislation

Lemos, Sara, 189–190

Leniency errors, 108–109

Levine, David, 39

Liberty Ashes, 199–200

Licensing, 17, 33–34, 232–233

Limbaugh, Rush, 13

Liquidated damages clauses, 75. *See also* Noncompetes

Living wage, 216, 246. *See also* Minimum wage

Loans, 88–89, 290n8

Loss aversion, 15

Lottery system, 3

Lowe, Peggy, 210

Loyalty, 255–256; relation with pay, 188, 190, 194, 197; transparency and, 68, 69, 72

Luck, 241

Lyft, 252–253

Mackey, John, 71–72

Managerial business model, 120, 122, 123

Managers: relation with shareholders, 120; surveys of, 19–20. *See also* Executives; Pay-setters

Mankiw, Greg, 26, 27

Manpower, 169–170, 172

Manual labor, 22; concentration and, 140. *See also* "Good jobs"; Manufacturing

Manufacturing, 22; automation in, 151–153, 160–161; changes in, 150–153, 174–175; competition in, 176; conditions in, 155–159; conflation with "good jobs," 148; decline in, 149; globalization and, 150–151, 152, 160–161, 174–175; labor cost for, 154–155; power in, 175–176; power shifts in, 153–157, 176; productivity in, 159; realities of, 149–150; return of, 153–157; safety standards / training in, 157–158; temp workers / staffing agencies in, 157–158, 170–174; turnover in, 156; union decline in, 159–161, 165–169; in US South, 157–158; wages in, 150, 154, 155, 156–158, 159–161, 163; worker alienation in, 150. *See also* "Good jobs"

Marginal productivity, 28–33, 90, 91, 243. *See also* Human capital model; Performance; Performance pay

Marinescu, Ioana, 240

Market, 18; anticompetitive practices and, 86; discipline by, 136 (*see also* Private equity model; Shareholder capitalism); linked with state, 243; minimum wage and, 27; power struggles in, 9; as site of pay-setting, belief in, 27; temporary help industry and, 172. *See also* Competition; Human capital model; Labor markets

Market adjustments, bonuses and, 48

Marketcraft, 243

Market failures, human capital model and, 31–32

Market rate of pay, 8–9, 16; importance of to pay-setters, 53; paying above, 19 (*see also* Efficiency wage theory); workers' perceptions of, 43. *See also* Equity; Labor markets; Mimicry

Market value, belief in, 20

Markovits, Daniel, 32

Marx, Matt, 76, 79

Matcor-Matsu Group, 157–158

Matsu Alabama, 157–158

Mayer Brown law firm, 111, 112

McCain, John, 147

McConnell, Mitch, 244, 245

McDonald's, 192

McKinney, Kevin, 255

Meatpacking, 185, 186, 207–213, 319n84. *See also* "Bad jobs"

Meckling, William, 122

Media: noncompetes in, 75. *See also* Journalism

Median wage, 221, 244. *See also* Inequality / inequity; Middle, expanding; Pay disparities

Medicaid, 216

Medicine. *See* Healthcare

Medtronic, 128

Men. *See* Gender; Gender pay gaps

Mental health, 246

Mergers, 134, 137–140; as mimicry, 138. *See also* Concentration; Private equity model

Merit. *See* Performance; Performance pay

Mexico: manufacturing moved to, 175; Walmart in, 187–188

Meyer, Herbert, 112

Michael, Maggie, 94

Michaels, David, 212

Microsoft, 109

Middle, expanding, 243, 254–262. *See also* Median wage

Milkman, Ruth, 179, 182

Mimicry, 5, 7–10, 19; bonuses and, 48; as collusion, 82; competition restriction and, 20–21, 80–82; equity concerns and, 10, 16; executive compensation and, 9–10; expanding middle and, 256; fissuring and, 239; importance of to pay-setters, 53; inequality and, 242; layoffs as, 138; market rate and, 8–9, 10, 16; mergers as, 138; no-hire rules and, 80–82; of offshore production, 160; performance measurement and, 100; power and, 16; power shifts and, 25; in retail, 190–191; shareholder capitalism and, 22, 126; union-negotiated contracts and, 168; wage surveys, 8

Minimills, 152

Minimum wage: abolition of, proposed, 27; benefits of raising, 248; effects of, 198–199, 245–247, 254; EITC and, 250; enforcement of, 251–252; equity effects of, 254; federal, 27, 230, 244–248; federal contractors and, 256; highest, 198; inequality and, 231; maintaining relative differentials and, 12–14; market and, 27; opposition to raising, 245, 246; preemption, 248; prices and, 189–190; real value of, 230–231; as reflection of performance, 27; relation with median wage, 244; states', 247; support for raising, 245; taking wages out of competition and, 255; wage boards and, 254. *See also* Living wage; Pay floor, raising

Minimum-wage legislation, 4; in Denver, 197; effects of, 198; fairness and, 11; living wage ordinances, 216; responses to, 115; retail workers and, 115. *See also* Labor laws; Law; Living wage

Mining work, 22, 149, 166. *See also* "Good jobs"

Mishel, Lawrence, 252

Missouri, noncompetes in, 78

Mobility, employee, 84. *See also* Competition; Job options; Labor markets

Models of pay-setting, 17–25. *See also* Human capital model; Occupational model

Mofty, Nariman El-, 94

Molinari, Donna, 246

Monopoloid situation, 224

Monopoly, 83. *See also* Concentration

Monopsony, 83–85, 283n4. *See also* Concentration

Monroe, John Stein, 99

Moore, Anthony, 197–198, 199

Morale: equity and, 48; pay cuts and, 11–12, 30; at Whole Foods, 72. *See also* Fairness

Morgan Stanley, 142

Mortgages, 88–89, 91

Motivation, 113

Motor Carrier Act, 179

Mozilo, John, 87, 88

Mud Bay, 13

Muller, Jerry, 95, 106

Murchison, Wallace, 85

Musk, Elon, 162–165

Nader, Ralph, 179

NAFTA (North American Free Trade Agreement), 174

Nakanishi Manufacturing Corporation, 158

NAM (National Association of Manufacturers), 179

Nation, 211

National Association of Manufacturers (NAM), 179

National Domestic Workers Alliance (NDWA), 215, 251–252

National Labor Relations Act (NLRA), 60–61

National Labor Relations Board (NLRB), 164

National Ophthalmology Board, 35

National Security Personnel System (NSPS), 98–99

Negotiations, as pay influencer, 43

Nelson, Sara, 139

Networks, role of in pay-setting, 44

News. *See* Journalism

New York City, 204–205

New York Times, 70, 149–150, 196, 197, 199

Nixon, Jeannine, 246

Nixon, Richard, 131

NLRA (National Labor Relations Act), 60–61

NLRB (National Labor Relations Board), 164

No Child Left Behind Act, 105

No-hire rules, 20, 58, 80–82, 84, 139, 240

Noncompetes, 20, 58, 74–79, 84, 90, 240, 286n51. *See also* Competition

Nonprofits: workers' views about pay-setting in, 45. *See also* Private sector

No-poaching agreements, 20, 58, 80–82, 84, 139, 240

Norms, pay, 16. *See also* Market rate of pay

North American Free Trade Agreement (NAFTA), 174

North Korea, 57

Norway, transparency in, 67, 72

NowThis, 74–75

NPR, 210

NSPS (National Security Personnel System), 98–99

Nursing assistants. *See* Home healthcare

Obama, Barack, 5, 59, 147, 154, 213, 217, 222, 262; on education, 227; on pay secrecy, 62

Obama administration, 26, 97, 104, 256

Occupation, 50; importance of to pay-setters, 51–52; subcontractors vs. core workers in, 52; workers' perceptions of, 42–43

Occupational model of pay, 17–18, 144, 222; barriers of entry in, 33–36; education in, 17; "equal pay for equal work" and, 46; inequality and, 232–233; licensing and, 33–34; rent-seeking and, 33–34; scholarship on, 27, 28, 33–37; workers' perceptions of, 42. *See also* "Bad jobs"; "Good jobs"

Occupational Safety and Health Administration (OSHA), 158, 201–202, 212

Occupations: pay disparities within, 221, 222, 233, 238, 255, 261; worth of, 36–37

Off-shoring. *See* Globalization; Outsourcing / offshoring

Oil shocks, 121, 151, 179

Oligopolies, 139–140, 288n81

One-percenters, 221–222

Ophthalmologists, 35–36

Organizational performance, 41, 50, 53

Organizational revenue, linking pay to, 259–261

Organizations: change in corporate culture, 235; inequality and, 24, 222, 233–237; power shifts toward, 233–234, 241; role of in pay-setting, 18–19, 144; segregation of high-skill workers into, 236–237; shareholder-value conception of, 235 (*see also* Shareholder capitalism; Shareholders); size of, 193–196. *See also* Pay-setters

Organized labor. *See* Unions

Orr, John, 111

OSHA (Occupational Safety and Health Administration), 158, 201–203, 212

Osterman, Paul, 214

Oswald, Andrew, 30

Outsourcing / offshoring, 160–161, 174–175, 234. *See also* Fissuring; Globalization; Manufacturing; Temp workers / staffing agencies

Overeducated American, The (Freeman), 228

Overeducation problem, 228–229

Overseas labor. *See* Globalization; Outsourcing / offshoring

Ovitz, Michael, 135

Owners, 124. *See also* Organizations; Pay-setters; Shareholders

Oxfam America, 210

Packers Sanitation Services, 212

Pandemic, 268–271

Parker, Doug, 118

Parker, Robert, 141

Path-dependence, 19

Paul, Rand, 35

Pay: base salary vs. performance-based pay, 4; consequences of, 265; as conversational taboo, 72; decline in, 183; growth in, 120; laws about, 183 (*see also* Minimum wage; Minimum-wage legislation); stagnation in, 137, 183, 232, 235, 241; wage stickiness, 11–12, 30, 47; wage theft, 201. *See also* Performance pay; Starting pay

Paycheck Fairness Act, 61

Pay cuts, 11–12, 15, 29–30, 47. *See also* Wage stickiness

Pay disparities, 333n62; concentration and, 240; between executives and workers, 16, 130–133, 223–224, 256, 323n13; within occupation, 221, 222, 233, 238, 255, 261; organizations as drivers of, 222; transparency and, 72–73. *See also* Discrimination; Equity; Gender pay gaps; Income distribution; Inequality / inequity; Racial / ethnic pay gap; Secrecy, pay

Payes, Julio, 198

Pay floor, raising, 230, 243. *See also* Minimum wage

Pay for performance. *See* Performance pay

Pay influencers: pay-setters' views about, 47–54; workers' views about, 39–46

Pay ratios, 16, 130–133, 223–224, 256, 323n13. *See also* Ceiling, lowering; Executive compensation; Income distribution; Shareholder capitalism

PayScale, 48

Pay-setters, 47–54. *See also* Executives; Shareholders

Pay-setting: beliefs about, 19–20 (*see also* Surveys); dominant understandings of, 20 (*see also* Human capital model; Occupational model); elements in, 5 (*see also* Equity; Inertia; Mimicry; Power); linked to inequality, 23–24; traditional explanations of, 4. *See also* Claims-making

Pearlstein, Steven, 119, 127

Performance: bonuses and, 48; defining, 96; importance of, 18, 53; motivation and, 113; in pay-setting, pay-setters' view of, 50–51; self-rating, 71; in workers' perception of pay influencers, 41. *See also* Commissions; Merit; Performance pay; Productivity; Productivity, marginal

Performance, organizational, 41, 50, 53

Performance measurement, 21, 24, 259; architecture of evaluation, 107–110; assumed objectivity of, 91; definitional disputes and, 90, 93–100; in education, 89, 90, 105–108, 109–110; fairness and, 111, 112; in healthcare, 101–102; imperfect measures, 100–110; inequality and, 32–33; inertia and, 103; in journalism, 93–94, 100; leniency errors, 108–109; mimicry and, 100; mission and, 90, 96; National Security Personnel System, 98–99; problems with, 91; research productivity and, 100; standardized tests, 103–108; stock price as, 129; subjective vs. objective measures, 109–110; use of one metric, 107. *See also* Human capital model

Performance pay, 290–291n15; belief in, 26–28, 54; cooperation and, 92, 109, 112; effects of, 21, 91–92, 106–107, 114; executive compensation and, 26; Facebook and, 95–96; fairness and, 111, 112; inequality / inequity and, 112, 236; in law firms, 111–112; pitfalls of, 92, 110–113; prevalence of, 92–93, 113; productivity and, 92; scholarship on, 27; support for, 259–261; in trucking industry, 178; at United Airlines, 3; at Wells Fargo, 3–4; workers' perceptions of, 42–45. *See also* Bonuses; Human capital model

Pfeffer, Jeffrey, 59, 113

Piece work, 156

Pierce, Brooks, 92

Piketty, Thomas, 262–263

Plastic surgeons, 36

Police, measuring performance of, 97–98

Policy options, for remedying inequality, 243. *See also* Ceiling, lowering; Middle, expanding; Pay floor, raising

Political participation, 265–266

Politics: "good jobs" and, 147–148; skill-biased technological change theory and, 226; small businesses and, 193

Poo, Ai-jen, 215, 251–252

Porter, Eduardo, 199

Potter, Roy, 215

Poverty: minimum wage and, 230; stress and, 246; working homeless, 247

Poverty wages, 244, 248–250. *See also* Minimum wage

Power, 5; actual / realized, 65–66; in "bad jobs," 217; coercive, 6; concentration and, 85, 139; defined, 6; of employees, 140, 257 (*see also* Unions); equity and, 14, 16; of executives, 133–134; fissuring and, 173–174; inertia and, 16; information and, 58, 59, 65–66; institutionalized, law as, 201–202; labor law and, 201; in labor markets, 30; lack of overt conflict and, 6; legitimate, 6–7; in manufacturing, 175–176; mimicry and, 16; monopsony, 83–85; as pay influencer, 44, 58 (*see also* No-hire rules; Noncompetes; Secrecy, pay); of pay-setters, 51; performance measurement and, 21; relation with other elements of pay-setting, 16; in sanitation industry, 203–204; scholarship on, 30; of shareholders, 22, 232, 264; unions and, 6, 230; Walmart's, 116. *See also* Information; Reclassification; Secrecy, pay; Shareholders

Power capability, 65

Power relations: dangerous jobs and, 206–207; equity and, 18, 216; in home healthcare, 216; law and, 203; market as site of, 9; in sanitation industry, 205; unequal, 6

Power shifts, 24, 25, 103, 115–144; in construction work, 182; disruption and, 103; between employers and unions, 167; "good jobs" and, 149–153, 167, 176, 183; inequality / inequity and, 233–237, 241–242; in manufacturing, 153–157, 176; mimicry and, 25; organizations and, 231–234, 241; temp work and, 169–174; toward employers and shareholders, 233–234, 241; in trucking industry, 179; union decline and, 164–169; wage stagnation and, 241. *See also* Private equity model; Shareholder capitalism

Power use, 65

Predestination, 129

Predistribution, 243

Presidential election, US (2016), 96

Prevailing wage laws, 183

Price, Dan, 13, 72

Prices, relation with wages, 189–190, 197, 199

Price takers, 58

Principal-agent problem, 122, 126, 129. *See also* Shareholder capitalism

Prisoners, former, 204, 246

Private equity firms, 26, 212

Private equity model, 132–134; creative destruction and, 135; effects on workers, 134–140; influence of, 136; promises of, 135–136. *See also* Shareholder capitalism

Private sector: pay secrecy and, 64; sanitation industry in, 204, 205, 206; views about pay-setting in, 41, 45

Productivity: definitional disputes regarding, 90; disclosure of workplace financial information and, 68–69; executive compensation and, 223, 232; in manufacturing, 159; measuring (*see* Performance measurement); motivation and, 113; pay ratios and, 223–224; relation with pay, 17–18, 190 (*see also* Performance pay)

Productivity, marginal, 28–33, 90, 91, 243. *See also* Human capital model; Performance; Performance pay

Productivity inequality, 23–24

Professors. *See* Universities

Profits, as goal, 137–138. *See also* Shareholder capitalism

Protestant Ethic and the Spirit of Capitalism, The (Weber), 129

Public companies, 119. *See also* Shareholder capitalism; Shareholders

Public sector. *See* Government sector

Publishing, 100

Pure Food and Drug Act, 207

Quality and Outcomes Framework (QOF), 102

Qualtrics, 40, 48

Questionnaires. *See* Surveys

Race Between Education and Technology, The (Goldin and Katz), 224

Race to the Top, 104, 105

Racial / ethnic pay gap, 8, 73, 333n62. *See also* Discrimination; Equity; Inequality / inequity; Pay disparities; Secrecy, pay

Raises, 98. *See also* Middle, expanding; Minimum wage; Performance pay

Raise the Wage Act, 244–245

Rand, Ayn, 27

Ratings systems, 108–110

Reagan, Ronald, 249

Recession, 88–89, 91, 104, 118, 153, 155, 161, 162

Recidivism, 246

Reclassification, 159–161, 171, 172–173, 175, 184. *See also* Fissuring; Independent contractors; Temp workers / staffing agencies

Recycling industry. *See* Sanitation industry

Relational inequality perspective, 18

Relational Investors, 125

Rent perspective, 23–24

Rents, 23–24, 31, 33–34, 231, 232

Reshoring, 153–157

Restaurants. *See* Fast food industry; Food service workers

Retail, 110–111, 185, 187–191, 312n1; Costco, 119–120, 188, 190, 191, 270; minimum wage legislation and, 115; wages in, 208, 319n87. *See also* "Bad jobs"; Walmart

Retention, 48. *See also* Turnover

Reuters, 76

Revenue, distribution of, 5. *See also* Pay

Reward structure, 98. *See also* Performance pay

Reward Work Act, 263–264

Ride share workers, 252–253, 331–332n43. *See also* Independent contractors

Ridley, Clarence, 106

Rigidity, wage, 12. *See also* Stickiness, wage

Risk, 125–126. *See also* Danger

Roberts, Matt, 173

Romney, George, 16, 131, 134, 140

Romney, Mitt, 132–133, 134

Roosevelt, Theodore, 207

Rothstein, Jesse, 107, 250

Rothwell, Jonathan, 32

Rubio, Marco, 265

Rule 10b-18, 142, 264

Russell-Kraft, Stephanie, 76

Sacramento Bee, 71

Saez, Emmanuel, 262–263

Safety standards / training, 157–158; penalties for violating, 203–204. *See also* Labor standards; Occupational Safety and Health Administration (OSHA)

Salary. *See* Pay; Pay-setting

Salary history, effects of, 8. *See also* Starting pay

Sales, tying pay to, 88–89, 110–111. *See also* Performance pay

Sanchez, Michael, 164

Sanders, Bernie, 263

San Francisco, 216–217

Sanitation industry, 185, 199–207; competition in, 200; conditions in, 186; danger in, 199–200, 203, 206; power in, 203–204; unions in, 205; wages in, 200–201; wage theft in, 201. *See also* "Bad jobs"

Sara Lee, 126

Satisfaction with pay, 39

Scale measures, 108–110

Scheiber, Noam, 32, 112

Schmidt, Eric, 237

Schoefer, Benjamin, 263

Scholarship, 100; on human capital model, 28–33; on pay-setters' approaches to pay-setting, 47–53; on power, 30. *See also* Surveys

Schwartz, Nelson, 127

Schwarzman, Steven, 26, 27

Scott, H. Lee, Jr., 189, 190

Sears, Roebuck, 120, 143

SeaWorld, 202

SEC (Securities and Exchange Commission), 142, 202, 223, 264

Secrecy, pay, 20; conversational taboos and, 72; discrimination and, 62, 64; impact of, 66–68; information and, 65, 66; legality of, 60–62, 64–65; pay disparities and, 59, 66, 67, 68; power and, 66, 73; prevalence of, 61, 63–64, 65; relation with wages, 66–68; restoring competition in labor markets and, 90; sector and, 64; support for, 65; surveys on, 63–64, 290–291n15; transparency and, 64; unionization and, 64; workers' compliance with, 66. *See also* Gender pay gaps; Inequality / inequity; Information; Racial / ethnic pay gap

Sector. *See* Government sector; Private sector

Securities and Exchange Commission (SEC), 142, 202, 223, 264

Security guards, 234

Senate, 244–245. *See also* Congress; Government

Seniority, 41, 44, 111, 258–259, 261, 333n62

Severance packages, 135, 203

Shadd, John, 142

Shareholder capitalism, 124–128, 136, 232; change in corporate culture and, 235; effects of, 134–140, 264–265; executive compensation and, 129–130; fissuring and, 238–239; healthcare under, 134; layoffs and, 137–138; mimicry and, 22, 126; power of CEOs and, 133–134; prevalence of, 128–134; profits and, 137–138; shift to, 22; short-termism of, 239, 263; stock buybacks, 141–142, 143, 260, 263. *See also* Ceiling, lowering; Private equity model

Shareholders, 119, 262; activist, 122–123, 124, 128; cost-cutting and, 175; focus on, 120–144, 189, 235; hostile takeovers, 123; lying to, 202; pay and, 118–120; power of, 22, 232, 264; power shifts toward, 233–234, 241; reaction to raising wages, 118–120, 143; relation with managers, 120; short-termism of, 239, 263; stock buybacks, 141–142, 143, 260, 263; tax cuts and, 141; Walmart and, 143–144. *See also* Ceiling, lowering; Elite, economic

Sherman Antitrust Act, 83

Shin, Taekjin, 137–138

Short-termism, 239, 263

Silva, Jennifer, 266

Simon, Herbert, 96–97, 106–107

Sinclair, Upton, 207, 208, 209, 319n84

Sinclair Broadcast Group, 75

Sinegal, James, 120

Sirkin, Hal, 155

Size, company, wages and, 119, 190–191, 193–196

Skill-biased technological change theory, 224–232

Skills, 18; emphasis on, 23–24 (*see also* Human capital model); executive compensation and, 232; inequality and, 23–24; market value and, 20; relation with pay, 225–232. *See also* Education; Occupational model; Performance; Productivity

Slaughterhouse jobs. *See* Meatpacking

Small businesses, 193

Smith, Noah, 31

Social institutions, 235

Socialism, 122

Social loafing, 39

Social responsibility, 121–122, 126

Society for Human Research Management, 37–38, 39

Solivan, Vanessa, 247

Sony Pictures disclosure, 57, 61, 66

South (region), 157–158

Southern, Kirsten, 156

Stability, 19

Staffing agencies. *See* Temp workers / staffing agencies

Stakeholders, internal, 120. *See also* Workers

Standardized tests, 103–108

Standards. *See* Labor standards; Wage and standards boards

Stantcheva, Stefanie, 262–263

Staples, 132

Starbucks, 223

Starting pay: inequality and, 71, 242; inertia and, 8, 43–44, 49; job shortages and, 159; noncompetes and, 79; for pilots, 139

State. *See* Congress; Government

Steel industry, 151, 152. *See also* "Good jobs"; Manufacturing

Steinbaum, Marshall, 83, 240

Stewart, Emily, 269

Stickiness, wage, 11–12, 30, 47

Stillwell, Robert, 153

Stock buybacks, 141–142, 143, 260, 263

Stockholders. *See* Shareholders

Stock options, 129–130, 135

Stock price, 129. *See also* Shareholder capitalism; Shareholders

Stockton, California, 161

Stout, Lynn, 127

Stress, 246

Strom, Andrew, 203

Subcontractors, 52, 239. *See also* Fissuring; Independent contractors; Outsourcing / offshoring; Temp workers / staffing agencies

Suicide rates, 246

Summers, Lawrence, 32–33, 224

Sun, Shengwei, 68

Suppliers, 116–117, 168, 174, 176, 187

Supply and demand, 28. *See also* Human capital model; Market

Surge Staffing, 157–158

Surveillance, of workers, 177

Surveys, 19–20; General Social Survey, 38, 92–93; on pay satisfaction, 37–38; pay secrecy and, 63–64, 65, 66, 93; of pay-setters, 48–54, 290–291n15; of wages, 8; on workers' views about pay influencers, 39–46

Target, 117

Tax Cuts and Jobs Act, 26, 140–143, 249

Taxes, 322n6; carried interest loophole, 26; EITC, 248–250; pretax distribution of income, 243; reducing inequality and, 262–263; Tax Cuts and Jobs Act, 26, 140–143, 249; Tax Reform Act, 249

Tax information, availability of, 67, 72

Tax Reform Act, 249

Taylor, Brook, 161

Teacher Incentive Fund, 104, 105

Teaching. *See* Education; Universities

Teaching evaluations, 108

Teamsters union, 179, 181, 205

Teamwork. *See* Cooperation

Technology / automation, 175, 226, 277–278n48; construction work and, 181; executive compensation and, 232; inequality and, 225–232; manufacturing and, 151–153, 160–161; in meatpacking, 213; in trucking industry, 176, 177–178; union decline and, 166. *See also* Skill-biased technological change theory

Temp workers / staffing agencies, 157–158, 169–174, 234, 237–239. *See also* Fissuring; Reclassification

10b-18 rule, 142, 264

Tesla Motors, 161–165

Texas A&M University, 89, 90, 100

Theory of compensating differentials, 200, 206, 208, 317n59

Theory of Wages, The (Hicks), 29

Theron, Charlize, 57, 66

Thoma, Mark, 31

Thompson, Derek, 100

Tilly, Chris, 187, 188, 190

Time Inc., 93, 94

Timken Company, 124–126, 127

Tinbergen, Jan, 223, 224

Tinbergen norm, 223–224

Tobacco companies, 82–83, 288n81

Toback, Steve, 206

Tomaskovic-Devey, Donald, 110

Training, 17, 157–158, 225–232. *See also* Education

Transparency, 67–73. *See also* Disclosure; Information; Secrecy, pay

Transportation, 166. *See also* Trucking industry

Trucking industry, 176–181, 270–271. *See also* "Good jobs"; Transportation

Trump, Donald, 133, 140, 147, 149, 193, 249, 270

Tull, Donald, 211

Turnover: in fast food industry, 196–197; in home healthcare, 214–215, 216, 217; in manufacturing, 156; relation with pay, 188; unions and, 257

UAW (United Auto Workers), 140, 165

Uber, 252–253, 331–332n43

Uncertainty, shifted to workers, 125–126

Undocumented workers. *See* Immigrants

Unemployment, 118, 268; during Great Recession, 155, 162; minimum wage and, 199

Unions, 282n48; in auto industry, 140, 156, 165; collective bargaining agreements, 253; in construction work, 166, 182; decline of, 140, 159–161, 164–169, 230, 231, 232; early, 156; effects of, 246; empowering workers and, 257; gender pay gaps and, 68; gig economy workers and, 252–253; globalization and, 166; "good jobs" and, 159–161, 164–169, 183; in home healthcare, 216; inequality and, 169, 231; inertia and, 168; internal labor markets and, 257–258; in meatpacking, 210–211; in mining work, 166; nonunion workers and, 169; opposition to, 164–165, 167, 174–175, 182, 210–211; outside US, 196, 253; pay secrecy

and, 64; performance pay and, 99; power in, 6; power of, 230; replaced by college degree as pay-setting resource, 230; in sanitation industry, 205; smaller firms and, 168; Teamsters, 179, 181, 205; in trucking industry, 179, 180, 181; turnover and, 257; UAW, 140, 165; wages and, 168. *See also* Collective action

United Airlines, 3, 10, 14

United Auto Workers (UAW), 140, 165

United Packinghouse Workers of America (UWPA), 211

Universities, 227, 228, 324n29; cost-effectiveness of faculty, 89, 90, 100; performance measurement at, 100–101; professors' salaries, 68; teaching evaluations, 108. *See also* Education

Vanity Fair, 109

Vaughn, Dezzimond, 164

Vertical comparisons, 14

Viking Sanitation, 200

Viscelli, Steve, 177–178, 180, 181

Vlasic, 116

Vox, 118

Wage and standards boards, 251–254

Wage decline, 183

Wage laws, 183. *See also* Minimum wage; Minimum-wage legislation

Wages. *See* Pay; Pay-setting

Wage stagnation, 137, 183, 232, 235, 241

Wage stickiness, 11–12, 30, 47

Wage surveys, 8

Wage theft, 201

Waldman, Peter, 158

Walker, Patricia, 215

Wall Street. *See* Shareholder capitalism; Shareholders

Walmart, 115–118, 127; conditions for workers, 186; healthcare and, 116; influence of, 174, 175, 190–191; number of employees, 149; outside US, 187–188; power of, 85, 116; shareholders and, 143–144; suppliers and, 116; wages in, 119, 182, 189; workers during pandemic, 270

Walton, Sam, 115

Warren, Elizabeth, 263

Wartzman, Rick, 127–128

Washington Post, 245

Wasserman, Bob, 162

Weber, Max, 129

Weil, David, 173, 194

Welfare. *See* Government assistance

Wells Fargo, 3–4, 21

Whitworth, Ralph, 125

Whole Foods, 71–72

Wiley Act, 207

Wilmers, Nathan, 85

Women: pay secrecy and, 66–67. *See also* Discrimination; Gender pay gaps; Inequality / inequity

Wood, Robert E., 120, 143

Worker board representation, 263–264

Workers, 143; alienation of, 150; beliefs about pay-setting, 37–46; empowering, 257; essential, 268–271; reclassification of (*see* Reclassification); representation of on corporate boards, 263–264; risk / uncertainty shifted to, 125–126; satisfaction with pay, 37–39; shareholder capitalism's effects on, 134–140; surveillance of, 177; surveys of, 19–20 (*see also* Surveys); undocumented (*see* Immigrants); well-paid, 190, 194

Working homeless, 247

Workplace fatalities, 206. *See also* Danger

Workplace relocation. *See* Globalization; Outsourcing / offshoring

Workplaces. *See* Organizations

World Trade Organization, 154

Yellen, Janet, 70

Yemen, 94

Zheo, Nellie, 255

Zikry, Maad al-, 94

Zipperer, Ben, 250